MANAGING PUBLIC PENSION PLANS

This book provides an in-depth explanation of public pension plan management and the decision-making processes surrounding pension policies within state and local governments in the United States. It addresses the intricate balance between securing retirement benefits for public employees and ensuring the fiscal sustainability of pension systems and their sponsoring governments. The book begins with an introduction to the purpose and significance of public pension systems, establishing a foundation for understanding key pension decisions. Using a logic model framework, the authors assess how environmental factors, stakeholders, and legal constraints shape decisions in pension management. The book identifies five core goals for public pension management – benefit sufficiency, cost affordability, funding sustainability, asset management efficiency, and governance quality – emphasizing the relationships among these objectives.

Detailed chapters cover investment policies, actuarial processes, and the design of benefits and contributions, explaining the financial and actuarial bases necessary for sound pension decisions. Pension reform efforts, including the transition from defined benefit plans to defined contribution, cash-balance, and hybrid plans, are examined in depth, highlighting the reasons for reforms and analyzing their impacts on employees and employers. The book concludes with ten takeaways for effective pension plan management and addresses emerging challenges such as fiscal pressures, inflation, and changing demographics. With practical implications grounded in research, this book serves as an essential resource for pension board members, pension system administrators, government officials, legislators and their staff, professionals, researchers, and students involved in public pension plan management.

Gang Chen is an associate professor of Public Administration and Policy at Rockefeller College, State University of New York, Albany, United States. He is the Co-Director of the State and Local Government Finance Project (SLGF) at the Center for Policy Research at Rockefeller College. Dr. Chen's research focuses on addressing critical financial management challenges confronting state and local governments. His work on state and local pension plans is widely published in top-tier journals in public administration and public finance. Dr. Chen's research has been supported by prominent associations and foundations, including the Governmental Accounting Standards Board (GASB), Society of Actuaries (SOA), Center for Retirement Research at Boston College, Equable Institute, Crane Foundation, Laura and John Arnold Foundation, Reason Foundation, and Pew Charitable Trusts.

Trang Hoang is an associate professor in the School of Public Administration, University of Nebraska at Omaha, United States. Her primary research interests include public pensions, public/nonprofit budgeting and financial management, health policy, and risk management. Dr. Hoang's work on public pension reform received the Network of Schools of Public Policy, Affairs, and Administration (NASPAA) Emerging Scholar Award in 2018 and the Best Dissertation Award in 2019. Her research projects have been supported by the IBM Center for the Business of Government and the Governmental Accounting Standards Board (GASB). Dr. Hoang is a recipient of the Rosemary O'Leary Award for excellent scholarship on women in public administration and public management.

Carol Ebdon is a professor emerita in the School of Public Administration at the University of Nebraska at Omaha, United States. Her research interests are in the areas of public budgeting and financial management. Dr. Ebdon has also worked in local government, including as the Director of Finance for the City of Omaha where her responsibilities included serving as the administrator and a member of the board of trustees for two defined benefit pension plans.

Routledge Public Budgeting and Finance

Editor

Bruce D. Mcdonald III

Professor of Public Budgeting and Finance, and Director of the School of Public Service

Old Dominion University, Norfolk VA

Public budgeting is a core function of public administration. Regardless of the level of government, size of government, type of management, or the socio-economic and political characteristics of the government, the execution of policies and programs requires the expenditure of resources, and important funding decisions must be made. Yet public officials are faced with policy and program implementation in an environment of limited resources. The Routledge Public Budgeting and Finance series explores issues related to effective, ethical, and equitable budgeting and financial management in the context of public administration. Topics of interest to the series include, but are not limited to:

- Budgeting for times of uncertainty
- Sales taxes
- Budget and revenue forecasting
- Management of local government debt
- Public pensions
- Financial analysis of public budgets
- Social equity budgeting
- Financing of subgovernment structures
- Financials of economic development
- Law enforcement budgeting
- Managing and organizing budget offices
- Transportation and infrastructure finance

Authors interested in discussing book project ideas on these and other public budgeting topics are encouraged to contact series general editor Bruce D. McDonald, III, Old Dominion University, at bmcdonal@odu.edu.

RECENTLY PUBLISHED BOOKS

Holding Government to Account
Democracy and the National Audit Office
Henry C Midgley, Laurence Ferry, and Aileen D Murphie

Managing Public Pension Plans
Decisions, Challenges, and Reforms
Gang Chen, Trang Hoang and Carol Ebdon

MANAGING PUBLIC PENSION PLANS

Decisions, Challenges, and Reforms

Gang Chen, Trang Hoang, and Carol Ebdon

Routledge
Taylor & Francis Group
NEW YORK AND LONDON

Designed cover image: Mihail Minea, Getty Images

First published 2025
by Routledge
605 Third Avenue, New York, NY 10158

and by Routledge
4 Park Square, Milton Park, Abingdon, Oxon OX14 4RN

Routledge is an imprint of the Taylor & Francis Group, an informa business

Open Access for Chapter 2 was funded by University at Albany, SUNY. Open Access for Chapter 3 was funded by University of Nebraska at Omaha.

Library of Congress Cataloging-in-Publication Data
Names: Chen, Gang (Public Administration) author | Hoang, Trang (Public Administration) author | Ebdon, Carol author
Title: Managing public pension plans : decisions, challenges, and reforms / Gang Chen, Trang Hoang and Carol Ebdon.
Other titles: Decisions, challenges, and reforms
Description: First edition. | New York, NY : Routledge, 2025. |
Series: Routledge Public Budgeting and Finance | Includes bibliographical references and index.
Identifiers: LCCN 2024060806 | ISBN 9781032671178 hbk |
ISBN 9781032671161 pbk | ISBN 9781032671185 ebk
Subjects: LCSH: State governments--Officials and employees--Pensions--United States | Local government--Officials and employees--United States--Pensions | Pensions--United States--States | United States--Officials and employees--Pensions
Classification: LCC JK2474 .C485 2025 | DDC 353.5/492130973--dc23/eng/20250415
LC record available at https://lccn.loc.gov/2024060806

ISBN: 978-1-032-67117-8 (hbk)
ISBN: 978-1-032-67116-1 (pbk)
ISBN: 978-1-032-67118-5 (ebk)

DOI: 10.4324/9781032671185

Typeset in Sabon
by KnowledgeWorks Global Ltd.

Gang Chen dedicates this book to his wife, Amy, and his two wonderful daughters, Lisa and Tina, for their unwavering support and encouragement.
Trang Hoang dedicates this book to her grandmother and mother, for their love and encouragement.
Carol Ebdon dedicates this book to the memory of her parents, Ann and Gerald Rotterdam, for all their love and support.

CONTENTS

List of Figures *xiii*
List of Tables *xv*
Acknowledgments *xvii*

1 Introduction to Public Pension Management 1

Introduction 1
Overview of retirement income in the United States 2
Public pension management 6
A logic model – the "black box" of public pension management 10
Organization of this book 12
References 13

2 A Logic Model Framework for Public Pension Management 17

Introduction 17
Existing framework and our model 18
Goals and outcomes 23
Inputs 25
Outputs and decisions 28
Summary 31
References 32

3 Balancing Goals for Public Pension Plans 37

Overview 37
Sufficiency of pension benefits 38
Affordability of pension costs 40
Sustainability of pension funding 42
Efficiency of asset management 44
Good governance of pension plans 45
Balancing the goals in pension plans 47
Mini case: overview of NYCTRS 48
Summary 51
References 52

4 How Environment, Stakeholders, and Constraints Shape Public Pension Decisions 55

Introduction 55
Environment 55
Stakeholders 60
Constraints 63
Summary 66
References 66

5 Investment Policies and Strategies for Public Pension Funds 71

Introduction 71
Investment policy 72
Asset classes and allocation strategy 75
Investment risk 79
Risk management 82
Investment performance 83
Divestments, ETIs, and ESG investments 84
A simulation of pension fund investment 85
Summary 89
References 90

6 Actuarial Processes and Assumptions in Public Pension Valuations 92

Introduction 92

The actuarial process: an overview 93
A summary of actuarial methods and assumptions used by U.S. public plans 97
A simulation of liabilities, assets, and required contributions 106
Summary 109
Glossary 110
References 112

7 Understanding Benefits Designs and Contributions Policies for Public Pension Plans 113

Introduction 113
Pension benefit decisions 114
Pension benefit formula 115
Eligibility rules for pension benefits 117
Adequacy of pension benefits and budget considerations 121
Pension contributions 129
Summary 136
References 137

8 Pathways to Public Pension Reforms 141

Current challenges and the path to reform 141
Internal factors 142
External factors 148
Decision-makers and stakeholders 149
Legal constraints and the role of the judiciary 150
Pension reforms 151
Summary 161
Mini case – state pension reforms in Illinois 162
Mini case – pension reforms at the local level – the case of the City of Omaha Police and Fire Retirement System (COPFRS) 164
References 167
Appendix A. Frequency of Pension Reforms by Types (2005–2023) 171

9 Defined Contribution, Cash-Balance, and Hybrid Plans in the Public Sector 172

Introduction 172
Features of DC, cash-balance, and hybrid plans 173
Advantages and disadvantages 175
Current status of DC plans in the public sector 177
Current status of risk-sharing, cash-balance, and hybrid plans in the public sector 179
Contingent employee contribution rates 179
Contingent cost-of-living adjustments 180
Cash-balance plans 181
DB-DC hybrid plans 181
Challenges in the transition from DB to other plans 183
References 185

10 Assessing the Impact and Trade-Offs of Public Pension Reforms 187

Introduction 187
Sufficiency of pension benefits 188
Affordability of pension costs 190
Sustainability of pension funding 194
Efficiency of asset management 196
Good governance of pension plans 198
Conclusion 200
References 201

11 Key Lessons and Emerging Issues in Public Pension Management 204

Introduction 204
Key takeaways 204
Emerging issues in the post-COVID era 208
Looking ahead 212
References 214

Index 216

FIGURES

5.1 U.S. Public Pension Plan Investments in All Asset Classes 78
5.2 U.S. Public Pension Plan Investments in Alternative Asset Classes 80
5.3 Distribution of Annual Asset Returns Based on the Hypothetical Portfolio 88
5.4 Distribution of the End-of-Tenth-Year Return 89
6.1 Actuarial Cost Methods Used by U.S. Public Pension Plans 98
6.2 Distribution of Asset Smoothing Period Used by U.S. Public Plans 101
6.3 Distribution of UAAL Amortization Period Used by U.S. Public Plans 101
6.4 Amortization Methods Used by U.S. Public Plans 102
6.5 Distribution of Blended Discount Rate Used by U.S. Public Plans 104
6.6 Distribution of Expected Rate of Return Used by U.S. Public Plans 104
6.7 Distribution of Inflation Rate Assumption Used by U.S. Public Plans 105
6.8 Simulation of an Individual Employee's Normal Cost 107
6.9 Simulation of an Individual Employee's Actuarial Accrued Liability 107
6.10 Required Contribution Rates under Various Funding Policies in an Asset Shock Scenario 108

6.11 Funded Ratios under Various Funding Policies in an Asset Shock Scenario 109
7.1 Benefits Factors for Employees in CalPERS 118
7.2 The Percentage of Pension Plans that Provide Social Security Coverage 121
7.3 State and Local Public Pension Revenues (2000–2014) (Presented in Billions of Dollars) 129
7.4 State Public Pension Revenues (2015–2022) 130
7.5 Local Public Pension Revenues (2015–2022) 130
7.6 Annual Contribution in the Florida Retirement System (2001–2022) 133
7.7 Average Actuarially Determined Contributions (ADC) and ADC Paid (2001–2022) 134
8.1 Normal Cost Rate (% of Payroll) from 2001 to 2021 144
8.2 Normal Cost Rate by Level of Administering Government 145
8.3 Normal Cost Rate by Employment Group 145
8.4 Required Contribution by Administering Government Type (2001–2021) 146
8.5 Pension Discount Rate (2001–2022) 150
8.6 State Pension Reform (2005–2023) 152
9.1 A Continuum of Risk-Sharing Arrangements in Public Pension Plans 174

TABLES

2.1 The Logic Model 21
3.1 Evaluation of Public Pension Plans' Replacement Ratios by Urban Institute 40
3.2 Goals of Public Pension Management 47
4.1 Inputs – Environment 56
4.2 Inputs – Stakeholders 60
4.3 Inputs – Constraints 64
5.1 Asset Allocation Targets (CRPTF) 74
5.2 List of Asset Classes Used by U.S. Public Pension Funds 76
5.3 2023 Survey of Capital Market Assumptions for Multiemployer Pension Plans 82
5.4 Asset Class Performance Benchmarks for CRPTF 84
5.5 Plan Asset Allocation and Capital Market Assumptions 86
5.6 Capital Market Assumptions – Asset Class Correlation Matrix 87
7.1 Employee Groups and FAS (Texas ERS) 115
7.2 Benefit Multipliers 117
7.3 Retirement Age and Full Retirement Requirements 118
7.4 Years of Services 119
7.5 Retirement Rules 119
7.6 Vesting Requirements 120
7.7 Legal Protections of Pension Benefits 124
8.1 Logic Model for Pension Reform 142

8.2 New York State and Local Retirement System Comparison of Employees' Retirement System (ERS) Benefits by Tiers 154
8.3 Pension Reform in the State Retirement System of Illinois 164
8.4 Pension Reform in City of Omaha Police and Firefighter Retirement System 166

Appendix A. Frequency of Pension Reforms by Types (2005–2023) 171
9.1 Advantages and Disadvantages of DB and DC Plans 175
9.2 Plan Types in PPD Plans (2019) 177
9.3 Key Features of Selected Cash-Balance Plans in the Public Sector 182
9.4 Key Features of Selected Hybrid Plans in the Public Sector 183
10.1 Effects of Public Pension Reforms 188

ACKNOWLEDGMENTS

We would like to express our sincere gratitude to the anonymous reviewers of this book, whose insights and feedback were invaluable in shaping its content and direction. Special thanks go to our editors at Routledge, who provided clear guidance and support throughout the manuscript preparation and publishing process. Our deepest appreciation goes to University at Albany, SUNY and the University of Nebraska Foundation for their generous grant, which made this work possible. We are also grateful to our colleagues and mentors at the Association for Budgeting and Financial Management (ABFM), whose expertise and encouragement were instrumental in the development of this book. Thank you all for your invaluable contributions.

1

INTRODUCTION TO PUBLIC PENSION MANAGEMENT

Introduction

In the United States, state and local governments establish employee retirement systems to provide pension benefits to public employees. According to the Annual Survey of Public Pensions (Census, 2023), there were 309 state-administered and 4,257 locally administered pension systems in 2023, covering 36 million members. Members include general-purpose government employees, public school teachers and administrators, police officers, and firefighters. Additionally, one retirement system may contain more than one pension plan that provides benefits to different employee groups.

These pension plans are funded by government contributions, member contributions, and investment returns generated from pension funds invested in capital markets. In 2023, state and local governments contributed $217 billion, while government employees contributed $69 billion to these systems (Census, 2023). Government contributions to pension systems come from the government budget. Future pension benefits promised to public employees are liabilities to the government and are backed by the government's taxing power. Therefore, effective management of these public pension plans is essential for ensuring fiscal sustainability for governments and retirement security for public employees. This book explains the decisions, challenges, and reforms associated with effectively managing these public pension plans.

In this chapter, we first introduce the various sources of retirement income for American workers, highlighting the role of public pension plans

DOI: 10.4324/9781032671185-1

in providing benefits for public employees. We then discuss the governance structures and current issues and challenges that we will explore further in the book. Additionally, we present the logic model, which we will use in this book to explain public pension plan management. Finally, we provide an overview of the chapters included in this book.

Overview of retirement income in the United States

In the United States, income for retirees mostly comes from three sources: Social Security; employer-sponsored pensions, including defined benefit (DB), defined contribution (DC), cash-balance, or hybrid plans; and private savings, including Individual Retirement Accounts (IRAs), state-facilitated retirement saving programs, and other non-IRA savings such as investments, home equity, annuities, etc. (Anguelov et al., 2012; Myers, 2020).

Social Security

The first source for retirement income is the federal Social Security system, which is funded by federal payroll taxes (6.2% for the employer and 6.2% for the employee in 2024). Social Security provides benefits to most public- and private-sector employees, covering about 96% of the jobs in the country (SSA, 2024a). Some state and local government employees are not covered by Social Security due to agreements between their state and the federal government. Government employees who are not covered by Social Security usually receive higher pension benefits from their government employer.

Social Security benefits are progressive (CBPP, 2024), meaning that they provide relatively greater benefit security to individuals with lower income levels. Nearly 60% of beneficiaries aged 65 or older rely on Social Security for at least 50% of their retirement income (SSA, 2024a), but the sufficiency of Social Security benefits varies by income levels. For example, a worker with annual earnings of $29,813 at age 65 would receive Social Security benefits of around $15,477 per year when they reach retirement, replacing over half of their previous earnings. In contrast, a worker with a higher annual income of $163,084 at the same age would receive $41,201 in Social Security benefits, which replaces nearly 25% of their prior income (CBPP, 2024). Social Security benefits are calculated based on Average Indexed Monthly Earnings (AIME), which represent the monthly average of the highest 35 years of earnings, adjusted – or "indexed" – to account for increases in general wage levels (SSA, 2024b). The AIME is then applied to the Primary Insurance Amount (PIA) formula, where different portions of the AIME are multiplied by three percentages to compute the benefit amount.

For instance, in 2024, the PIA is the sum of (1) 90% of the first $1,174 of AIME, (2) 32% of the AIME portion between $1,174 and $7,078, and (3) 15% of any AIME exceeding $7,078 (SSA, 2024c). This tiered approach to the calculation ensures the progressive nature of Social Security benefits.

Employer-sponsored pension plans

DB plans

The second source of retirement income comes from employer-sponsored pension plans. A Congressional Research Service (CRS) report (Isaacs et al., 2024) shows that 72% of civilian workers in the United States have access to and 56% of them participated in employer-sponsored pension plans. DB and DC are the two major types of employer-sponsored pension plans. In the public sector, most state and local government employees are covered primarily by DB pension plans, while in the private sector, DC plans such as 401(k) plans are more common.

In a DB plan, benefits are calculated by a benefit formula, which usually takes into account the years of service, the final average salary, and a multiplier. For example, if the benefit multiplier is 2% and the final average salary is based on the last five years before retirement, a plan member who works for 30 years will receive 60% (2% multiplied by 30) of their average salary in the last five years as their starting annual pension benefit. Most DB plans also provide postretirement benefit adjustments, called cost-of-living adjustments (COLAs), to help pension benefits keep up with inflation. If the plan also has a 2% automatic COLA, this person's benefit will increase by 2% every year; if the plan's COLA is linked to inflation, the benefit adjustments will track the inflation rate.

In the United States, 86% of public-sector employees have access to a DB plan while 39% have access to DC plans (Isaacs et al., 2024). While DB plans provide secure benefits because of the benefit formula and COLA adjustments, this benefit security comes with the disadvantage of a lack of mobility and flexibility. If plan members leave the plan before reaching a certain number of working years, called the "vesting period," they may lose a portion of their benefits. In contrast, DC plans offer more flexibility and mobility, making them an attractive option for workers who prioritize these plan features.

DC plans

A DC plan is another major type of employer-sponsored pension plan. In a DC plan, the employer only promises the regular contribution amounts to the pension plan, but not the final pension benefit amounts. For example, if the employer agrees to contribute 6% of an employee's salary, and the employee is also required to contribute 6%, the total annual contributions to the employee's retirement account would amount to 12% of their salary. These contributions will be maintained in these accounts and will generate investment returns based on the investment options provided by the employer and chosen by the individual employee. Contribution amounts grow as salaries increase, and investment returns are reinvested to gain compounded interest. When the employee retires, the balance in their retirement account is converted to annual retirement income. If the employee switches jobs before retirement age, they can transfer their accumulated funds to another DC plan or a similar retirement account.

In the United States, most private-sector pension plans are DC plans, commonly referred to as 401(k) plans, while the majority of public employees are covered by DB plans. In 2022, 86% of state and local government employees had access to a DB pension plan, while only 15% of private-sector workers had access to a DB plan (Zook, 2024). However, a growing number of state and local governments now offer DC plans, cash-balance plans, or DB-DC hybrid plans as either supplementary or primary pension options for their employees (Munnell et al., 2014). Cash-balance or DB-DC hybrid plans will be discussed in later chapters.

Private savings

Besides Social Security and employer-sponsored pension plans, the third source for retirement income is an individual's own personal savings or income earnings. One of the important tools for retirement savings in the United States is the IRA, which provides tax advantages to encourage personal saving for retirement income. The two most common types of IRAs are traditional IRAs and Roth IRAs. With traditional IRAs, contributions are tax-deductible, but withdrawals from the accounts are taxable. In contrast, with Roth IRAs, contributions are not tax-deductible, but qualified distributions or withdrawals are not taxable (IRS, 2024). The 2024 contribution limits for both traditional and Roth IRAs range from $7,000 to $8,000, depending on age (IRS, 2024).

Participation in and contributions to IRAs are entirely voluntary. A CRS report (Myers, 2020) shows that in 2019, 25.4% of households had an IRA account, with a median balance of $70,000 and an average balance of $253,088. However, the participation rate and account balance vary significantly by income level. Among households with an income greater than $125,000, 54.2% had IRAs with an average balance of $405,000. In contrast, for the lowest quintile (less than $30,000 annual income), only 6.7% had IRAs, with an average balance of $95,306, highlighting significant inequity in retirement savings in the United States.

Most contributions to IRAs come from rollovers from workplace pension plans, while overall contributions to IRAs remain low (Holden, 2023; Isaacs et al., 2024). The generally low levels of participation and savings, along with the inequity in retirement savings, raise concerns about retirement security. One study (Myers, 2020) found that the level of retirement income satisfaction varies greatly across wealth groups. In the lowest net worth quintile, 64.1% of households with IRAs rate their perceived retirement income as "adequate," compared with only 49.1% of households without IRAs. Additionally, a 2018 National Financial Capability Study (Lin et al., 2018) reported that 51% of Americans worry they will run out of money in retirement.

Financial security and the importance of public pension plans

When examining the adequacy of retirement income, a useful measurement to consider is the replacement rate, which is the ratio of postretirement income to preretirement income. For example, if the replacement rate is 90%, it means that the annual retirement income is 90% of the annual earnings before retirement, or in other words, the retirement income can "replace" 90% of the preretirement earnings. Most financial advisors recommend that a replacement rate of 75–80% is an appropriate retirement income level (Peng, 2008; Young & Theodore, 2023).

According to recent research (Burkhalter & Rose, 2024), the replacement rate for Social Security benefits at normal retirement age varies from 27.2 to 76.4%, depending on the level of income. For individuals in the lowest income quantile, the replacement rate can be as high as 70–80%. For those with median to high incomes, the replacement rate is around 30–40%, indicating that Social Security alone is not sufficient for retirement income.

Public-sector employees in the United States often have more secure and sufficient pension benefits compared to their private-sector counterparts. Assuming a 2% benefit factor, a DB public pension plan can provide up to a 60% replacement rate for a public employee with 30 years of service in the government. When combining this 60% replacement rate from public pensions with the assumed 30–40% replacement rate from Social Security, this hypothetical public employee can achieve a sufficient and stable retirement income.

Due to the significance of public pension benefits as the main retirement income for state and local government retirees, the substantial impact of pension contributions on government budgets, and the critical importance of pension plan liabilities to fiscal sustainability, this book focuses on the public pension plans sponsored by state and local governments. The next sections will provide an overall discussion of public pension management, including governance structures and the current issues for public pension management.

Public pension management

Pension system governance

Public DB pension plans are overseen by a board or individual that has a fiduciary responsibility to make decisions that are in the best interest of the plan participants. There are three standard structures that are used for pension governance. In the first governance structure, a board provides oversight for both administration and investments. In this single-board approach, the board typically has an investment committee that focuses on investment performance and options and recommends actions to the board as appropriate. This is by far the most common governance structure. One study found that, as of 2017, 74% of plans have a single pension board. The second governance structure is to have two separate boards: one to oversee investments and the other for administrative oversight. As of 2017, 16% of plans used this structure. The third governance structure operates with a sole individual fiduciary. This is far less common, with only 9% of plans having this governance method (Aubry & Crawford, 2019).

Pension boards vary in size. The range in one study was from 5 to 19 board members, with 33% of boards having between eight to ten members (Aubry & Crawford, 2019). The composition of pension boards also varies between plans. Members may bring different important skills, such as investment, legal, or actuarial expertise. Pension board members also represent various stakeholder groups and may be elected or appointed. For example, a board might have several members who are appointed by the government, such as elected officials and/or government officials (these may be considered ex officio), members who are elected by the membership or the public, and members who are appointed by the board. "Adequate stakeholder representation – i.e., plan participants, government officials, and general public members with a voting presence on the board – contributes to board efficacy by promoting board legitimacy to various stakeholders" (Aubry & Crawford, 2019, p. 3). As of 2018, one study found that 54% of board members were participants of the pension plan, 31% represented the general public, and 15% were ex officio government representatives (Aubry & Crawford, 2019).

Boards and sole fiduciaries commonly have authority over decisions related to investments, such as developing an investment policy, determining goals for allocation of assets across various classes of investments, and hiring/firing investment managers. Determining actuarial assumptions is another important area of decision making for pension system fiduciaries. These assumptions are estimates about demographic and economic trends that are used to project assets and liabilities of the plan over time to understand the plan's fiscal condition. Key actuarial assumptions include, for example, the expected rate of return on investments, annual payroll growth rates, and mortality rates. Boards may also play a role in other activities, such as determining COLAs to pension payments and approving disability retirements (Brainard & Brown, 2019).

Pension systems often have staff to provide administrative duties such as paying pension benefits, accounting and legal functions, monitoring investment performance, and preparing reports for board review. Boards may also hire external managers and consultants. For example, external actuarial firms commonly assist in developing and recommending appropriate actuarial assumptions to the board. Outside legal expertise may also be sought on occasion (Aubry & Crawford, 2019).

Many pension systems also contract for investment management. Historically, public pension plans invested in relatively safe and straightforward assets such as government bonds that could be managed internally. Beginning in the 1980s, plans began to allocate growing shares of their assets to other investments such as equities and alternative investments. With this transition, plans have increasingly hired external asset managers. One study found, for example, that the average number of external managers used by public pension plans increased from 28 in 2006 to 55 in 2018 (although there are variations between plans). About one-quarter of plans continue to manage some assets internally (Aubry & Wandrei, 2020).

Government pension plan sponsors also play an important role in public pension plans. The sponsoring governments establish the retirement system and make decisions about the pension benefits. They also generally set the employer and employee contribution policies, while the plan actuaries recommend the actuarially determined contributions (ADC). Elected officials may also serve as ex officio pension board members and/or appoint board members (Brainard & Brown, 2020).

Some state and local governments use DC plans in addition to, or in place of, DB plans. While these DC plans may be overseen by boards, many are within the purview of a government official such as the finance or human resource director. One study of DC plans in one state with relatively small local governments found that the governments typically hired third-party service providers to administer the plans (e.g., local banks or insurance companies). The third-party providers provided the investment options to the participants, provided regular reports, and offered financial education to employees. The government oversight role was fairly limited (Chen et al., 2013).

Public pension plan governance is challenging. The decisions made by board members have vitally important short- and long-term consequences for the plan participants, government, and taxpayers. For example, poor investment decisions can lead to decreased assets that may ultimately require pension benefit cuts that reduce a retiree's standard of living or necessitate working longer than expected, and/or employer contribution increases that can have a negative ripple effect on other government services.

While board members may have different areas of expertise, they are expected to become knowledgeable about the complex areas of actuarial assumptions and investment practices. In addition, there are changes such as volatile financial markets, changes in financial reporting standards, and new laws that may impact pension governance, and boards are also navigating tensions between goals and constituencies that may be at odds. It takes time and training to acquire an understanding of these factors, but the average tenure for board members is only six years (Aubry & Crawford, 2019), which reduces the important institutional knowledge needed for pension oversight. Providing resources to assist in pension governance is therefore critical.

Challenges and current issues of the public pension management

Public-sector retirement systems, along with their pension boards, administrators, and sponsored governments, face multiple financial and management challenges. On the one hand, the public retirement systems serve an important goal of providing sufficient and adequate retirement benefits for their employees. Pension benefits play an important role in addressing the public- and private-sector wage gap, which helps state and local governments to recruit and retain talent. On the other hand, state and local governments, facing revenue constraints and general trends of budget austerity, find it increasingly difficult to keep up with the rising costs in their public pension systems. From 2002 to 2015, pension contributions as a share of state budgets more than doubled, from 2.3% in 2002 to 4.8% in 2015 (NASRA, 2018). Moreover, state unfunded pension liabilities continued to rise, reaching over $1.4 trillion in 2016 (Pew Charitable Trusts, 2018). At the same time, pension contributions directly compete with other government spending priorities. This led to some state and local governments not adequately paying their contributions to the pension systems, which contributed to the alarming growth of pension debt. In addition, the low market returns with the decline in the stock market during 2000–2002, and the economic recession of 2007–2009, sharply affected the funding level of many pension plans (Boyd & Yin, 2017; Norcross & Biggs, 2010; Peng & Wang, 2017; Seligman, 2013).

Facing rising concerns over the financial sustainability of public retirement systems, many state and local governments have implemented pension reforms to slow down the growth of pension costs and unfunded liabilities. Those movements started in the early 2000s, but there were drastic increases in the number of states implementing pension reforms following the 2007–2009 economic recession. Reforms vary in design, but generally target pension reductions, including decreases/cuts or suspension of COLAs, contribution increases, raising full retirement eligibility (i.e., retirement age, length of service, vesting period, etc.), and the adoption of DC, cash-balance, or hybrid pension plans. Reforms might help the states to improve funding levels to an extent. Pension unfunded liabilities decreased to $1.25 trillion by the end of fiscal year 2019 and the average funded ratio increased to 71% (Pew Charitable Trusts, 2021). Boosted with some federal funds and unprecedented high market returns (above 20% in many cases), state pension funds decreased unfunded liabilities to below $1.0 trillion and increased the funded ratio to 82% in fiscal year 2021 (Pew Charitable Trusts, 2023). Despite that, the volatility of the financial markets and budget austerity continue to raise concerns about pension contributions and funding status.

Notwithstanding, pension reforms did not come without a cost. While pension reforms might have addressed some fiscal concerns, they undoubtedly have made public pension benefits less sufficient and less secure than they were before. This phenomenon has implications for the retirement security of public employees and overall issues of recruitment and retention for the governments. In terms of the former, pension benefits have been part of the traditional three-legged stool discussed earlier of employer pensions, Social Security, and personal savings. A reduction of pension benefits can make it harder for public employees to maintain their financial security upon retirement, especially in systems where governments are not part of the Social Security system. In terms of the latter, some research has found negative impacts of pension reforms on worker retention in the public sector (Goldhaber et al., 2017; Gorina & Hoang, 2020; Lewis & Stoycheva, 2016). Reduction of pension benefits can increase worker dissatisfaction and raise equity issues among different generations or different groups of the public-sector workforce. Also, DB pension plans have been considered golden handcuffs to help the public sector retain its workers.

The adoption of alternative forms of benefits (such as DC or cash-balance plans) could negatively affect workers' retention. As some governments continue facing hiring difficulties, changes to pension benefits make it even more challenging to recruit and retain employees.

A logic model – the "black box" of public pension management

To explain the current issues with public pension systems, previous studies have identified different factors responsible for the growing unfunded pension liabilities and the decreasing pension funding ratio. For example, public-sector unions have been blamed for generous pension benefit packages and the increase in pension unfunded liabilities (Frandsen & Webb, 2019; Kearney, 2003; Zax & Ichniowski, 1988). In response to this, many states (i.e., Wisconsin, Michigan, Alaska, Oklahoma) have taken steps to curb collective bargaining and the union power (Munnell, 2012). Other studies identified the main cause of the public pension problems as stemming from the undisciplined fiscal actions taken by state and local governments by forgoing, delaying, or not fully paying their ADC (Hoang & Goodman, 2018; Munnell, 2012; Splinter, 2017). In practice, some pension systems are required to increase their pension contribution or make one-time payments to make up for the funding gap. Other scholars point to decreases in investment returns (some due to economic crises) or risky investment actions taken by public pension plans as driving forces behind the decrease in pension funding ratios (Novy-Marx & Rauh, 2014; Peng & Wang, 2017). On a related point, some research asserts that the structure of the pension discount rate and pension accounting contribute to risky investment strategies, lack of transparency and consistency of pension reporting, and pension funding issues (Allen & Petacchi, 2023; Mortimer & Henderson, 2014; Stalebrink & Donatella, 2021). Still others have criticized the political interests of elected officials in extending pension benefits and politically appointed pension boards who put their own interests above their fiduciary duties to the pension fund when they direct pension fund investments toward in-state economic initiatives (Andonov et al., 2018).

A major problem with this approach to the study of pensions and pension decisions is the lack of a system approach that enables researchers and practitioners to grasp the full complexity of pension management. Those pension concerns (i.e., pension funding, unfunded liabilities, and pension reforms) are multidimensional issues that cannot be adequately addressed by solely addressing one group of stakeholders or one factor. For instance, even though pension funding issues have been a focus of media coverage, legislative discussions, think-tank reports, and academic research, this funding issue is only the tip of the iceberg, or (arguably) one of the most visible outcomes of pension management. There remain other goals that need to be considered and balanced by public pension plans, including the role of public pensions as a tool for recruitment, the financial security of public-sector employees, and the long-term financial sustainability of the pension system. In addition, there are various management actions and multiple groups of stakeholders that either directly or indirectly influence pension management decisions and outcomes. Therefore, looking at solely the public-sector unions or the politically elected officials will not yield the optimal solutions to pension management.

We suggest that, to address current challenges and issues of public retirement systems, the first step is to understand how the systems are managed and the factors that influence pension decisions. With a goal to provide a comprehensive review of pension management, or the "black box" of pension funding issues and reform options, this book introduces a logic model (described in detail in Chapter 2) that describes (1) the legal, political, social, and economic environments of the public pension systems and groups of stakeholders and their influences, (2) pension decisions related to investment strategies, actuarial practices, pension benefits, and contributions, and (3) different goals and outcomes of public pension systems. This logic model will enable readers to understand the ecosystem around public pension management, how pension decisions are made, and will broaden the scope of understanding of pension goals, measurements, and actions. It is not only pension funding but also other important goals that public pension systems have to balance. Not only the public-sector unions and elected officials, but also pension plan administrators, credit rating agencies, state legislatures, courts, standard-setting agencies, and the public play important roles in influencing pension decisions. And it is not only internal decisions (such as setting benefits and contributions) but also the external environment (such as investment markets, economic conditions, and fiscal conditions) that can impact pension outcomes. This system approach to public pension management is critical because it gives the readers (i.e., researchers, pension administrators, pension boards, pension beneficiaries, union leaders, and the public) an overall view of the decision flows within pension systems, who is involved, and the constraints that bind pension decisions.

Furthermore, using real-world case studies, the book explains principles and issues around pension benefits, contributions, investment strategies, and actuarial practices. The logic model, cases, and findings from pension studies shed light on major issues in public pension management, recent reforms as well as the impacts of those reforms on different goals of the public pension systems. While most current books or journal articles have focused on the problems in public pensions, this book sets out to explore the path to more sustainable pension systems. The book also addresses some new topics in public pension management that have emerged in recent years, including actuarial changes, risk management, governments' budgetary stress due to pension costs, and the relationship between pension management and government employment. The book is written using plain language to explain pension management to a wide audience, including pension board members, plan administrators, government officials, legislators and their staff, and researchers, who are interested in public pension research.

Organization of this book

The book is organized as follows. The first two chapters provide some background information about the public pension landscape and our logic model framework. The current chapter offers an overview of retirement income sources in the United States, public pension systems and trends, governance structures, and current challenges and issues. *Chapter 2* synthesizes major themes in public pension research and identifies the shortfalls of the existing frameworks. The chapter moves on to introduce our logic model that illustrates a comprehensive review of the main decisions and influencing factors of pension management and the decision-making process, from the consideration of pension environments and different groups of stakeholders (inputs) to pension decisions (outputs), and how those decisions contribute to the overall pension goals (outcomes).

The following chapters provide a more detailed description and explanation of pension management. *Chapter 3* discusses the five main goals of pension systems, including sufficiency of pension benefits, affordability of pension costs, sustainability of pension funding, efficiency of asset management, and good governance practices. *Chapter 4* describes input factors that may influence decisions: the legal/political/economic environments surrounding the pension system, the groups of stakeholders (government employers, political leaders, various groups of public employees, interest groups (i.e., public-sector unions)), and constraints that pension decision-makers are bound by. *Chapter 5* describes the main components of investment policies, different investment risks and risk management, and the process to measure and assess investment performance. The chapter also discusses current investment trends and special policies on divestments and environmental, social, and governance (ESG). *Chapter 6* describes and explains the actuarial processes and assumptions used by public pension plans to determine their assets, liabilities, funded ratios, and ADC. Actuarial processes are often the most complicated hurdles to understand pension reports and management decisions because they involve complex procedures integrating actuarial models, financial theories, and plan statistics. To assist pension board members, policymakers, and other stakeholders of public plans, as well as researchers, in understanding the actuarial process, this chapter unpacks the major components and explains the key economic and demographic assumptions used in the valuation. *Chapter 7* discusses pension benefits and contributions, and related factors, including legal constraints and the involvement of different groups of stakeholders in the decision-making process. *Chapter 8* describes major challenges of financing public pension retirement systems and the pension reforms implemented by state and local governments in responding to the growth of pension unfunded liabilities. *Chapter 9* focuses on alternative forms of employer-sponsored pension plans, including DC, cash-balance, and DB-DC hybrid plans. *Chapter 10* provides an overall assessment of the impacts of pension reforms on the various goals of pension management, pension governance, benefit levels to employees, and financial responsibilities of state and local governments. The book concludes with *Chapter 11*, which provides lessons learned and some emerging issues for public-sector retirement systems.

References

Allen, A., & Petacchi, R. C. (2023). Preparer opposition and strategic implementation of governmental accounting standards: Evidence from public pension accounting reform. *Management Science*, *69*(7), 4259–4282. https://doi.org/10.1287/mnsc.2022.4515

Andonov, A., Hochberg, Y. V., & Rauh, J. D. (2018). Political representation and governance: Evidence from the investment decisions of public pension funds. *The Journal of Finance*, *73*(5), 2041–2086. https://doi.org/10.1111/jofi.12706

Anguelov, C. E., Iams, H. M., & Purcell, P. J. (2012) *Shifting income sources of the aged.* Social Security Administration Research, Statistics, and Policy Analysis. Retrieved September 17, 2024, from https://www.ssa.gov/policy/docs/ssb/v72n3/v72n3p59.html

Aubry, J.-P., & Crawford, C. V. (2019). *Does public pension board composition impact returns?* Center for Retirement Research Brief, Number 67.

Aubry, J.-P., & Wandrei, K. (2020). *Internal vs. external management for state and local pension plans.* Center for Retirement Research Brief, Number 75.

Boyd, D., & Yin, Y. (2017). *How public pension plan investment risk affects funding and contribution risk.* The Rockefeller Institute of Government State University of New York - Pension Simulation Project. https://doi.org/10.1177/0022146513479002

Brainard, K., & Brown, A. (2019, November). *Overview of public pension governance.* National Association of State Retirement Administrators. https://www.nasra.org/files/Topical%20Reports/Governance%20and%20Legislation/NASRA%20governance%20overview.pdf

Brainard, K., & Brown, A. (2020, May). *Public pension governance stakeholder roles.* National Association of State Retirement Administrators. https://www.

nasra.org/files/Topical%20Reports/Governance%20and%20Legislation/NASRA%20governance%20roles.pdf

Burkhalter, K., & Rose, K. (2024). *Replacement rates for hypothetical retired workers*. Actuarial Note Number 2024.9. https://www.ssa.gov/OACT/NOTES/ran9/an2024-9.pdf

Center on Budget and Policy Priorities (CBPP). (2024). *Policy basics: Top ten facts about Social Security*. https://www.cbpp.org/research/social-security/top-ten-facts-about-social-security

Chen, G., Ebdon, C., Kriz, K., & Laforge, O. M. (2013). The management of defined contribution pension plans in local government. *Public Budgeting and Finance*, *33*(3), 75–95.

Frandsen, B. R., & Webb, M. (2019). Public employee pensions and collective bargaining rights: Evidence from state and local government finances. *Journal of Law, Economics & Policy*, 15, 163.

Goldhaber, D., Grout, C., & Holden, K. L. (2017). Pension structure and employee turnover: Evidence from a large public pension system. *ILR Review*, *70*(4), 976–1007. https://doi.org/10.1177/0019793916678424

Gorina, E., & Hoang, T. (2020). Pension reforms and public sector turnover. *Journal of Public Administration Research and Theory*, *30*(1), 96–112. https://doi.org/10.1093/jopart/muz009

Hoang, T., & Goodman, D. (2018). Public pensions and collective bargaining rights: Evidence from state and local governments. *Public Administration Review*, *78*(5), 772–784. https://doi.org/10.1111/puar.12936

IRS. (2024). *Traditional and Roth IRAs*. https://www.irs.gov/retirement-plans/traditional-and-roth-iras

Isaacs, K. P., Myers, E. A., & Topoleski, J. J. (2024). *Pensions and Individual Retirement Accounts (IRAs): Investment issues*. https://crsreports.congress.gov/product/pdf/R/R47996

Kearney, R. C. (2003). The determinants of state employee compensation. *Review of Public Personnel Administration*, 23(4), 305–322. https://doi.org/10.1177/0734371X03259279

Lewis, G. B., & Stoycheva, R. L. (2016). Does pension plan structure affect turnover patterns? *Journal of Public Administration Research and Theory*, *26*(4), 787–799. https://doi.org/10.1093/jopart/muw035

Lin, J. T., Bumcrot, C., Ulicny, T., Mottola, G., Walsh, G., Ganem, R., Kieffer, C., Lusardi, A., Gatz, J., Larrimore, J., Melford, G., & Zepp, P. (2018). *The state of U.S. financial capability: The 2018 National Financial Capability Study*. https://finrafoundation.org/sites/finrafoundation/files/NFCS-2018-Report-Natl-Findings.pdf

Mortimer, J. W., & Henderson, L. R. (2014). Measuring pension liabilities under GASB statement no. 68. *Accounting Horizons*, *28*(3), 421–454. https://doi.org/10.2308/acch-50710

Munnell, A. H. (2012). *State and local pensions: What now?* Brookings Institution Press.

Munnell, A. H., Aubry, J.-P., & Cafarelli, M. 2014. *Defined contribution plans in the public sector: An update*. https://crr.bc.edu/wp-content/uploads/2014/04/SLP_37_508rev.pdf

Myers, E. A. (2020). *Individual Retirement Account (IRA) ownership: Data and policy issues*. Congressional Research Service (CRS) Report R46635. https://crsreports.congress.gov/product/pdf/R/R46635/3

NASRA. (2018). *NASRA issue brief: State and local government spending on public employee retirement systems*. National Association of State Retirement Administrators, March, 1–5.

Norcross, E., & Biggs, A. (2010). *The crisis in public sector pension plans: A blueprint from reform in New Jersey*. Mercatus Center - George Masion University, 10.

Novy-Marx, R., & Rauh, J. D. (2014). Linking benefits to investment performance in US public pension systems. *Journal of Public Economics*, 116, 47–61. https://doi.org/10.1016/j.jpubeco.2014.01.007

Peng, J. (2008). *State and local pension fund management*. CRC Press/Taylor & Francis Group.

Peng, J., & Wang, Q. (2017). Affordability of public pension benefit: A historical and empirical analysis of US state and local government pension contributions. *Journal of Pension Economics and Finance*, 16(1), 21–42. https://doi.org/10.1017/S1474747215000268

Pew Charitable Trusts. (2018). *The state pension funding gap: 2016*. https://www.pewtrusts.org/en/research-and-analysis/issue-briefs/2018/04/the-state-pension-funding-gap-2016

Pew Charitable Trusts. (2021). *The state pension funding gap: Plans have stabilized in wake of pandemic*. https://www.pewtrusts.org/en/research-and-analysis/issue-briefs/2021/09/the-state-pension-funding-gap-plans-have-stabilized-in-wake-of-pandemic

Pew Charitable Trusts. (2023). *Public retirement systems need sustainable policies to navigate volatile financial markets*. https://www.pewtrusts.org/en/research-and-analysis/issue-briefs/2023/11/public-retirement-systems-need-sustainable-policies-to-navigate-volatile-financial-markets

Seligman, J. S. (2013). State pension funding practices and the great recession of 2007-2009. *Journal of Public Budgeting and Financial Management*, 25(2), 346–390.

Social Security Administration (SSA). (2024a). *Social Security programs in the United States*. https://www.ssa.gov/policy/docs/progdesc/sspus/social-insurance-programs.html

Social Security Administration (SSA). (2024b). *Social Security benefit amounts*. https://www-origin.ssa.gov/oact/COLA/Benefits.html

Social Security Administration (SSA). (2024c). *Primary Insurance Amount*. https://www-origin.ssa.gov/oact/COLA/piaformula.html

Splinter, D. (2017). State pension contributions and fiscal stress. *Journal of Pension Economics and Finance*, 16(1), 65–80. https://doi.org/10.1017/S1474747215000189

Stalebrink, O. J., & Donatella, P. (2021). Public pension governance and opportunistic accounting choice: A politico-economic approach. *The American Review of Public Administration*, 51(3), 227–245. https://doi.org/10.1177/0275074020954397

Urban Institute. (2024). *Project: State and local backgrounders*. https://www.urban.org/policy-centers/cross-center-initiatives/state-and-local-finance-initiative/projects/state-and-local-backgrounders/state-and-local-government-pensions

U.S. Census. (2023). *Annual survey of public pensions: State & local tables*. https://www.census.gov/data/tables/2023/econ/aspp/aspp-historical-tables.html

Young, R., & Theodore, L. (2023, August 3). *How to determine the amount of income you will need at retirement*. T. Rowe Price insights on retirement. https://www.troweprice.com/personal-investing/resources/insights/how-to-determine-amount-of-income-you-will-need-at-retirement.html

Zax, J., & Ichniowski, C. (1988). The effects of public sector unionism on pay, employment, department budgets, and municipal expenditures. In R. B. Freeman & C. Ichniowski (Eds.), *When public sector workers unionize* (pp. 323–364). University of Chicago Press. https://www.nber.org/

books-and-chapters/when-public-sector-workers-unionize/effects-public-sector-unionism-pay-employment-department-budgets-and-municipal-expenditures

Zook, D. (2024). *How do retirement plans for private industry and state and local government workers compare?* https://www.bls.gov/opub/btn/volume-12/how-do-retirement-plans-for-private-industry-and-state-and-local-government-workers-compare.htm

2

A LOGIC MODEL FRAMEWORK FOR PUBLIC PENSION MANAGEMENT

Introduction

Most state and local government employees in the United States are covered by government-sponsored pension plans. As of March 2021, 92% of all state and local government workers had access to a pension plan, with 86% having access to defined benefit (DB) plans, and 75% of those participating in DB plans (CRS, 2022). Not only do employees demand pension benefits, but employers also have incentives to provide pensions to recruit, retain, motivate, and even retire workers (Clark & Schieber, 2004; Koedel et al., 2013). Given that public-sector salaries are generally less competitive than those in the private sector, pension benefits have been identified as one of the critical factors to attract workers and retain public employees with the government (Goldhaber et al., 2017; Lewis & Stoycheva, 2016). Also, pension benefits have fiscal implications for state and local governments. Many public employee retirement systems are currently underfunded – the assets accumulated are not sufficient to meet the pension liabilities over time. To shore up pension funding, government and retirement plan officials often adopt pension reforms to reduce future liabilities and increase pension assets. Despite those efforts, the accrued unfunded liabilities of state DB plans were still around $1 trillion at the end of fiscal year 2021 (Pew Charitable Trusts, 2023).

Even though the importance of public pensions and their funding issues is widely recognized, the systems within which key decisions are made are not well understood by many policymakers and stakeholders. The governance structure, along with the institutions, constraints, processes, and

DOI: 10.4324/9781032671185-2

professional standards, all influence the decisions that are made. These decisions ultimately determine the outcomes of pension systems. Without understanding how these components work together, developing successful reforms and making appropriate decisions that can best fit the needs of employees in the most cost-efficient way would be more difficult.

This chapter builds on current literature to develop a framework for public pension plan management. We use a logic model approach to identify the various **inputs** that influence the decision-makers, the relevant **decisions (outputs)** that are made by pension system trustees and by officials in the administering governments, and the resulting performance **outcomes (or the aligned goals)** for the system. This comprehensive approach will assist in scholarly efforts to build and test theories related to pension systems. In addition, it will benefit practitioners who are dealing with pension issues and seeking solutions to enhance system sustainability.

Existing framework and our model

There is a robust literature on the management of public pension plans. The central theme in the literature is the funding level of the plans, that is, the appropriate funding level and how to ensure that plans can meet those funding targets. Prior research focused on funding-related topics because many pension plans have been seriously underfunded and the sponsoring governments have faced challenges in meeting their contribution requirements. Around this theme, previous studies use frameworks from different fields to explain the contributing factors to plans' funding performance. The frameworks in prior studies include political economy (Mitchell & Hsin, 1994; Norcross & Smith, 2021), institutional theory (Matkin et al., 2019; Stalebrink, 2017; Stalebrink & Donatella, 2021), and cutback management (Chen, 2018). These frameworks generally fall under two streams of literature according to the types of contributing factors they focus on.

The first stream of literature follows the political economy perspective and focuses on the role of the political system (law, politics, governments) in determining pension funding decisions. This approach views pension funding performance as an outcome of a political process in which the laws function as the constraints while government officials and elected politicians make decisions to maximize their interests within those constraints – a central tenet of Public Choice Theory (Schneider & Damanpour, 2002). Employee unions and the general public are the interest groups in this process, in which the former are more likely to advocate and negotiate for more generous pension benefits on behalf of their union members, and the latter are more likely to be against benefit increases as they ultimately have to foot the bill to fund the pension systems through their tax dollars.

The underfunding issue is found to be caused by laws that prevent benefit decreases and self-interest-maximizing public officials who do not have a long-term vision of the sustainability of pension plans and often delay or make inadequate pension contributions to the system under fiscal stress conditions. This is best summarized in Norcross and Smith (2021):

> With constitutional or legislative guarantees for funding their public pension, public employees lobby for increased benefits even when they might understand that the state or local government will struggle to procure the resources to meet those promises in the future. With their legal protection, they can rely on their lobbying power vis-à-vis the general public to help ensure that any future funding gaps will fall on future taxpayers at the local or federal level and not result in reduced benefits for themselves. (p. 2)

Empirical studies follow this approach and use the funded ratio or the government's contribution rate as the outcome of public pension policies. Those studies find that pension benefits are highly protected by state laws and union contracts and that government management capacity, public employee union density, legislative professionalism, political ideology, and public opinions/attention significantly influence pension funding and performance (Coggburn & Kearney, 2010; Glaeser & Ponzetto, 2014; Thom & Randazzo, 2015). Besides funding, prior studies find that these political-economic factors also explain investment decisions and discount rates in pension plans (Peng & Wang, 2017; Stalebrink, 2014; Stalebrink & Donatella, 2021).

The second stream of literature mostly derives from the field of public financial management. In this stream, researchers pay special attention to the interaction between public pension funding and the finances of the governments that sponsor these plans. The difference between this approach and the political economy approach is the focus on financial management and fiscal rules within the government. This approach assumes that public pension decisions interact with other fiscal decisions made by the government, while the government contributions to pension plans compete with other spending needs for public services. Therefore, pension plan underfunding problems will lead to great fiscal issues for the government. This is best summarized in Peng (2008):

> The management of public pension plans has a direct impact on the overall fiscal health of government finance. Increases in pension contribution reduce the amount available for other popular government services, such as education, healthcare, and public safety, and thus, has

> the potential to contribute to or exacerbate fiscal pressure on state and local governments… Therefore, understanding how pension contribution is determined and what factors will cause it to decrease or increase over time is critical to understanding the linkage between public pension plans and the rest of government finance. (p. 5)

Research in the field of public budgeting and financial management has found empirical evidence that pension underfunding, just like issuing debt, is one way to create a "fiscal illusion" so that the government can reduce the cost of public services, postpone the cost to the future, and gain public support for its current budget (Hoang & Maher, 2022; Peng, 2004). Studies also demonstrate that when facing fiscal stress, governments have a tendency to cut pension benefits, adjust their actuarial assumptions, and reduce employers' contributions to pension plans (Chen, 2018; Eaton & Nofsinger, 2004). Fiscal constraints and the dynamic of revenue sources can also impact pension plan management practices; more stringent withdrawal rules from budget stabilization funds, or stricter balanced budget requirements and debt limits, or city fiscal autonomy and reliance on property taxes are found to be negatively associated with pension contributions and funding ratios (Gorina, 2018; St. Clair, 2013; Wang, 2017).

In this book, we aim to connect these two streams of literature and use a logic model approach (the inputs, outputs, and goals/outcomes) to explain decision making in public pension plans (see Table 2.1). The retirement system, which is divided into the categories of pension system and administering government, is the focus of this logic model framework. The retirement system has several goals and outcomes to pursue. Those goals include the sufficiency of pension benefits, the affordability of pension costs, the sustainability of pension funding, the efficiency of asset management, and the good governance of pension plans. Several key decisions are made by different decision-makers within the retirement systems, including benefits, contributions, investments, and actuarial assumptions. These decisions are influenced by the political and economic environments, as well as the stakeholder motivations, and are constrained by laws and other rules under which the pension plans operate.

The use of the logic model framework to explain the management of public pension plans overcomes several shortcomings in previous discussions. First, using the logic model, our study aims to provide a broader consideration of pension funding goals and decisions. In prior studies, the outcome of pension plan management has been too narrowly defined to only focus on the funding level (see a review in Davidyan, 2021), which leads to a series of studies looking into the determinants of the pension funding ratio, while ignoring the fact that the pension funding level might

TABLE 2.1 The Logic Model

	Inputs			*Outputs*	*Outcomes (goals)*
	Environment	**Stakeholders**	**Constraints**	**Decisions**	**Performance**
Pension system	Capital markets Fiscal health of system Political embeddedness	Administrators pension Trustees Advisors	Regulations and laws related to investments and actuarial practices	Investments Actuarial practices	Sufficiency Affordability
Administering government	Fiscal health of government Credit ratings Political ideology Electoral politics	Participating employers Elected officials Unions/employees Retirees taxpayers	State laws on benefit protection Court rules on benefits Union contracts	Benefits Contributions	Sustainability Efficiency Good governance

be an interactive consequence of various stakeholders and their management or fiscal decisions. For employees or union representatives, the level of pension benefits is an even more visible or implicit criterion for them to consider in labor contracts or negotiations. For governments who are under tight fiscal austerity or fiscal stress, the fluctuation of pension contributions might attract more of their attention since those contributions directly compete with other government spending obligations. Also, the increase or decrease of the pension funding ratio is highly correlated with the ups and downs of financial markets (or external factors) and might not always precisely reflect the management and funding decisions of the plan sponsors. For instance, a decrease in pension funding level in the second quarter of 2020 and an increase in pension funding at the end of 2021 were largely affected by the fluctuation of the capital markets and do not indicate poor or good management decisions. In this case, failing to consider pension investment decisions, such as investment portfolio or asset allocations, might lead to misunderstanding the causes of pension underfunding.

Second, by presenting a comprehensive consideration of the goals of pension systems and their stakeholders, our framework illustrates the complex trade-offs or balancing act, along with varying power dynamics, in the pension decision-making process. On the one hand, public pension systems exist to meet government needs to provide employment benefits to recruit and retain employees. A competitive pension package can help governments attract a skilled workforce and keep them in the public sector. On the other hand, governments need to consider the cost of funding pension systems, in relation to other funding needs. In addition, pension stakeholders (pension beneficiaries, active employees, public-sector unions, pension administrators, elected officials, the general public, etc.) have different opinions toward public pensions, and through direct or indirect mechanisms, they want to influence pension decisions to serve their interests.

Furthermore, the constraints and resources have been studied in prior studies as contributing factors. However, the relationships between those factors and the funding performance have been in large part considered a "black box." That is, we know that these are contributing factors, but do not clearly understand at which point, to which stakeholders, and in what decision(s) the factors are effective. Our framework enables us to overcome these shortcomings of previous studies while providing a more comprehensive understanding of pension outcomes, different pension stakeholders and their interests, the interaction of complex pension management and funding decisions, and a broader consideration of the pension's internal and external environment.

The following section provides an overview of the major factors of the pension logic model framework. More detailed discussions of pension goals, inputs, and decisions (benefits, contributions, investments, and actuarial practices) are presented in the following chapters.

Goals and outcomes

In this section, we focus on describing the five main goals of pension systems. These include sufficiency, affordability, sustainability, efficiency, and good governance as the goals of decision making in public pension systems. The priorities among these goals may vary over time and across plans.

Sufficiency of pension benefits

Sufficiency is the goal to provide enough retirement benefits to public employees. For employees, retirees, and their union representatives who are involved with pension plan decision making, improving or maintaining the sufficiency of pension benefits is their primary goal. Political officials, depending on their ideological position, might also have an agenda to maintain a certain level of pension benefit sufficiency.

Sufficiency of pension benefits can be measured in various ways through the examination of normal cost, the replacement rate, or the lifetime take-home income. The normal cost, which is the cost to cover benefits accrued in a single year, and the cost-of-living adjustments (COLAs), are used to measure the level of pension benefits (Munnell, 2012). Two other related concepts are replacement rate and lifetime take-home income. The replacement rate is the ratio of postretirement income to preretirement income. A higher replacement rate means that pension income is able to replace a greater portion of a person's annual income before he or she retires and thus helps to maintain their quality of life. Lifetime take-home income is concerned with the long-term net income for a particular member who participates in a pension plan. Most public plans require plan members to make contributions when they are working. Lifetime take-home income considers both the contributions a member has made when they are working and the total benefits they receive after they retire, discounted to a present value.

Affordability of pension costs

Affordability of pension cost is about keeping the annual employer contribution amount at a reasonable level, especially when compared to the government's budget. Pension plans require government employers to make annual contributions that are calculated by plan actuaries, called actuarially determined contributions (ADC).[1] Most governments are required to fully pay ADC, but some experience legislative constraints on the amount of ADC paid (especially in the case of increases). Some governments are able to smooth the payments from ADC over a number of years, but postponing ADC will likely reduce the funding level and lead to higher contributions in future years. The affordability of employers' costs is measured by the ADC rate (often scaled by payrolls or in some cases by general fund revenues). The higher the ratio, the more expensive it is to fund pension systems.

Since government officials have to balance their budgets while meeting other spending needs, they are mostly concerned about the affordability of pension costs. Citizens are also concerned about the pension cost because it can crowd out other public services or require extra tax dollars. Regulators from governments or elsewhere are concerned about the possibility that pension costs may lead to fiscal stress. When assessing a government's credit rating, rating agencies (such as Standard & Poor's) pay attention to the ADC, especially when the increases in ADC outpace the financial capacity to pay for those obligations.

Sustainability of pension funding

Sustainability of pension plan funding is about keeping sufficient assets to cover the plan's liabilities. Pension liabilities come from the future benefits that are promised to employees. Pension assets come from contributions from governments and members as well as investment returns. The ratio of assets to liabilities, called the funded ratio, is the measurement of sustainability of pension plan funding.

Sustainability of pension funding matters for all stakeholders of pension plans, although sustainability is more of a long-term goal than a short-term concern. When the pension funding ratio decreases, a plan will have sustainability concerns but will not experience immediate consequences as long as pension contributions and benefits are kept at the previous levels. However, when the funded ratio drops to a critical level, the sustainability issue becomes a red flag to credit rating agencies or regulators, and plans may have to adopt changes such as increasing contributions or cutting benefits. Therefore, pension board members, pension fund managers, government officials, elected politicians, and unions all share the long-term goal of maintaining the sustainability of pension funding, while their short-term goals might differ.

Efficiency of asset management

Efficiency of asset management is about getting the most net investment returns from the pension assets invested in the capital markets. Investment returns are the largest source of income for most public pension plans. When investments are managed efficiently, returns can bring in extra income, so that pension costs can be lower and pension benefits can be higher. The efficiency of asset management is a common goal shared by most stakeholders of pension plans.

To improve asset management efficiency, pension plans establish investment policies that specify the asset classes they want to invest in and the risk tolerance level. Pension boards also hire and supervise fund managers to implement the investment policies and monitor the day-to-day operations of pension funds. Investment management is one of the most important tasks for pension boards. They review investment performance and approve major changes in investments. State laws might also set rules for pension investments, such as prohibiting investments in certain regions for geopolitical reasons or encouraging investment in certain areas for socioeconomic considerations.

Good governance of pension plans

Public pension plans can benefit from good governance practices. Different stakeholders might place emphasis on different aspects of good governance. For instance, pension trustees hold the fiduciary responsibilities to represent members of the plan and make decisions in the interest of the beneficiaries. Most plans have the so-called "prudent person rule" which requires that trustees must make decisions "with the reasonable care and skill" (OECD, 2010). Pension plans also follow sets of regulations and professional standards put forward by professional organizations such as the Governmental Accounting Standards Board (GASB) and the Society of Actuaries (SOA). Frequently mentioned good practices include transparency (timely and accurate reporting of plan financial position), stability of policies, equity, oversight, due process to avoid conflict of interest, and also to ensure the prudent principles in managing pension assets (control risks and avoid risky investment for the purposes of chasing returns).

Inputs

Three primary types of input factors for the management of public pension plans may influence pension decisions: the environment, stakeholders, and constraints. Several components are included in each of these three categories. These factors also may differ for the two different groups of decision-makers: pension board trustees and administering government officials.

Environment

Three major factors influence the decisions of *pension trustees*. First, *capital markets* are critical. Most pension systems heavily invest their assets in the capital markets, and therefore, market performance is an important component of the system's environment. Investment performance is greater when markets are strong, while declining markets may lead to investment concerns for pension systems (Brown et al., 2011; Coggburn & Kearney, 2010). During the Great Recession, many pension systems lost a significant portion of their pension assets. Market declines often result in decisions to make changes to investments and/or actuarial practices. Under the pressure of growing unfunded pension liabilities and a low market return environment, some pension systems have taken action to reduce pension benefits and/or increase pension contributions (Brainard & Brown, 2018; St. Clair & Martinez Guzman, 2018; Thom, 2017).

Second, the *overall fiscal health of the pension system* is a major consideration for pension boards of trustees. If the system is not sustainable (i.e., continual decreases in pension funding ratios), there is pressure on decision-makers to make changes. In many cases, the poor-performing capital markets go hand-in-hand with the drop in funded ratios (e.g., many pension systems experienced significant negative returns and low funded ratios during the 2007–2009 economic recession). This situation creates urgency for pension boards to initiate actions to restore pension funding sustainability.

In addition to economic, social, and institutional factors, the *political embeddedness* perspective is an important element that can influence the pension board of trustees' decisions and actions. A strong alignment between the pension board and the government can increase the flow of information and cooperation, which can help foster smoother adoption and implementation of certain pension decisions (i.e., policies or reforms) (Moe 1985; Wang & Peng, 2018). However, these close relationships between pension governance and governments can raise concerns that pension decisions are made based on political interests, instead of the best interests of pension plan participants (Andonov et al., 2018; Anzia & Moe, 2017; Brown et al., 2015; Dobra & Lubich, 2013; Eaton & Nofsinger, 2004; Stalebrink & Donatella, 2021).

Four major factors affect the decisions of the *administering government*. First, the *fiscal health of the government* is also an important factor for pension benefits and contributions (Giertz & Papke, 2007; Gorina, 2018; Peng, 2004). Governments with a more stable financial condition (i.e., having more reserve funds or operating balances) are less likely to initiate pension benefit cuts, while governments experiencing high volatility in pension contribution payments are more likely to make changes (i.e., benefit cuts or contribution increases) to pension systems (Hoang, 2022; St. Clair & Martinez Guzman, 2018).

Second, the *credit rating* of the governments is another important factor for administering governments. Since credit rating agencies consider pension unfunded liabilities as part of governments' overall financial obligations, higher levels of unfunded liabilities might trigger a negative credit outlook or even potential downgrades. A credit rating downgrade may lead governments to reduce pension benefits or increase contributions to the system to strengthen the system's financial sustainability (Hoang, 2023; Martell et al., 2013).

Third, *political ideology* and overall perceptions of government operations also impact pension decisions. Conservatives who prefer small government are more likely to adopt actions to scale down pension benefits and overall government spending, while liberals, who are more in favor of adequate labor benefits, may be more likely to support generous pension benefits for public employees (Anzia & Moe, 2017; Thom, 2013).

Finally, *electoral politics* sometimes play a role in pension-related decisions. Some governments or groups of public employees with more political resources can exert influence on public officials to adopt certain pension reforms to support their election agenda (Frandsen, 2016; Hoang & Goodman, 2018; Schneider, 2005).

Stakeholders

Multiple stakeholders also influence public pension decisions. Internally, pension systems rely on *administrators* to monitor investments and finances, pay benefits appropriately, prepare reports, etc. Administrators may have differing perspectives than trustees. The roles of pension administrators and their influence on pension decisions can vary depending on the structure of the pension system (i.e., single versus multiple employer systems). *Trustees* are the decision-makers for the pension system. Trustees may represent different constituencies, such as retirees, employers, and current employees/unions. These groups may have different agendas which may lead to disagreement among trustees. Externally, the primary external stakeholders for the pension system are the various *advisors* hired to assist the trustees. For instance, investment managers and other investment consultants are hired to advise pension trustees on asset selection and allocation, as well as broader investment strategies. Actuaries conduct and make recommendations related to actuarial policies.

The administering government also needs to consider various stakeholders in their decisions. The various *employer governments* and their *elected officials* may have different preferences on pension contributions, benefit levels, or other pension policies (Albrecht & Hingorani, 2004; Mitchell & Yang, 2005; Useem & Mitchell, 2000). *Public unions*, who represent the interests of public employees, different groups of *public employees* (e.g., civilian employees, public safety, teachers), or *retirees* who receive benefits from the pension systems, might have different concerns related to investment risks, pension benefits, contribution levels, or other decisions related to earlier retirement or postretirement employment options (Kelley, 2014; Pennacchi & Rastad, 2011). Finally, *taxpayers* may have a very different perspective from the covered employees and retirees. Most private-sector employees are not covered by DB plans, so taxpayers and voters may resent having their tax dollars used to provide high retirement benefits that they themselves will not receive.

Constraints

Pension boards and administering government officials do not have complete autonomy. They are constrained by laws, regulations and standards, court decisions, and contracts. Pension systems should follow *actuarial and financial reporting practices*. For example, accounting standards are determined by the GASB. These policies may change over time, which can affect pension decisions and outcomes; for example, GASB Statements No. 67 and 68 affected the reporting and measurement of pension data in financial statements. Systems also need to consider applicable *state and local laws* related to investments and asset allocations. Some states have restrictions on how public funds (including public pensions) invest their money.

Administering governments are also constrained in various ways. *State statutes or constitutions* can hinder governments' ability to make changes to pension benefits and contributions (Brown, 2014; Munnell & Quinby, 2012; Thom, 2017). Union contracts generally cannot be changed without negotiation and bilateral agreement. In addition, *courts* may weigh in to restrict actions of governments related to pension benefits and contributions.

Outputs and decisions

There are four categories of pension decisions as outputs of decision making in pension plan management. Decisions related to investments and actuarial practices are generally made by pension trustees and professionals they hire, while pension benefits and employee/employer contributions are usually determined by the administering government (often in negotiation with unions). Each of these four areas will be considered in turn.

Investments

Pension board trustees have fiduciary duties to prudently manage the pension fund (NASRA, 2023). One of their most important decisions involves deciding on asset allocation and investment strategy. A sound investment strategy and asset allocation decisions are critical to ensure adequate revenues for the pension fund and release the governments from the pressure of increasing pension contributions. The pension board's decisions related to investments often involve balancing the trade-off between risks and returns through the process of asset allocation or portfolio selection more broadly (Blake et al., 1999; Coronado et al., 2003; Hoang & Nguyen, 2023).

Actuarial practices

Pension boards also review and make decisions on pension actuarial practices based on actuaries' recommendations and in compliance with GASB requirements and other professional standards. The board's review of actuarial assumptions, including the discount rate, is important to determine the funding level of the plan and the pension contribution rates. The *discount rate*, arguably the most important and debated actuarial practice, is used to calculate or discount the future pension benefits to the present value. The higher the discount rate, the lower the liabilities and the higher the funded ratio, and vice versa. Many pension boards have lowered the discount rate in recent years. This has been due to factors such as low investment returns as well as the implementation of GASB Statements No. 67/68 with the requirement of lower blended discount rates. Pension boards also make decisions about actuarial cost methods, the amortization period, and smoothing. Several optional *actuarial cost methods* are available that have varying effects on the calculation of normal costs over time.

Economic assumptions are also made to evaluate pension fund liabilities. The three main economic assumptions are salary growth rate, inflation rate, and investment return assumption. *Demographic assumptions* include retirement rates, disability rates, and mortality rates. These assumptions can be determined using actuarial professional standards and the SOA mortality table and studies. Experience studies are usually conducted every few years to determine the pension plan's actual demographic trends and can be used to adjust the assumptions. These assumptions are important for the calculation of future benefits and liabilities.

Benefits

Pension benefits are contractual agreements between governments and their employees, and these benefits are protected by laws or in some cases by the state constitution. The defined pension benefit is typically calculated based on three factors: (a) the number of years of service of the employee, (b) the final average salary of the employee, and (c) a benefit multiplier. Changes in any of these factors can affect the benefit levels. In some governments, contracts that determine compensation and pension benefits are negotiated with employee unions. Decisions related to pension benefits include the requirements for normal (full) retirement eligibility (retirement age, years of service, and vesting period), the level of benefit generosity (benefit multiplier, calculation of pensionable salaries, COLA, and period used to calculate final average salary) as well as any earlier retirement benefits.

One unique aspect of public pension benefits is whether the governments opt-in to the Social Security system for their employees. Federal law allows state and local governments to exclude employees from Social Security coverage if the employees are provided with a sufficiently generous pension. This is important because it can impact the generosity of pension benefits as state and local governments outside the Social Security System tend to provide larger pension benefits to compensate employees for the lack of Social Security benefits (Kelley, 2014). Concerns have been raised, though, that given the recent waves of benefit reduction and longer vesting periods, the pension benefits in those governments that do not offer Social Security benefits fall short of Social Security equivalence for noncovered workers (Aubry et al., 2022).

In addition, in many states, pension benefits for public employees are protected by state statutes and under the Contract Clause or state constitutions, such as in the state of Illinois (Munnell & Quinby, 2012; Thom, 2017). These legal standards limit the power of state and local governments to reduce pension benefits. Furthermore, increases in union collective bargaining power can lead to pension benefit growth (Anzia & Moe, 2019; Frandsen & Webb, 2019; Kearney, 2003; Zax & Ichniowski, 1988). Powerful groups such as municipal police unions or teacher unions can capitalize on their political power to influence negotiations in favor of more generous benefit packages.

Contributions

To fund annual normal cost and reduce the unfunded liabilities, sponsor governments should pay the annual ADC. The financial discipline of paying full ADC is important to maintain a sustainable pension funding level. However, scholars have also observed that some governments have used pension contributions as a countercyclical budgetary tool as they delay or reduce pension contributions below required levels when faced with budget deficits (Bifulco et al., 2012; Giertz & Papke, 2007; Hoang & Maher, 2022; Peng, 2004; Thom & Randazzo, 2015). Failure to meet those pension contribution obligations can lead to severe consequences of raising unfunded pension liabilities and threatening the financial health of both the pension fund and the government.

It is noteworthy that ADC is the required contribution recommended by the actuaries. While the majority of state policies authorize fully funded ADC, some states impose limits on annual increases of the employer contribution rate or only allow payment of a fixed percentage of compensation specified in statutes, which is often lower than the amount recommended by actuaries (Brainard & Brown, 2018; Munnell et al., 2008). In some cases, municipal codes require a substantially equal contribution between employers and employees, which implies that governments cannot unilaterally increase their pension contributions to meet ADC requirements in the case of a pension shortfall, even if they have financial resources to do so.

Recent pension reforms aim to increase employer and employee contributions to raise pension funding levels. In many cases, raising employee contributions requires labor contract negotiation and/or legislative approval. Additionally, some pension plans implement cost-sharing policies that provide a longer term approach to pension contribution issues and give plans more flexibility in making adjustments to the employee contribution rate or post-employment benefits based on the rate of investment return or funding level. These approaches can include splitting some or all of the total annual costs between the employer and the employees or adjusting the employee contribution in response to investment returns (Pew Charitable Trusts, 2017).

Summary

Public pension management decisions are critical for the fiscal health of these systems and the sponsoring governments. Several types of decisions are made by pension trustees and by officials of the administering governments. Our model outlines those decisions, and we also explain the major inputs that influence them. Decision-makers have to consider environmental factors, agendas of various stakeholders, and the constraints that limit their authority. The decisions that they make then affect the outcomes. Also, pension systems have various goals that they have to balance. Using the framework, we identified several important ways in which the goals of pension systems are measured.

The existing literature is generally focused on narrow aspects of public pension management, such as funding level, investment decisions or reform efforts. Our framework contributes to the literature by developing a holistic systems model that takes into consideration current issues and is centered around key pension decisions. In addition, we distinguish between decisions made by pension system trustees and those made by the administering government; these decision-makers may also be influenced by different environments, stakeholders, and constraints. This logic model will be helpful for scholars to conduct empirical tests of the relationships between the various components to build normative and positive theories.

This model can also be useful for government officials and public pension stakeholders. Many plans are dealing with underfunding issues and seeking ways to decrease pension liabilities and increase assets. Our framework provides an overview of the various levers that influence decisions, and how decisions then can affect the outcomes. Decision-makers can use this understanding to devise reforms that may be successfully implemented to improve the fiscal health of public pension systems. More discussions on the goals, environments, stakeholders, constraints, and decisions are presented in the following chapters.

Note

1 The actuarially determined contribution (ADC) was formally referred to as ARC (annual or actuarially required contribution) prior to 2014. Some scholars and reports used the terms actuarially determined employer contribution (ADEC) to refer to the ADC.

References

Albrecht, W. G., & Hingorani, V. L. (2004). Effects of governance practices and investment strategies on state and local government pension fund financial performance. *International Journal of Public Administration*, *27*(8–9), 673–700. https://doi.org/10.1081/PAD-120030261

Andonov, A., Hochberg, Y. V., & Rauh, J. D. (2018). Political representation and governance: Evidence from the investment decisions of public pension funds. *The Journal of Finance*, *73*(5), 2041–2086. https://doi.org/10.1111/jofi.12706

Anzia, S. F., & Moe, T. M. (2017). Polarization and policy: The politics of public-sector pensions. *Legislative Studies Quarterly*, *42*(1), 33–62. https://doi.org/10.1111/lsq.12145

Anzia, S. F., & Moe, T. M. (2019). Interest groups on the inside: The governance of public pension funds. *Perspectives on Politics*, *17*(4), 1059–1078. https://doi.org/10.1017/S1537592718003468

Aubry, J.-P., Liu, S., Munnell, A. H., Quinby, L., & Springstead. (2022). State and local government employees without Social Security coverage: What percentage will earn pension benefits that fall short of Social Security equivalence? *Social Security Bulletin*, *82*(3). https://www.ssa.gov/policy/docs/ssb/v82n3/v82n3p1.html

Bifulco, R., Bunch, B., Duncombe, W., Robbins, M., & Simonsen, W. (2012). Debt and deception: How states avoid making hard fiscal decisions. *Public Administration Review*, *72*(5), 659–667. https://doi.org/10.1111/j.1540-6210.2012.02533.x

Blake, D., Lehmann, B. N., & Timmermann, A. (1999). Asset allocation dynamics and pension fund performance. *The Journal of Business*, 72(4), 429–461.

Brainard, K., & Brown, A. (2018). *Significant reforms to state retirement systems.* National Association of State Retirement Administrators. https://www.nasra.org/files/Spotlight/Significant%20Reforms.pdf

Brown, J. R. (2014). Reforming public pensions subject to political and legal constraints: The Illinois experience. *National Tax Journal*, *67*(4), 941–963. https://doi.org/10.17310/ntj.2014.4.09

Brown, J. R., Clark, R., & Rauh, J. (2011). The economics of state and local pensions. *Journal of Pension Economics and Finance*, *10*(2), 161–172. https://doi.org/10.1017/S1474747211000138

Brown, J. R., Pollet, J. M., & Weisbenner, S. J. (2015). *The in-state equity bias of state pension plans* (Working Paper 21020). National Bureau of Economic Research. https://doi.org/10.3386/w21020

Chen, G. (2018). Understanding decisions in state pension systems: A system framework. *The American Review of Public Administration*, *48*(3), 260–273. https://doi.org/10.1177/0275074016675242

Clark, R. L., & Schieber, S. J. (2004). Adopting cash balance pension plans: Implications and issues. *Journal of Pension Economics and Finance*, *3*(3), 271–295. https://doi.org/10.1017/S1474747204001738

Coggburn, J. D., & Kearney, R. C. (2010). Trouble keeping promises? An analysis of underfunding in state retiree benefits. *Public Administration Review*, *70*(1), 97–108.

Coronado, J. L., Engen, E. M., & Knight, B. (2003). Public funds and private capital markets: The investment practices and performance of state and local pension funds. *National Tax Journal*, *56*(3), 579–594. https://doi.org/10.17310/ntj.2003.3.09

Congressional Research Service (CRS). (2022). *Pensions and Individual Retirement Accounts (IRAs): An overview.* https://crsreports.congress.gov/product/pdf/R/R47119/2

Davidyan, J. Y. (2021). Defined benefit public pension funding determinants and consequences: A review of the literature. *Public Finance and Management*, *20*(2), 214–242. https://doi.org/10.1177/152397212102000204

Dobra, M., & Lubich, B. H. (2013). Public pension governance and asset allocation. *Journal of CENTRUM Cathedra: The Business and Economics Research Journal*, 6(1). https://papers.ssrn.com/sol3/papers.cfm?abstract_id=2236469

Eaton, T. V., & Nofsinger, J. R. (2004). The effect of financial constraints and political pressure on the management of public pension plans. *Journal of Accounting and Public Policy*, *23*(3), 161–189. https://doi.org/10.1016/j.jaccpubpol.2004.04.001

Frandsen, B. R. (2016). The effects of collective bargaining rights on public employee compensation: Evidence from teachers, firefighters, and police. *ILR Review*, *69*(1), 84–112.

Frandsen, B. R., & Webb, M. (2019). Public employee pensions and collective bargaining rights: Evidence from state and local government finances. *Journal of Law, Economics & Policy*, *15*, 163.

Giertz, J. F., & Papke, L. E. (2007). Public pension plans: Myths and realities for state budgets. *National Tax Journal*, *60*(2), 305–323.

Glaeser, E. L., & Ponzetto, G. A. M. (2014). Shrouded costs of government: The political economy of state and local public pensions. *Journal of Public Economics*, *116*, 89–105. https://doi.org/10.1016/j.jpubeco.2014.03.005

Goldhaber, D., Grout, C., & Holden, K. L. (2017). Pension structure and employee turnover: Evidence from a large public pension system. *ILR Review*, *70*(4), 976–1007. https://doi.org/10.1177/0019793916678424

Gorina, E. (2018). City Revenue structure and unfunded pension liabilities. *State and Local Government Review*, *50*(3), 189–202. https://doi.org/10.1177/0160323X18817806

Hoang, T. (2022). Fiscal competition and state pension reforms. *Public Budgeting & Finance*, *42*(3), 41–70. https://doi.org/10.1111/pbaf.12315

Hoang, T. (2023). Public pension reform and credit quality of state governments. *Public Finance Review*, *51*(3), 368–431. https://doi.org/10.1177/10911421221143569

Hoang, T., & Goodman, D. (2018). Public pensions and collective bargaining rights: Evidence from state and local governments. *Public Administration Review*, *78*(5), 772–784. https://doi.org/10.1111/puar.12936

Hoang, T., & Maher, C. S. (2022). Fiscal condition, institutional constraints, and public pension contribution: Are pension contribution shortfalls fiscal illusion? *Public Budgeting & Finance*, *42*(4), 93–124. https://doi.org/10.1111/pbaf.12328

Hoang, T., & Nguyen, A. T. (2023). Navigating the public pension landscape: An examination of asset allocations. *Public Finance and Management*, *22*(1), 1–34. https://doi.org/10.37808/pfm.22.1.1

Kearney, R. C. (2003). The determinants of state employee compensation. *Review of Public Personnel Administration*, *23*(4), 305–322. https://doi.org/10.1177/0734371X03259279

Kelley, D. G. (2014). The political economy of unfunded public pension liabilities. *Public Choice*, *158*(1–2), 21–38. https://doi.org/10.1007/s11127-012-0049-3

Koedel, C., Podgursky, M., & Shi, S. (2013). Teacher pension systems, the composition of the teaching workforce, and teacher quality: Teacher pension systems. *Journal of Policy Analysis and Management*, *32*(3), 574–596. https://doi.org/10.1002/pam.21699

Lewis, G. B., & Stoycheva, R. L. (2016). Does pension plan structure affect turnover patterns? *Journal of Public Administration Research and Theory*, *26*(4), 787–799. https://doi.org/10.1093/jopart/muw035

Martell, C. R., Kioko, S. N., & Moldogaziev, T. (2013). Impact of unfunded pension obligations on credit quality of state governments. *Public Budgeting & Finance*, *33*(3), 24–54. https://doi.org/10.1111/j.1540-5850.2013.12013.x

Matkin, D. S. T., Chen, G., & Khalid, H. (2019). The governance of public pensions: An institutional framework. *Administration & Society*, *51*(1), 91–119. https://doi.org/10.1177/0095399715621945

Mitchell, O. S., & Hsin, P. L. (1994). *Public pension governance and performance.* National Bureau of Economic Research (NBER). 10.3386/w4632. https://www.nber.org/papers/w4632

Mitchell, O. S., & Yang, T. (2005). *Public pension governance, funding, and performance: A longitudinal appraisal* (WP2005_2). Wharton Pension Research Council Working Papers. https://repository.upenn.edu/entities/publication/aa323447-95d3-410c-a943-12e240ee59fc

Moe, T. M. (1985). Control and feedback in economic regulation: The case of the NLRB. *American Political Science Review*. *79*(4):1094–1116. https://doi.org/10.2307/1956250

Munnell, A. H. (2012). *State and local pensions: What now?* Brookings Institute Press.

Munnell, A. H., Haverstick, K., Aubry, J.-P., & Golub-Sass, A. (2008). *Why don't some states and localities pay their required pension contributions?* Center for Retirement Research. https://crr.bc.edu/wp-content/uploads/2008/05/slp_7-508.pdf

Munnell, A. H., & Quinby, L. (2012). *Legal constraints on changes in state and local pensions.* Center for Retirement Research at Boston College. https://crr.bc.edu/wp-content/uploads/2012/08/slp_25.pdf

NASRA. (2023). *NASRA issue brief: State and local government contributions to statewide pension plans: FY22.* https://www.nasra.org/files/Issue%20Briefs/NASRAADCBrief.pdf

Norcross, E., & Smith, D. J. (2021). *The political economy of public pensions. Elements in Austrian economics.* Cambridge: Cambridge University Press. https://doi.org/10.1017/9781009019965

OECD. (2010). *Managing investment risk in defined benefit pension funds.* OCED Working Paper on Insurance and Private Pensions. https://www.oecd.org/en/publications/managing-investment-risk-in-defined-benefit-pension-funds_5kmjnr3sr2f3-en.html

Peng, J. (2004). Public pension funds and operating budgets: A tale of three States. *Public Budgeting & Finance*, *24*(2), 59–73. https://doi.org/10.1111/j.0275-1100.2004.02402004.x

Peng, J. (2008). *State and local pension fund management.* CRC Press/Taylor & Francis Group.

Peng, J., & Wang, Q. (2017). Affordability of public pension benefit: A historical and empirical analysis of US state and local government pension contributions. *Journal of Pension Economics and Finance*, *16*(1), 21–42. https://doi.org/10.1017/S1474747215000268

Pennacchi, G., & Rastad, M. (2011). Portfolio allocation for public pension funds. *Journal of Pension Economics and Finance*, *10*(2), 221–245. https://doi.org/10.1017/S1474747211000102

Pew Charitable Trusts. (2017). *Cost-sharing among state defined benefit pension plans.* https://www.pewtrusts.org/en/research-and-analysis/articles/2017/01/18/cost-sharing-among-state-defined-benefit-pension-plans

Pew Charitable Trusts. (2023). *Public retirement systems need sustainable policies to navigate volatile financial markets.* https://www.pewtrusts.org/-/media/assets/2023/11/public-retirement-systems-need-sustainable-policies_v5.pdf

Schneider, M. (2005). The status of U.S. public pension plans: A review with policy considerations. *Review of Public Personnel Administration*, *25*(2), 107–137. https://doi.org/10.1177/0734371X04271062

Schneider, M., & Damanpour, F. (2002). Public choice economics and public pension plan funding: An empirical test. *Administration & Society*, *34*(1), 57–86. https://doi.org/10.1177/0095399702034001005

Stalebrink, O. J. (2014). Public pension funds and assumed rates of return: An empirical examination of public sector defined benefit pension plans. *The American Review of Public Administration*, *44*(1), 92–111. https://doi.org/10.1177/0275074012458826

Stalebrink, O. J. (2017). Public pension fund investments: The role of governance structures. *Journal of Law, Economics & Policy*, *14*, 35.

Stalebrink, O. J., & Donatella, P. (2021). Public pension governance and opportunistic accounting choice: A politico-economic approach. *The American Review of Public Administration*, *51*(3), 227–245. https://doi.org/10.1177/0275074020954397

St. Clair, T. (2013). The impact of budget stabilization funds on state pension contributions. *Public Budgeting & Finance*, *33*(3), 55–74. https://doi.org/10.1111/j.1540-5850.2013.12014.x

St. Clair, T., & Martinez Guzman, J. P. (2018). Contribution volatility and public pension reform. *Journal of Pension Economics and Finance*, *17*(4), 513–533. https://doi.org/10.1017/S1474747217000129

Thom, M. (2013). All of the above: How fiscal, political, and workforce traits affect pension funding. *State and Local Government Review*, *45*(3), 163–171. https://doi.org/10.1177/0160323X13499733

Thom, M. (2017). The drivers of public sector pension reform across the U.S. states. *The American Review of Public Administration*, *47*(4), 431–442. https://doi.org/10.1177/0275074015589342

Thom, M., & Randazzo, A. (2015). Underfunding annual pension contributions: Examining the factors behind an ongoing fiscal phenomenon. *State and Local Government Review*, *47*(1), 35–44. https://doi.org/10.1177/0160323X14568025

Useem, M., & Mitchell, O. S. (2000). *Holders of the purse strings*. Pension Research Council.

Wang, Q. (2017). Fiscal institutions and the funding of US state and local pension plans. *Public Money & Management*, *37*(7), 507–514. https://doi.org/10.1080/09540962.2017.1372112

Wang, Q., & Peng, J. (2018). Political embeddedness of public pension governance: An event history analysis of discount rate changes. *Public Administration Review*, *78*(5), 785–794. https://doi.org/10.1111/puar.12968

Zax, J., & Ichniowski, C. (1988). The effects of public sector unionism on pay, employment, department budgets, and municipal expenditures. In R. B. Freeman & C. Ichniowski (Eds.), *When public sector workers unionize* (pp. 323–364). University of Chicago Press.

3

BALANCING GOALS FOR PUBLIC PENSION PLANS

Overview

When government employees' pension plans were established in the early twentieth century in the United States, they were designed to provide sufficient pension benefits to attract and retain public employees (Clark et al., 2003). Public-sector jobs are generally perceived to be more secure and with better benefits than private-sector jobs. Public school teachers, police officers, firefighters, and general government employees enjoy secure and guaranteed pension benefits at a level that many private-sector employees do not have. Most employees also consider sufficient pension benefits to be one of the advantages of public-sector jobs.

For public employees and retirees, it is obvious that providing sufficient pension benefits is the primary goal of public pension plans. However, sufficient benefits are not the only policy goal for pension policymakers and managers of public pension plans to consider as they make decisions on the management of the plan. Pension plan management is an area where many stakeholders have interests and voices. Without considering all the policymakers' and stakeholders' goals and motivations, pension-related policies cannot be successful.

Take the sponsoring governments for example. In many state-administered, multiple-employer pension systems, state and local governments join these systems with the expectation that as long as they keep paying the required contributions, their employees will get sufficient pension benefits. They make the decision to join these systems because they believe in the efficiency of pooled pension assets. The efficiency of asset

DOI: 10.4324/9781032671185-3

management and the affordability of the required contribution amount become these participating employers' primary concerns. Participating employers would also prefer stable annual contributions at a lower level so it would be easier for them to budget for annual pension expenses.

Other stakeholders, such as politicians, government administrators, and taxpayers, also have preferences when it comes to public pension plan management. Many politicians are aware of the current challenges in funding public pensions and might have political motivations to either improve the funding of pension plans and/or protect pension benefits. Administrators bring their expertise or experience in decision making and may emphasize certain policy goals or best practices. Taxpayers, as the ultimate payers and the recipients of public services, are concerned about the overall costs of providing public pension benefits, which could crowd out expenditures for other public services.

When all policymakers' and stakeholders' perspectives are considered, we see that there are generally five goals public pension plans are balancing. They are: sufficiency of pension benefits, affordability of pension costs, sustainability of pension funding, efficiency of asset management, and good governance of pension plans. Stakeholders may pay attention to one or more of these goals and prioritize them in different ways. Keeping these goals in consideration when making pension plan management decisions is important for the success of pension policies and reforms. These five goals will each be discussed in detail in the following sections.

Sufficiency of pension benefits

The goal of sufficiency can be described by the notion that public pension plans should provide benefits at a competitive level to effectively attract and retain high-quality public employees committed to government service. Most people perceive that pension benefits for public-sector employees are more generous than those for private-sector employees. Research on pension plans and public-sector employment shows that keeping public pension benefits at a sufficient level is helpful for the recruitment and retention of public employees (Munnell et al., 2015; Quinby & Sanzenbacher, 2020; Quinby et al., 2018).

It is not an easy task to define "competitive" or "sufficient" pension benefits. As mentioned in Chapter 2, there are several indicators for the level of pension benefits, such as the normal cost, replacement rate, and lifetime take-home income. In this chapter, we focus on the replacement rate as a measurement of the generosity level of pension benefits because it is more straightforward. The replacement rate is the ratio of an individual's preretirement income to the same individual's retirement income.

A replacement rate of 100% means that this person's retirement income can fully "replace" their preretirement income and thus can sustain the same living standards before and after retirement. Although the sufficiency of pension benefits depends on individual circumstances such as lifestyle and living expenses, most financial advisors consider that a replacement rate of 75–80% is a desirable retirement income level (Peng, 2008; Young & Theodore, 2023).

In public defined-benefit plans, the typical benefit multiplier is around 2% (according to Urban Institute, 2014a). Assuming a public employee works for a total of 25 years in the public sector, the replacement rate for this defined benefit (DB) pension benefit would be 50%. If this employee also receives Social Security benefits, which could provide around 30% of preretirement income depending on the individual's earning level (Clingman et al., 2021), a sufficient level of pension benefits can be achieved as the total replacement rate for this employee is around 80%. Note that some state and local government employees are not covered by Social Security. Those employees will need higher pension benefits to attain a sufficient level of retirement income. In comparison, the replacement rate for private-sector pension benefits is on average around 15–20 percentage points lower than public pensions (Foster, 1997).

Stable and sufficient pension benefits are the primary concern for public employees and their union representatives when they consider pension-related policies. If employees have collective bargaining rights, pension benefit changes are subject to negotiation with employee unions. Pension policy changes that aim to reduce current employee benefit levels often receive resistance from employee groups and might be challenged in court.

Politicians and government administrators have diverse opinions on the sufficiency of public pension benefits. On the one hand, benefit levels help to recruit and retain a high-quality public workforce, whose support is crucial for any political agenda. Public employee morale and motivation are vital for the provision of public services. It is politically unpopular to propose policies to cut employee pension benefits. On the other hand, high pension benefits also mean higher pension expenses and fewer resources for other public service programs and projects. When pension benefits are overly generous without funding support, there will also be concerns over government officials' ability to make responsible fiscal decisions, which politicians and government administrators seek to avoid.

The Urban Institute (2014b) conducted an evaluation of U.S. state and local pension plans. One focus of this evaluation was on the retirement income security for both short- and long-term government employees. Using a simulation based on benefit rules and financial information from state and local pension plans, they conclude that "traditional pension plans

TABLE 3.1 Evaluation of Public Pension Plans' Replacement Ratios by Urban Institute

Grades	*Long-term employees*	*Short-term employees*
A (replacement rate ≥ 80%)	MT, OH, KY, OK, UT, MS, SD, WI, SC, MO, MD, OR, ID, IA, MN, AZ, AR, TX, KS, VA, WY, AL, CO, GA, PA, TN, NY, NM, VT, HI, ND, NH, NJ, LA, NC, NE, WV, CA, DE	MS, SD, WI, UT, NM, WY, ID, WV, NE, ND
B (70% ≤ replacement rate < 80%)	IL, IN, ME, CT, MI, WA, FL, RI, AK	SC, MT, MO, MD, OR, AR, IA, MN, PA, TN, AZ, CA, DE, NC
C (60% ≤ replacement rate < 70%)	DC, NV, MA	IL, KY, NY, VA, TX, FL, VT, HI
D (50% ≤ replacement rate < 60%)	None	OK, OH, CT, WA, ME, AK, CO, KS, DC, LA, NV
F (replacement rate < 50%)	None	MA, IN, AL, GA, MI, NH, NJ, RI

Source: Urban Institute (2014b).

sponsored by most state and local governments generally provide lucrative retirement incomes to long-term employees but offer little retirement security to workers who change employers several times over their career." The detailed grades for each state's replacement rate for long- and short-term employees are shown in Table 3.1. Note that in the Urban Institute's simulation, long-term employees are assumed to work for 30–40 years with the same employer, while short-term employees are assumed to also work for 30–40 years over their lifetime but change their jobs with different employers.

Affordability of pension costs

The affordability goal is focused on maintaining pension expenses at a reasonable level in comparison to the financial resources of the sponsoring governments for funding these plans. Public pension plans are funded by both contributions from the government and the employees. Keeping those annual pension expenses affordable is an important goal for many policymakers and stakeholders because higher pension expenses lead to higher taxes or less financial resources for other public service programs.

The definition of pension cost affordability can vary among governments with different financial conditions and capacities. When discussing pension affordability, we often compare the annual pension expenses with other spending or revenue benchmarks. The first approach is to compare the annual required employer contributions with the total payroll, which is the sum of salaries received by employees of a government in a given year. On average in the fiscal year 2021, employer contributions were 22.3% of the payroll in state-administered plans and 35.6% of the payroll in local-administered plans (according to the authors' calculation based on the CRR, 2022). Another approach is to compare the annual pension expenses with a government's overall budget. Pension expenses for state governments on average comprise around 2.7% of state total revenues, while for local governments on average, pension costs are 7.5% of local total revenues (according to the authors' calculation based on the Public Plans Database, 2022 and U.S. Census data on government payrolls and total revenues). NASRA (2023a) also estimates that in aggregate, state and local governments spend 5.2% of their direct general spending on public pensions.

Whether pension expenses at this level are affordable is a debatable question depending on the government's other spending needs and revenue sources. If we compare the expense of public DB plans with defined contribution (DC) plans in the public or private sector, we can see that public DB plan expenses are much higher than DC plans. Private DC plans' employer match is at a much lower rate of 4.8% of employee salaries (Fidelity, 2023). The National Compensation Survey (Stoltzfus, 2016) also shows that employer costs for providing DC plans to private-sector employees average 4% of workers' wages and salaries in large establishments with 100 or more employees. However, private DC plans also provide much lower benefits, which are likely not acceptable to public employees. According to a survey (Giesecke & Rauh, 2022), if the public sector were to freeze DB plans and introduce DC plans, the acceptable contribution rate for public employees would be around 18.2% of payroll, which is much higher than the private DC plan employer cost but still lower than the current pension cost in many systems.

We can also compare pension costs with other spending items in a government budget. For state governments in the fiscal year 2023, National Association of State Budget Officers (NASBO) (White, 2023) estimates that the rainy-day fund balance averages 12.4% of general fund expenditures, which is roughly twice as much as the spending on public pensions. The U.S. Census Annual Survey of State and Local Government Finances also shows that interest expenses on debt take up 4% of state and local direct general expenditures (Urban Institute, n.d.), which is still less than spending on pensions.

When credit rating agencies assign ratings to government entities, the affordability of pension costs is an important factor (Aon Hewitt, 2017). Fitch's expenditure framework defines the carrying cost metric as the sum of governmental debt service, pension required contributions, and other post-employment benefit (OPEB) payments as a percentage of governmental expenditures. Fitch considers a carrying cost metric of less than 10% as an "aaa" rating and less than 20% as an "aa" rating (FitchRatings, 2021).

In addition to the affordability level of pension expenses, the fluctuations in these expenses from one year to the next also pose fiscal challenges for sponsoring governments. A sudden increase in pension costs in a year, which could be due to investment losses in a recession year or policy-related contribution increases, might cause fiscal stress to governments. Most governments have legal requirements to balance their budget on a yearly basis, and many plans also use smoothing methods to reduce the annual volatility of pension expenses. Such smoothing methods include using an asset smoothing period and the amortization of unfunded liabilities, which will be discussed in Chapter 6.

Public opinions on the costs of public pensions have also changed over time, which might reflect the fact that pension plans are getting more expensive for governments. In the 1990s, pension costs were 3.4% of state and local direct general spending, but this percentage has increased to above 5% in the 2020s (NASRA, 2023a). The negative public opinions toward high pension costs are also reflected in the media. As a response to the shifting public opinion, many politicians have incorporated plans to change state retirement systems as they campaign for public office (Degen, 2022).

Sustainability of pension funding

Sustainability of pension funding refers to whether pension plans have adequate and sustainable funding to meet the liabilities associated with the benefits promised to employees and retirees. The funding ratio of public pension plans is defined as the ratio of pension assets to pension liabilities. The decline of funding ratios for public pension plans following the Great Recession has raised serious concerns for many governments. The media have used the term "pension crisis" to describe the phenomenon when many public pension plans do not have enough funding to cover pension liabilities (e.g., see Brown, 2023). Unlike pension benefit decreases or cost increases, a drop in pension funding level does not have immediate consequences as long as the pension plan can still make benefit payments, but if the funding level keeps dropping, pension plans will have short- or long-term solvency concerns. Also, for credit rating agencies, a pension plan's funding level indicates whether the plan has accumulated sufficient assets to cover its liabilities and, thus, is also an important indicator of the plan's fiscal health and long-term sustainability when determining credit ratings.

Analysts of public pension plans have different ideas about the definition of a healthy and sustainable funding level. Ideally, pension plans should have enough assets to fully (100%) cover their future liabilities. Many regulators or analysts still regard the 100% funded ratio as a goal that should be pursued by pension plans. For example, Standard & Poor's (S&P) states that "the funding target for public pension and OPEB plans should typically be at least 100%. We view funding targets of less than 100% as a credit weakness because these plans carry higher interest costs associated with the unfunded liability" (S&P, 2016, p. 25). However, because pension asset values fluctuate following the ups and downs of capital market returns, it is difficult for pension plans to always maintain a 100% funded ratio. Many analysts agree that if a pension plan maintains a reasonable funding level, such as around 80%, the plan is still sustainable in the long term. The Government Accountability Office (GAO, 2007) states that "A funded ratio of 80% or more is within the range that many public-sector experts, union officials, and advocates view as a healthy pension system." The 2007 GAO report has been cited by other studies, including a Pew report in 2010 as the standard to determine a healthy pension funding level. S&P rating methodology (2016) considers a three-year average pension-funded ratio of 80–90% to be "good" and above 90% to be "strong."

We should also note that the pension funding level is calculated in an actuarial process with various cost methods and assumptions. Future benefit payments are discounted to their present values using a discount rate that could vary by pension systems. Pension plans also use the actuarial value of assets, which could be smoothed over several years, rather than the market value, to report and calculate required contributions and unfunded liabilities. Accounting and actuarial standards have changed over the years to make these assumptions more transparent and consistent across plans (see GASB, 2012a, 2012b). When evaluating the funding level of pension plans, these assumptions, especially the discount rate, should be taken into consideration. In fact, when the reporting standards were inconsistent, Moody's developed its own adjusted pension assets and liabilities when assessing the solvency of public pension plans (Moody's, 2013).

Maintaining the sustainable funding of public pension plans is a goal that is shared by many policymakers and stakeholders. Because of the rising concerns over the public pension funding crisis, politicians have increasingly paid more attention to the underfunding problems and called for actions to improve pension funding. Administrators and participating government employers are concerned about the funding level because a low funding ratio provides pressure to increase contributions to the plans. Low pension funding also creates unfunded liabilities in financial reports and might affect credit ratings. At the same time, governments are also concerned about the short-term goal to balance the budget, and thus, especially during a recession when there are immediate needs to pay for other public services, they might be willing to underfund the pensions in order to meet these other needs. Pension plan members are also concerned about pension funding; low funding ratios might lead to pressure to reduce benefits or increase employee contributions. Nonetheless, because most employees have benefits that are predetermined and protected by law, plan members' primary concern is still on the benefit level.

Efficiency of asset management

Besides contributions from employers and employees, investment returns are also a major income source for pension plans. In fact, looking at the data from 1992 to 2021, on average investment returns account for 64% of public pension revenue sources, while employer contributions account for 25% and employee contributions account for 11% (NASRA, 2023b). If public pension plans meet or exceed their expected investment return targets, there may be no pressure for employers and employees to raise contributions or reduce benefits. Thus, the efficiency of asset management, which indicates high investment returns and low fees, is a goal that is widely shared by pension policymakers and stakeholders.

Many pension plans have set a rate of return goal in their investment policy. The long-term expected rate of return (ERR) assumption in many plans was around 7.5% for some time. Historically, this rate (ERR) was also used as the discount rate to calculate the present value of pension liabilities with the anticipation that assets will grow at this rate to meet future benefits. A higher discount rate means lower pension liabilities and lower required contributions. When ERR was used as the discount rate, plans might have been motivated to pursue a high rate of return assumption so they could reduce pension contributions. Since 2012, new accounting standards have led to the separation of the ERR from the discount rate used for financial reporting, which has reduced this motivation (GASB, 2012a, 2012b; also see Chapter 4 for a more detailed discussion).

Looking back to the longer history of pension asset management, we see that plans have increasingly shifted from fixed-income investments to riskier asset classes such as equities and alternative investments. Pew (2014) shows that public pension funds historically invested the majority of their assets in government and corporate bonds, but the allocation of assets to equities and alternatives increased from below 30% in the 1970s and 1980s to around 50% in the 1990s, and eventually reached around 73% in 2012.

The pursuit of high yields also creates concerns about investment risk and investment fees. While seeking high returns, controlling investment risk is also important. Some plans have set up a legal list of investments and prescribe the percentage of assets that can be invested in a certain asset class in their investment policies, although many plans have changed this practice and follow a "prudent person rule," which gives more discretion to the fund managers.

The fees that are associated with the investment and management of pension assets have received more attention, especially as pension plans increasingly invest in alternative investments, such as private equities and venture capital, which usually come with higher investment fees. Potentially, multi-employer cost-sharing systems can create a large asset pool that has more investment opportunities and lower investment fees as fees are shared among participating employers. However, the fee structure may become more complicated for employers to understand and supervise.

Some public pension plans have also included environmental, social, and governance (ESG) goals in their investment strategies. ESG investments are sensitive to the economic, social, and governance aspects of the investment. The consideration of ESG could serve the purpose of protecting pension assets. However, there is still no empirical finding supporting how ESG investing improves returns or reduces risks (Aubry et al., 2023). Other related goals are to prevent investments in certain assets that bring damage to society or to invest in certain businesses that pursue certain social or economic goals, such as businesses that are locally run or managed by underrepresented minority groups. There is still no consensus on whether these social and economic goals should be prioritized when managing pension funds.

Good governance of pension plans

Unlike the goals of benefits, costs, funding, and investment returns, which have more objective and quantitative measurements, the goal of good governance can only be assessed in a qualitative way. This goal is also very important, though, as the governance rules and structure safeguard the management of a pension plan and will eventually affect the other goals.

Good governance of pension plans can be broadly defined as designing appropriate processes and organizational structures for the operation of pension plans. Rating agencies consider pension plan management and governance when they assign ratings to governments (Aon Hewitt,

2017). The governance factors mostly relate to the plan's practices in following accounting and actuarial standards, setting up the due process to control risk, avoiding conflict of interests, and ensuring balanced representation of diverse stakeholders on the board. The guidelines and best practices for good governance have been put forward by professional associations.

The Government Finance Officers Association's (GFOA) best practices in pension and benefit administration include guidance for preparing pension plan summary documents, educating employees about retirement benefits, selecting investment professionals, reviewing actuarial valuation reports, and disclosing pension funding obligations. According to these best practices, a good pension system "completely, accurately, and clearly describes the significant components of the pension plan for participants" and should "educate employees about retirement income," "exercise appropriate due diligence in their selection of investment professionals," and "implement appropriate procedures when determining the level of information that needs to be disclosed about their pension funding obligations relative to their financial position" (GFOA, 2022).

Miller and Funston (2014) developed six principles for effective public pension fund governance, which include effective and capable fiduciaries to manage investments and operate funds; ethical leaders that comply with laws, regulations, and policies; open and accountable decision-making processes; intelligent and insightful risk management; a long-term view to ensure financial soundness and effective retirement solutions; and continuous adaptation to changing conditions. They also suggest that public pension funds conduct regular, independent fiduciary reviews to provide an objective evaluation of fund governance and operations.

The American Federation of State, County and Municipal Employees (AFSCME), which represents public-sector employees and retirees, also provides best practice guidance on selecting and educating pension board members, and setting ethical standards and fiduciary duties (AFSCME, 2020).

Finally, Aubry and Crawford (2019) from the Center for Retirement Research at Boston College suggest that the composition of board members is an important component of board effectiveness. They argue that a pension board should have the collective skills, experience, and subject-matter expertise to oversee a pension fund's various activities. Additionally, an effective pension board should have adequate stakeholder representation, including plan participants, government officials, and members of the general public. In 2018, 54% of public pension board members were plan participants, 15% were ex officio members, and 31% were from the general public (Aubry & Crawford, 2019).

Balancing the goals in pension plans

The five goals and the current consensus regarding appropriate targets for each goal are summarized in Table 3.2, which can help policymakers and stakeholders in public pension plans understand the goals and benchmarks discussed in the literature. However, it is equally important to balance these five goals, as there are always trade-offs among them. Pension policies that focus on certain goals, such as reducing pension costs or increasing pension funding, might involve measures to reduce pension benefits,

TABLE 3.2 Goals of Public Pension Management

Goals	*Current consensus on the targets*	*Notes*	*Sources*
Sufficiency of pension benefits	Replacement ratio ≥ 75–80%	If employees are not covered by Social Security, the expected replacement ratio would be higher.	Urban Institute (2014b), Peng (2008), and Young & Theodore (2023)
Affordability of pension costs	The sum of debt service, pension, and OPEB expenses < 20% of governmental expenditures for "aa" rating	Other cost measures include pension costs as a percent of total payroll.	FitchRatings (2021)
Sustainability of pension funding	Funding ratio ≥ 80%	The 80% rule is not a consensus. Some argue that 100% should be the goal.	GAO (2007) and S&P (2016)
Efficiency of asset management	Meeting the long-term expected rate of return (ERR)	ERR varies by plan. For most plans, this rate is around 7.5%.	Authors' opinion
Good governance of pension plans	Following best practices in plan governance, accounting and financial reporting standards, processes, and board composition	Best practices are recommended by professional associations.	GFOA (2022), Miller and Funston (2014), AFSCME (2020), and Aubry and Crawford (2019)

which compromise the goal of benefit sufficiency. Effective pension plan management should assess the plan's current status against these targets and carefully consider how any policy changes impact each goal.

Mini case: overview of NYCTRS

The New York City Teachers' Retirement System (NYCTRS) is one of New York City's five major pension systems. NYCTRS provides pension benefits to New York City public school teachers, certain other school employees, and college teachers in the City University of New York (CUNY) system. The system contains two major pension plans: a cost-sharing, multiple-employer defined-benefit plan called the Qualified Pension Plan (QPP), and a voluntary defined-contribution plan called the tax-deferred annuity (TDA). As of 2022, the system has approximately 124,000 in-service members and 92,000 retired members and beneficiaries. This section discusses how the five goals for public pension plan management were achieved in NYCTRS.

Sufficiency: the replacement rate

As discussed above, one of the measurements for the sufficiency of pension benefits is the replacement rate. It is not straightforward, however, to calculate the average replacement rate for NYCTRS members. Members receive benefits mainly from the defined-benefit plan QPP, but some of them also participate in the voluntary DC plan TDA, which provides guaranteed investment returns. In QPP, there are five benefit tiers with different formulas, contribution requirements, and retirement eligibility rules. The different tiers are due to benefit changes (mostly reductions) in 1973, 1976, 1983, and 2012. Members receive different benefit levels depending on the date they joined the system.

Here we provide a simple estimation of the replacement rate based on the benefit formula in the defined-benefit QPP plan. The benefits are calculated based on total service credit and the final average salary (FAS). FAS is generally the highest average of wages earned during any continuous five-year period of employment. The benefit factors are calculated following the rules summarized in NYCTRS 2022 Annual Comprehensive Financial Report.

> Benefits: (1) For a member with fewer than 20 years of service, the benefit is 1.67% times FAS multiplied by years of service. (2) For a member with at least 20 (Tier VI) but fewer than 30 years of service (Tier III/IV), the benefit is 2% times FAS multiplied by years of service (Tier III/IV) or

> 35% plus 2% times FAS multiplied by each additional year exceeding 20 years of service (Tier VI). (3) For a member with 30 or more years of service, the benefit is 2% times FAS for each of the first 30 years of service plus 1.5% times FAS for each additional year (Tier III/IV). (p. 11)

For an employee who started working for a public school in New York City at the age of 25 and retired at the normal retirement age of 63 (i.e., 38 years of service), the replacement rate is around 72% (30 * 2% + 8 * 1.5% = 72%). With fewer years of service such as 25 years, the replacement rate will decrease to 45% (35% + 5 * 2% = 45%). Members are also required to contribute 3–6% of their payroll depending on their salary level. With higher members' contributions, the lifetime take-home income for a member is reduced. Increasing members' contributions is a way of reducing benefit levels.

NYCTRS also provides automatic cost-of-living adjustments (COLAs), which are one-half of the increase in the Consumer Price Index for All Urban Consumers (CPI-U) with a floor of 1% and a cap of 3% of the first $18,000 of the sum of the maximum retirement allowance and prior COLAs (NYCTRS, 2022). This automatic COLA helps preserve the purchasing power of pension benefits after retirement.

Affordability: the employers' contribution rates

The system's actuary calculates the actuarially determined contributions (ADC) in the actuarial process. In the fiscal year 2022, the NYCTRS required employers' contribution was $3.3 billion, which is around 29.6% of payroll. Employers are legally required to fully pay the annual contribution amount.

The Department of Education (DOE) is the largest contributing employer in the system, which pays $3.2 billion to the system. Considering that NYC's general revenues were approximately $69.7 billion in the fiscal year 2022 (NYC, 2022), the pension contributions are around 4.58% of the city's general revenues. For NYCTRS, the high contribution rate has been a concern for many years. Looking at the contribution rates in the past ten years (2013–2022), the average rate is above 37.7% of payroll with a high of 44.8% of payroll in 2016.

Sustainability: the funded ratio

NYCTRS also reports the funded ratios of the QPP-DB plan as part of their actuarial valuation process. In the fiscal year 2020, the reported funded ratio for the QPP plan was 80.4%. This funded ratio has gradually increased over the last decade from 58.2% in the fiscal year 2011, and finally reaching above 80% for the first time in the decade from 2011 to 2020 (NYCTRS 2022). Comparing the funded ratios with the goals listed in Table 3.2, we see that NYCTRS has made substantial improvements toward reaching the funding goal. Its funded ratio has improved by more than 20% in the last decade.

The actuarial funded ratio is influenced by the actuarial methods used to calculate liabilities and assets. The various cost methods and discount rates, along with their impact on liabilities and funded ratios, will be discussed further in Chapter 6.

Efficiency: expected rate of return

As of 2022, the system's ERR on investments is 7.0%, which represents the long-term investment return goal set by NYCTRS for its pension funds. NYCTRS invests its pension assets in several funds. As of June 30, 2022, QPP assets were invested 26% in U.S. equities, 17% in non-U.S. equities, 20% in alternative investments, and 37% in fixed-income and short-term investments. The gross investment returns in the years 2020, 2021, and 2022 were 5.1, 25.1, and −9.39%. In the fiscal year 2022, the annualized three-, five-, and ten-year returns were 6.02, 6.82, and 8.06%, respectively (NYCTRS, 2022). Because the ERR is based on a long-term horizon, we should use the long-term perspective to examine whether the pension fund has met its return goals. In the past ten years (2013–2022), the investment returns fell below the 7% expected rate in four years (2015, 2016, 2020, and 2022), but the overall annualized rate is still at 8.06%, one percentage point above the expected rate.

Governance and policies

New York City's credit rating was Aa2 (Moody's) and AA (S&P) in the fiscal year 2022. NYCTRS is governed by the Teachers' Retirement Board, which consists of seven trustees that represent members and employers. Among the seven trustees, three are elected by members, two are appointed by the Mayor of New York City, and the other two are ex officio trustees (the City Comptroller and the Chair of the Panel for Education Policy). The Board holds monthly meetings, which are open to the public, and the meeting minutes are published on the system's website. NYCTRS sends semiannual newsletters to members, which report their investment returns and new policies.

NYCTRS follows generally accepted accounting principles to prepare their annual financial reports. They have received GFOA's Certificate of Achievement for Excellence in Financial Reporting, which recognizes that the financial reports have followed GASB standards to report necessary information and are readable.

In sum, by comparing NYCTRS's performance with the goals and targets summarized in Table 3.2, we can conclude that the system has provided sufficient retirement benefits for long-term employees, employer contribution rates are relatively high, the funded ratio has improved and reached sustainable funding in 2022, investment goals have been met, and the system has maintained a good credit rating while following financial reporting standards.

Summary

In this chapter, we describe and explain the five goals for public pension plan governance. Pension plan policymakers and stakeholders consider these goals as they make pension policies, but they might place different emphasis on these goals depending on their interests or preferences at a point in time. Debates over which goals to prioritize often occur when pension policy changes are discussed.

For example, when the sponsoring governments face high pension liabilities and costs, pension plans often face pressure to reduce pension costs. Policy options for cutting pension costs often entail cutting pension benefits by creating a new tier with lower benefits or asking active employees to increase their contributions. The creation of new tiers with lower benefit levels and higher employee contribution rates will help to lower pension costs in the long run. However, employees under the new tier have less benefit sufficiency and retirement security. Policymakers need to work with employee groups to negotiate over these multiple goals of benefit sufficiency, cost affordability, and fiscal sustainability.

Another typical example of a compromise over the goals occurs over contribution changes during a recession. When economic recessions occur, pension assets often receive lower-than-expected returns, which will lower funding levels and increase required contributions. During recessions, governments also often have lower tax revenues and often face pressure to increase spending in other public service areas either to create jobs or to provide assistance to citizens. This can lead to pressure to reduce pension contributions in a recession year for other more immediate needs, if their contribution policies allow them to do so. However, lower pension contributions will impact the fiscal sustainability of the pension plan. Facing this decision, policymakers in different governments make different choices depending on the information they have or their policy agenda. Lawmakers in some states have set up policies to mandate governments to fully pay their required contributions to public pension plans. In fact, we observe different contribution practices across governments and pension plans, which will be discussed further in Chapter 7.

As a summary, we suggest that these five goals are important for public pension plan management and for discussions over pension policy changes. Current issues in pension management, such as low pension funding ratios and high pension costs, are usually due to previous decisions that emphasized certain goals but sacrificed other goals. Successful policy changes or reforms in pension plans are usually the result of balancing these goals.

References

American Federation of State, County and Municipal Employees (AFSCME). (2020). *Best practice policies for trustees and pension systems*. https://afscmestaff.org/wp-content/uploads/2020/03/AFSCME-report-pension-best-practices-1.pdf

Aon Hewitt. (2017). *How do public pension plans impact credit ratings?* https://insights-north-america.aon.com/investment/how-do-pensions-impact-credit-ratings-whitepaper-201710-v2

Aubry, J.-P., Chen, A., Hubbard, P., & Munnell, A. H. (2023). ESG investing and public pensions: An update. Retrieved October 17, 2023, from https://publicplansdata.org/issue_brief/esg-investing-and-public-pensions-an-update/

Aubry, J.-P., & Crawford, C. V. (2019). *Does public pension board composition impact returns?* Center for Retirement Research at Boston College. https://crr.bc.edu/wp-content/uploads/2019/08/SLP67_.pdf

Brown, A. (2023, February 14). Time bomb of public pension funding ticks louder. *Washington Post*. https://www.washingtonpost.com/business/energy/time-bomb-of-public-pension-funding-ticks-louder/2023/02/13/a9cbcfae-ab94-11ed-b0ba-9f4244c6e5da_story.html

Center for Retirement Research (CRR). (2022). Public Plans Database. https://publicplansdata.org/.

Clark, R. L., Craig, L. A., & Wilson, J. W. (2003). *A history of public sector pensions in the United States*. University of Pennsylvania Press.

Clingman, M., Burkhalter, K., & Chaplain, C. (2021). *Replacement rates for hypothetical retired workers*. Actuarial Note No. 2021.9. Social Security Administration, Office of the Chief Actuary Baltimore, Maryland.

Degen, C. (2022). *Several governor races could have impact on state retirement plans*. Pensions & Investments. Retrieved October 16, 2023, from https://www.pionline.com/elections/several-governor-races-could-have-impact-state-retirement-plans

Fidelity. (2023). *How does a 401(k) match work?* https://www.fidelity.com/learning-center/smart-money/average-401k-match

FitchRatings. (2021). *U.S. public finance tax-supported rating criteria: Master criteria*. https://www.nasra.org//Files/Topical%20Reports/Credit%20Effects/Fitch%20Methodology.pdf

Foster, A. (1997). *Public and private sector defined benefit pensions: A comparison*. https://www.bls.gov/opub/mlr/1997/article/public-and-private-sector-defined-benefit-pensions-a-comparison.htm

Giesecke, O., & Rauh, J. D. (2022). *How much do public employees value defined benefit versus defined contribution retirement benefits?* SSRN Scholarly Paper 4308471. https://doi.org/10.2139/ssrn.4308471

Governmental Accounting Standards Board (GASB). (2012a). *Statement No. 67: Financial reporting for pension plans—an amendment of GASB Statement No. 25*. https://www.gasb.org/standards-and-guidance/pronouncements.

Governmental Accounting Standards Board (GASB). (2012b). *Statement No. 68: Accounting and financial reporting for pensions—an amendment of GASB Statement No. 27*. https://www.gasb.org/standards-and-guidance/pronouncements.

Government Finance Officers Association (GFOA). (2022). *Pension and benefit administration best practices*. https://www.gfoa.org/best-practices/pension-policy-governance-and-management

Miller, R., & Funston, R. (2014). *Public pension governance that works*. Funston Advisory Services LLC. https://www.nasra.org/Files/Topical%20Reports/Governance%20and%20Legislation/FunstonGovernance1403.pdf

Moody's Investors Service. (2013). *Adjustments to US state and local government reported pension data*. https://www.nasra.org/Files/Topical%20Reports/Credit%20Effects/Moodysfinal1304.pdf

Munnell, A. H., Aubry, J. P., & Sanzenbacher, G. (2015). *Recruiting and retaining high-quality state and local workers: Do pensions matter?* Center for Retirement Research at Boston College Working Paper (2015-1).

National Association of State Retirement Administrators (NASRA). (2023a). *NASRA issue brief: State and local government spending on public employee retirement systems*. https://www.nasra.org/files/Issue%20Briefs/NASRACostsBrief.pdf

National Association of State Retirement Administrators (NASRA). (2023b). *NASRA issue brief: Public pension plan investment return assumptions*. https://www.nasra.org/files/Issue%20Briefs/NASRAInvReturnAssumptBrief.pdf

New York City. (2022). *Annual comprehensive financial report of the comptroller*. https://comptroller.nyc.gov/wp-content/uploads/documents/ACFR-2022.pdf

New York City Teachers' Retirement System (NYCTRS). (2022). *Annual comprehensive financial report for fiscal years ended June 30, 2022 and June 30, 2021*. https://www.trsnyc.org/memberportal/Publications/finance

Peng, J. (2008). *State and local pension fund management*. CRC Press/Taylor & Francis Group.

Pew Charitable Trusts. (2014). *State public pension investments shift over past 30 years*. https://www.pewtrusts.org/~/media/assets/2014/06/state_public_pension_investments_shift_over_past_30_years.pdf

Quinby, L. D., & Sanzenbacher, G. T. (2020). Do pensions matter for recruiting state and local workers? *State and Local Government Review*, 52(1), 6–17.

Quinby, L. D., Sanzenbacher, G. T., & Aubry, J. P. (2018). *How have pension cuts affected public sector competitiveness?* Center for Retirement Research at Boston College. https://crr.bc.edu/wp-content/uploads/2018/04/slp_59.pdf

S&P Global Rating. (2016). *U.S. state ratings methodology*. https://www.nasra.org//Files/Topical%20Reports/Credit%20Effects/RatingsDirector_USStateRatingsMethodology.pdf

Stoltzfus, E. R. (2016, December). *Defined contribution retirement plans: Who has them and what do they cost?* Beyond the Numbers: Pay and Benefits (Vol. 5, No. 17). U.S. Bureau of Labor Statistics. https://www.bls.gov/opub/btn/volume-5/defined-contribution-retirement-plans-who-has-them-and-what-do-they-cost.htm

Urban Institute. (n.d.). *State and local backgrounders*. https://www.urban.org/policy-centers/cross-center-initiatives/state-and-local-finance-initiative/state-and-local-backgrounders/state-and-local-expenditures#:~:text=Most%20state%20and%20local%20government,%2C%20and%20courts)%2C%20and%20housing

Urban Institute. (2014a). *State and local employee pension plan database*. https://apps.urban.org/features/SLEPP/data.html

Urban Institute. (2014b). *The state of retirement: Grading America's public pension plans*. https://apps.urban.org/features/SLEPP/index.html

U.S. Government Accountability Office. (2007, September 2007). *State and local government retiree benefits—Current status of benefit structures, protections, and fiscal outlook for funding future costs*. https://www.gao.gov/assets/gao-07-1156.pdf

White, K. (2023, January 25). *Rainy day funds reach historic levels, leaving states more prepared than ever for a future downturn*. https://community.nasbo.org/budgetblogs/blogs/kathryn-white/2023/01/25/rainy-day-funds-reach-historic-levels

Young, R., & Theodore, L. (2023, August 3). *How to determine the amount of income you will need at retirement. T. Rowe Price insights on retirement*. https://www.troweprice.com/personal-investing/resources/insights/how-to-determine-amount-of-income-you-will-need-at-retirement.html

4

HOW ENVIRONMENT, STAKEHOLDERS, AND CONSTRAINTS SHAPE PUBLIC PENSION DECISIONS

Introduction

Pension boards and administering government officials make a variety of decisions related to public pensions, including pension benefits, contribution rates, investment policies, and actuarial assumptions. These decisions are not made in a vacuum. Decision-makers have a variety of available options, but their choices depend to some extent on a variety of factors both internal and external to the pension system. This chapter identifies three types of input factors that may influence pension decisions. These include the environment (e.g., fiscal health of the government and politics), stakeholders (e.g., employees and retirees), and constraints (e.g., legal requirements and labor union contracts). Each of these categories comprises several components, which vary between the two groups of decision-makers in governments and pension systems. The three types of factors, and the reasons they may affect pension decisions, will be addressed in turn.

Environment

The pension system operates within an environment that encompasses fiscal health of the government and the pension system, the state of the economy and financial markets, and politics. These variables can change over time with the economic cycle and political leadership transitions. In addition, previous decisions made by pension trustees and elected officials have a feedback loop. The results of those decisions can affect the

DOI: 10.4324/9781032671185-4

current environment. For example, if a government does not make actuarially determined contributions over a period of time, the pension system will become underfunded. This then will be an important environmental factor for trustees as they consider changes to actuarial assumptions and investments. The underpayment of contributions may be related to the government's fiscal health and may also result in credit rating downgrades. Elected officials of the administering government may then seek to change pension benefits and contributions. Maintaining awareness of the internal and external environment and understanding how it can affect their decisions, as well as how their decisions can affect the future environment and therefore future decisions, is important for officials in fulfilling their duties to the system and its beneficiaries, and to the government and its citizens.

We identify seven major environmental factors that can affect pension decisions (see Table 4.1). Three of these are relevant for pension system trustees: capital markets, the overall fiscal health of the pension system, and political embeddedness. The other four environmental factors are more relevant to officials of the administering government: fiscal health of the government, credit ratings, political ideology, and electoral politics. While we discuss these as discrete factors, they are often interrelated.

Capital markets

Capital markets are critical considerations for pension systems, as they typically rely on invested assets for a significant portion of current and/or future pension payments. For plans included in the NASRA Public Fund Survey, for example, investment returns comprised 63% of revenues over the last 30 years (NASRA, 2023). Market performance is therefore an important component of the system. Investment performance is greater when markets are strong, while declining markets may lead to investment concerns for pension systems (Baker, 2011; Brown et al., 2011; Coggburn & Kearney, 2010). For example, during the Great Recession, "…the collapse of the stock market reduced the value of equities held by state and local

TABLE 4.1 Inputs – Environment

Decision-makers	*Factors*
Pension system trustees	• Capital markets • Fiscal health of pension system • Political embeddedness
Administering government officials	• Fiscal health of government • Credit ratings • Political ideology • Electoral politics

plans by about $1 trillion, substantially undermining the funded status of virtually all state and local plans" (Munnell et al., 2010, p. 1). To put this in perspective, the 2008 loss in valuation was the equivalent of eight years of employer and employee pension contributions (Clark & Sabelhaus, 2009). Under the pressure of growing unfunded pension liabilities and low market return environments, some governments have taken action to reduce pension benefits and/or increase pension contributions (Brainard & Brown, 2018; St. Clair & Martinez-Guzman, 2017; Thom, 2017).

Fiscal health of pension system

The strength of capital markets then has a direct effect on the overall fiscal health of the pension system, which is often measured by the funded ratio of the system. Reduced asset values of investments lead to lower funded ratios. These losses can cause more distress to pension systems that were already underfunded than to systems that were fully funded. The funded ratio for state and local pension plans rose in the 1990s with a strong stock market, but then declined between 2001 and 2011 as a result of two market downturns. The aggregate funded ratio for plans in the Public Plans Database was 103% in 2001 (Aubry & Crawford, 2019a) but only about 74% in 2022 (Aubry, 2022). If the system is not sustainable, there may be pressure on decision-makers to make changes to investments, contributions, benefits, or actuarial assumptions, especially in times of poor-performing capital markets.

Political embeddedness

Governments not only oversee and regulate pension benefits and contributions but are also involved in pension governance through their appointed pension board trustees. Examining the political embeddedness of public pension boards is critical to understanding the extent to which state and local governments' political ideology and fiscal goals/priorities influence pension board decisions (Wang & Peng, 2018). Strong ties between the pension board and the government can reduce uncertainties and increase the flow of information and cooperation between different pension stakeholders, interest groups, and voters, which can help foster smoother adoption and implementation of pension policies or reforms (Moe, 1985; Wang & Peng, 2018). However, strong ties between pension governance and governments can also cause pension board decisions to align with the political and fiscal goals of government officials, while being less attentive to the interests of pension plan participants and long-term benefits of pension financial sustainability (Anzia & Moe, 2019). One way this can be manifested is through trustees adopting accounting and actuarial policies to underestimate the true cost of funding public pension promises (Chaney et al., 2002; Eaton & Nofsinger, 2004; Novy-Marx & Rauh, 2011; Stalebrink & Donatella, 2021). Eaton and Nofsinger (2004) found evidence that governments in fiscal stress use actuarial assumptions that make the plan look more highly funded and lower the required contributions to the pension system. An earlier study found that almost two-thirds of states altered actuarial assumptions during times of budget deficits (Mitchell & Smith, 1994).

In addition, embeddedness can lead boards into investment strategies to enhance economic development or social investments that are politically popular and provide state/local benefits. These decisions, though, could lead to asset allocations that violate the asset diversification principle and possibly yield lower returns (Andonov et al., 2017; Brown et al., 2009; Dobra & Lubich, 2013). For example, Pennsylvania state pension funds were pressured to provide partial financing for a new Volkswagen plant that closed a decade later, and over one-half of the loan was forgiven (Eaton & Nofsinger, 2004), an effort to help Colt Industries led to a loss of $25 million for the Connecticut state pension fund, and the Kansas state pension fund lost $100–200 million from a state investment program (Aubry et al., 2020). Over the last decade, environmental, social, and governance (ESG) investing has increased substantially, although these policies may also result in lower returns (Aubry et al., 2020).

Fiscal health of government

The administering government also considers several environmental factors in its decisions. The fiscal health of the government itself is important in determination of benefits and contributions (Giertz & Papke, 2007; Gorina, 2018; Peng, 2008; St. Clair, 2013). Governments in fiscal stress have less capacity to increase pension benefits or employer contributions, for example, than those that are fiscally healthy. Pension contributions are funded by the same sources that pay for other essential state/local services, such as public safety and education. When resources are scarce, competition for funds is intense, and pension contributions may be seen as being less urgent than maintaining other programs, so elected officials may find it easier in the short term to delay these payments (Peng, 2004). State fiscal conditions have generally been found to affect pension benefit funding levels (Coggburn & Kearney, 2010).

In addition, the fiscal health of the government and the pension system often go hand in hand. When the stock market is doing well, pension assets increase, which may require fewer government contributions. In a bear market, though, asset values decrease, requiring higher contributions.

This situation is often due to an economic slowdown, in which the government is also experiencing lower tax revenues, making it even harder to maintain or increase pension contributions. The Kentucky Retirement System, for example, became seriously underfunded by 2012; a significant portion of the underfunding was due to not making the actuarially determined retirement contributions and not paying for cost-of-living adjustments (Pew, 2013).

Credit ratings

The fiscal health of the government is also related to credit ratings. Governments seek ratings from bond rating agencies when they issue debt as a signal of their creditworthiness. Bonds that are more highly rated generally pay lower interest rates, which makes them less expensive for the issuing government. Rating agencies consider a variety of factors in their ratings, including long-term obligations. High levels of unfunded pension liabilities may result in lower credit ratings (Aubry & Crawford, 2017; Martell et al., 2013). This concern over credit downgrades may lead these governments to seek to reduce pension benefits or increase contributions to the system to reduce the unfunded liabilities.

Political ideology

Political ideology may also be a factor in governmental decisions. For example, conservatives may be more inclined to prefer defined contribution pension plans to the defined benefit plans that are more generous to employees and riskier for employers. Liberals, on the other hand, may favor generous defined benefit plans that offer more stability to retirees (Anzia & Moe, 2019; Thom, 2013). One study found that states controlled by Republicans were more likely to implement defined contribution plans (Munnell et al., 2008).

Electoral politics

Finally, electoral politics sometimes play a role in pension-related decisions (this may or may not be related to political ideology). Some governments have unionized employee groups with human and financial resources that they use to influence the public and elected officials through campaign contributions and political ads, for example (Frandsen & Webb, 2019; Hoang & Goodman, 2018; Schneider, 2005). Recipients of donations, or those seeking support from the unions, may feel beholden to the unions and willing to increase pension benefits when possible. During the 2021–2022 election cycle alone, the four largest national public employee unions spent over $700 million on election-related activities (Smith, 2023). In addition, the pressure to keep campaign promises and increase reelection chances can provide an added incentive, especially in times of fiscal stress, for elected officials to make less than the actuarially determined contributions in order to fund other public services (Eaton & Nofsinger, 2004). Some studies have found unfunded pension liability levels to be higher in unionized states than in those that are not unionized (Coggburn & Kearney, 2010).

Stakeholders

In addition to environmental factors, public pension decisions are also influenced by multiple stakeholders. These stakeholder groups may have different, competing interests which can lead to conflicts for decision-makers. The major relevant stakeholders vary between the two types of decision-makers: pension system trustees and administering government officials. However, there is some overlap in stakeholder groups between the two decision-makers. We identify three stakeholders for pension system trustees: constituency groups represented by trustees, pension administrators, and advisors. Stakeholder groups for the administering government officials include the employer governments, elected officials, unions and employees, retirees, and taxpayers. Table 4.2 summarizes the stakeholder groups. We will discuss each of these stakeholders and their general interests related to the pension system.

Trustees' constituencies

Pension boards have one of three structures: a single board that is responsible for administration and investments (about 74% of plans are in this category), separate investment and administrative boards (about 16% of plans), or a sole individual fiduciary who may also have a support board of

TABLE 4.2 Inputs – Stakeholders

Decision-makers	*Stakeholders*
Pension system trustees	• Trustees' constituencies • Pension administrators • Advisors
Administering government officials	• Employer governments • Elected officials • Unions/employees • Retirees • Taxpayers

members without voting rights (9% of plans) (Aubry & Crawford, 2019b). Trustees are the decision-makers for the pension system. However, they may represent different constituencies, such as retirees, employers, and current employees/unions. These groups may have different agendas which may lead to disagreement among trustees, even though they have a fiduciary duty to act in the best interests of the system and its members (Chen et al., 2015). Over one-half of board members in state/local plans are plan participants, while 15% are ex-officio members (e.g., representatives of the sponsoring government) and 31% represent the general public. Experts suggest having six to ten board members to allow for broad representation of stakeholders but to also be able to work efficiently. Plans range in board size. For example, the Idaho Public Employees Retirement System has five members, while the Tennessee State and Teachers Retirement system has a board of 19 members (Aubry & Crawford, 2019b). The effects of having plan participants (current workers and retirees) on the board are not clear (Munnell et al., 2010). These participants may be more interested in benefit expansion or increased cost-of-living adjustments than in funding the system adequately, and they may have less expertise to oversee investments, but on the other hand, they have more of a stake in the outcomes than other board members so may be more inclined to advocate for full funding. In addition, elected officials may try to gain control of pension boards. For example, California's Governor Wilson proposed replacing the state system CalPERS board with political appointees in the 1990s; the system offered up to $1.6 billion to help balance the state budget to forestall this effort (Eaton & Nofsinger, 2004).

Pension administrators

Internally, pension systems rely on pension administrators for activities such as monitoring investments and finances, paying benefits, and preparing reports. Administrators may have differing perspectives from trustees. For example, single-employer systems where pension administrators are employees of the sponsoring government may be influenced by elected officials who seek to make the system appear healthier than it is or desire higher investment returns despite the added risks, in an effort to reduce required employer contributions. The State of Wisconsin is a positive example of a system that insulates pension administration from political influence (Randazzo & Alexander, 2020).

Advisors

The primary external stakeholders for the pension system are the various advisors hired to assist the trustees, including actuaries and investment consultants. Actuaries conduct and make recommendations related to actuarial policies. They have a professional responsibility to follow accepted actuarial practices, but the changes they recommend may result in higher unfunded liabilities than are desirable (Chen, 2018; Gunz et al., 2009; Hoang & Maher, 2022). For example, if an actuary recommends that assumptions regarding expected mortality rates be changed because the population is living longer, this will increase the estimated pension liabilities as retirees will live and receive benefits for a longer period.

Many pension trustees do not have expertise in investment management. In some cases, a separate investment council, whose members have familiarity with this area, makes the investment decisions. Otherwise, it is common for boards to hire external advisors and managers to assist them with their various investments which may include a portfolio with a variety of equities, bonds, and alternative investments such as private equity and hedge funds. Investment managers and other investment consultants are interested in obtaining and retaining business with the pension system, which may mean overselling expected returns and minimizing actual investment risks (Chen et al., 2013; Clark & Monk, 2019). In addition, fees paid to these managers reduce the net investment returns. Studies have found that external managers reduce investment performance, largely because of these fees (Aubry & Wandrei, 2020).

Employer governments

The previously discussed stakeholders related to considerations of the pension board. The administering government also has several different stakeholder groups that may influence their decisions. In a multiemployer system, the individual employer governments may have different interests (Albrecht & Hingorani, 2004; Albrecht et al., 2007; Harper, 2008; Useem & Mitchell, 2000; Yang & Mitchell, 2005). For example, one in better fiscal health may prefer different levels of benefits for their employees than one experiencing fiscal stress.

Elected officials

Elected officials within the administering government may also have differing perspectives. As noted earlier, for example, ideological differences and partisan politics can lead to conflicts related to pension policies and decisions (Andonov et al., 2017; Brown et al., 2009; Schneider & Damanpour, 2001; Wang & Peng, 2018). This is particularly challenging during times of government fiscal stress when governments are struggling to balance the budget, and when pension plans are underfunded. For example, a study of pension reform efforts in Utah, Rhode Island, New Jersey, and Illinois illustrates the role of political and ideological conflicts (McGuinn, 2014).

Unions/employees

Employees generally prefer higher benefits with little or no employee contributions, so they may put pressure on elected officials to seek these objectives. Unions may have more influence than other public employees because they may make campaign contributions to candidates for office and have other means for strong advocacy for their agenda. About 32.5% of public-sector employees are union members, but there is variation across states and by type of job; for example, public safety employees and teachers tend to be more heavily unionized than general employees (U.S. Department of Labor, 2024). There may be conflicts between various employee groups if they have different pension plans and compete against each other for government budget dollars (e.g., civilian employees versus public safety, or public safety versus teachers) (Anzia & Moe, 2015; Kelley, 2014; Pennacchi & Rastad, 2011).

Taxpayers

Finally, taxpayers may have a very different perspective from the covered employees and retirees. Most private-sector employees are not covered by defined benefit plans, so taxpayers and voters may resent having their tax dollars used to provide retirement benefits that they themselves will not receive. This may put countervailing pressure on government officials to offset that of the system members. For example, the City of Omaha mayor faced a recall election in 2011. Contributing reasons for this effort were the deals he negotiated with the police and fire unions, and a proposed new restaurant tax to address significant unfunded pension liabilities (Hoang & Ebdon, 2021).

Constraints

Pension boards and administering government officials do not have complete autonomy in their decision making. Legal constraints and professional standards and practices limit what they can do (see Table 4.3). For pension systems, these constraints include actuarial and financial reporting standards, as well as state and local laws that relate to their investment decisions. Administering governments may be limited by state laws that protect pension benefits, as well as by court decisions. In addition, many governments are bound by contractual agreements with labor unions under which pension benefits are negotiated.

TABLE 4.3 Inputs – Constraints

Decision-makers	*Constraints*
Pension system trustees	• Actuarial standards of practice • Generally accepted accounting principles • State and local laws on investments
Administering government officials	• State legal protections of pension benefits • Labor union contracts • Court decisions

Actuarial standards of practice (ASOP)

There is a great deal of uncertainty about the cost estimates of providing a pension to an individual. For example, wage growth for that employee over time will affect the pension amount as well as contributions from the employer/employee, and the return on asset investments over time is critical in determining the required employer contributions. These are just two of many assumptions that are required to estimate the financial costs of a plan. Even small changes in these assumptions can have major effects on the system's fiscal health (Eaton & Nofsinger, 2004; Giertz & Papke, 2007). Pension systems generally hire an actuary to assess and recommend these assumptions and estimate the funded level of the system. Actuaries in the United States follow professional standards (actuarial standards of practice, ASOP) developed by the Actuarial Standards Board (ASB). These standards ensure that actuarial assumptions are professionally sound, though pension boards may retain some discretion in their final adoption.

Generally accepted accounting principles

Generally accepted accounting principles (GAAP) for state and local governments are developed by the Governmental Accounting Standards Board (GASB). As with actuarial policies, accounting standards can also affect the estimated assets, liabilities, and funded levels of pension plans. Not all governments follow GAAP, but many states require public pension plans to use GASB standards (Munnell et al., 2010). GAAP also change over time, which can affect pension decisions and outcomes. For example, GASB Statements No. 67 and 68 took effect beginning in 2014 and had a substantial effect on the reporting and measurement of pension data in financial statements. Assets are now reported at market value, rather than with a smoothing method, and estimated benefits are discounted with a blended rate of the expected rate of return on assets and the return on high-grade municipal bonds (which is generally lower and considered more conservative). In addition, local governments in cost-sharing plans now report their share of the unfunded liability. Munnell and Aubry (2016) found that the unfunded liability for a sample of 92 cities increased from 37% of own-source revenue to 70% as a result of GASB Statement No. 68.

State and local laws

Systems also need to consider applicable laws related to investment options. In the past, some states only allowed pension systems to invest in conservative investments with low risk and low returns, such as U.S. Treasury instruments, but this changed in the 1980s and 1990s (Peng, 2004). Many now follow the "prudent person" rule which allows for more discretion on the part of the pension systems while requiring trustees to make decisions with consideration of risk. Some states also use "legal lists" of specific types of investment options available to pensions (e.g., some can invest in alternatives such as hedge funds and private equity, while others cannot) and may include restrictions on the percentages of assets that can be allocated to certain asset classes (Aubry & Crawford, 2019b).

State legal protections of pension benefits

Administering governments are also constrained in various ways, especially related to making changes in pension benefits. The three constraints we discuss related to administering governments are somewhat interrelated. First, many states protect pension benefits either in state statutes or constitutions, but the type and level of protections vary. Alaska, Illinois, and New York protect past and future benefits in their state constitutions, while Indiana and Texas have no such protections (Aubry & Crawford, 2017), and Hawaii, Louisiana, and Michigan constitutions protect only benefits to date, rather than future benefits (Munnell & Quinby, 2012). Benefits for new employees are not protected in any states, so it is easier for governments to reform pensions for these employees by creating tiered systems (Aubry & Crawford, 2017).

Labor union contracts

In addition, many governments use collective bargaining with their employees. Union contracts are developed through negotiation between the government and the employee group(s) (Munnell & Quinby, 2012; Thom, 2017). Union contracts may cover pension benefits and generally cannot be changed without negotiation and bilateral agreement (or some type of arbitration or court process when the parties are at impasse).

Governments with labor contracts, therefore, are limited in the decisions they can make to increase or reduce benefits or contributions.

Court decisions

If governments and employee groups and/or retirees are at odds, lawsuits may be filed, and courts make decisions that may affect the ability of governments to change pension benefits and contributions. These court decisions vary across states depending on the facts of the cases and the specific language in state and local laws and constitutions (Monahan, 2013). It was rare in the past for pensioner benefits to be reduced; for example, this did not occur under severe fiscal stress in the 1975 New York City or 1994 Orange County California cases (Brown et al., 2011). After the Great Recession, though, some sponsoring governments sought to make dramatic changes to benefits through bankruptcy or unilateral changes to plans. One example is the 2014 City of Detroit bankruptcy agreement that froze pension systems, reduced pension benefits, eliminated cost of living adjustments for nonuniform employees, and reduced cost of living adjustments for uniformed employees (Tompor, 2018).

Summary

There are two groups of pension decision-makers: pension system trustees and officials of the administering government. They make a variety of decisions related to pension investments, actuarial assumptions, benefits, and contribution policies. The context within which these decisions are made is important to understand and may be quite different across systems. This chapter identified three different types of input factors that may affect these decisions: the environment, stakeholders, and constraints. An overview of the inputs and how they may be relevant was provided. The next several chapters will focus on the decisions that are made by the pension board and government officials. The first of these chapters, Chapter 5, discusses decisions related to pension fund investment.

References

Albrecht, W. G., & Hingorani, V. L. (2004). Effects of governance practices and investment strategies on state and local government pension fund financial performance. *International Journal of Public Administration*, *27*(8–9), 673–700. https://doi.org/10.1081/PAD-120030261

Albrecht, W. G., Shamsub, H., & Giannatasio, N. A. (2007). Public pension fund governance practices and financial performance. *Journal of Public Budgeting, Accounting & Financial Management*, *19*(2), 245–267.

Andonov, A., Bauer, R. M. M. J., & Cremers, K. J. M. (2017). Pension fund asset allocation and liability discount rates. *The Review of Financial Studies*, *30*(8), 2555–2595. https://doi.org/10.1093/rfs/hhx020

Anzia, S. F., & Moe, T. M. (2015). Public sector unions and the costs of government. *The Journal of Politics*, *77*(1), 114–127. https://doi.org/10.1086/678311

Anzia, S. F., & Moe, T. M. (2019). Interest groups on the inside: The governance of public pension funds. *Perspectives on Politics*, *17*(4), 1059–1078. https://doi.org/10.1017/S1537592718003468

Aubry, J.-P. (2022). *Public pensions contend with falling markets and rising inflation*. Center for Retirement Research Brief, Number 22-13.

Aubry, J.-P., Chen, A., Hubbard, P. M., & Munnell, A. H. (2020). *ESG investing and public pensions: An update*. Center for Retirement Research Brief, Number 74.

Aubry, J.-P., & Crawford, C. V. (2017). *State and local pension reform since the financial crisis*. Center for Retirement Research Brief, Number 54.

Aubry, J.-P., & Crawford, C. V. (2019a). *Update on the funded status of state and local pension plans – FY 2018*. Center for Retirement Research Brief.

Aubry, J.-P., & Crawford, C. V. (2019b). *Does public pension board composition impact returns?* Center for Retirement Research Brief, Number 67.

Aubry, J.-P., & Wandrei, K. (2020). *Internal vs. external management for state and local pension plans*. Center for Retirement Research Brief, Number 75.

Baker, D. (2011). *The origins and severity of the public pension crisis*. Center for Economic and Policy Research (CEPR). https://www.policyarchive.org/handle/10207/96093

Brainard, K., & Brown, A. (2018). *Significant reforms to State Retirement Systems*. National Association of State Retirement Administrators. https://www.nasra.org/reforms

Brown, J., Pollet, J., & Weisbenner, S. (2009). *The investment behavior of state pension plans* (No. onb09-12). National Bureau of Economic Research (NBER). https://www.nber.org/sites/default/files/2020-08/orrc09-12_0.pdf

Brown, J. B., Clark, R., & Rauh, J. (2011). The economics of state and local pensions. *PEF*, *10*(2), 161–172.

Chaney, B. A., Copley, P. A., & Stone, M. S. (2002). The effect of fiscal stress and balanced budget requirements on the funding and measurement of state pension obligations. *Journal of Accounting and Public Policy*, *21*(4), 287–313. https://doi.org/10.1016/S0278-4254(02)00064-9

Chen, G. (2018). Understanding decisions in state pension systems: A system framework. *The American Review of Public Administration*, 48(3), 260–273. https://doi.org/10.1177/0275074016675242

Chen, G., Ebdon, C., Kriz, K. A., & Laforge, O. M. (2013). The management of defined contribution pension plans in local government. *Public Budgeting & Finance*, *33*(3), 75–95. https://doi.org/10.1111/j.1540-5850.2013.12015.x

Chen, G., Kriz, K., & Ebdon, C. (2015). The effect of board composition on public sector pension funding. *Journal of Public Budgeting, Accounting & Financial Management*, *27*(3), 352–376. https://doi.org/10.1108/JPBAFM-27-03-2015-B003

Clark, G. L., & Monk, A. H. B. (2019). Asset owners, investment management, and commitment: An organizational framework. *The Journal of Retirement*, *6*(3), 9–22. https://doi.org/10.3905/jor.2019.6.3.009

Clark, R. L., & Sabelhaus, J. (2009). How will the stock market crash affect the choice of pension plans? *National Tax Journal*, *62*(3), 477–496. https://doi.org/10.17310/ntj.2009.3.08

Coggburn, J. D., & Kearney, R. C. (2010). Trouble keeping promises? An analysis of underfunding in state retiree benefits. *Public Administration Review*, *70*(1), 97–108.

Dobra, M., & Lubich, B. H. (2013). Public pension governance and asset allocation. *Journal of CENTRUM Cathedra*, *6*(1), 83–101. https://papers.ssrn.com/sol3/papers.cfm?abstract_id=2236469

Eaton, T. V., & Nofsinger, J. R. (2004). The effect of financial constraints and political pressure on the management of public pension plans. *Journal of Accounting and Public Policy*, *23*, 161–189.

Frandsen, B. R., & Webb, M. (2019). Public employee pensions and collective bargaining rights: Evidence from state and local government finances. *Journal of Law, Economics, & Policy*, *15*(2), 163–186.

Giertz, J. F., & Papke, L. E. (2007). Public pension plans: Myths and realities for state budgets. *National Tax Journal*, *60*(2), 305–323. https://doi.org/10.17310/ntj.2007.2.07

Gorina, E. (2018). City revenue structure and unfunded pension liabilities. *State and Local Government Review*, *50*(3), 189–202. https://doi.org/10.1177/0160323X18817806

Gunz, S., McCutcheon, J., & Reynolds, F. (2009). Independence, conflict of interest and the actuarial profession. *Journal of Business Ethics*, *89*, 77–89. https://doi.org/10.1007/s10551-008-9985-8

Harper, J. T. (2008). Public sector pension governance in the United States: Up to the task? *Rotman International Journal of Pension Management*, *1*(1), 22–28. https://ssrn.com/abstract=1290601

Hoang, T., & Ebdon, C. (2021). *Institutional framework and path dependence in pension reform: A case study* (Working Paper).

Hoang, T., & Goodman, D. (2018). Public pensions and collective bargaining rights: Evidence from state and local governments. *Public Admin Review*, *78*(5), 772–784. https://doi.org/10.1111/puar.12936

Hoang, T., & Maher, C. S. (2022). Fiscal condition, institutional constraints, and public pension contribution: Are pension contribution shortfalls fiscal illusion? *Public Budgeting & Finance*, 42(4), 93–124. https://doi.org/10.1111/pbaf.12328

Kelley, D. G. (2014). The political economy of unfunded public pension liabilities. *Public Choice*, *158*(1/2), 21–38. https://doi.org/10.1007/s11127-012-0049-3

Martell, C. R., Kioko, S. N., & Moldogaziev, T. (2013). Impact of unfunded pension obligations on credit quality of state governments. *Public Budgeting & Finance*, *33*(3), 24–54. https://doi.org/10.1111/j.1540-5850.2013.12013.x

McGuinn, P. (2014, February). *Pension politics: Public employee retirement system reform in four states*. Brown Center on Education Policy at Brookings. https://www.brookings.edu/wp-content/uploads/2016/06/Pension-Politics_FINAL_225.pdf

Mitchell, O. S., & Smith, R. S. (1994). Pension funding in the public sector. *The Review of Economics and Statistics*, *76*(2), 278–290.

Moe, T. M. (1985). Control and feedback in economic regulation: The case of the NLRB. *American Political Science Review*, *79*(4), 1094–1116. https://doi.org/10.2307/1956250

Monahan, A. (2013). *Understanding the legal limits on public pension reform*. American Enterprise Institute. https://www.nasra.org/Files/Topical%20Reports/Legal/Monahan1305.pdf

Munnell, A. H., & Aubry, J.-P. (2016). *GASB 68: How will state unfunded pension liabilities affect big cities?* Center for Retirement Research Brief, Number 47.

Munnell, A. H., Aubry, J.-P., & Quinby, L. (2010). *Public pension funding in practice* (Working Paper 16442). National Bureau of Economic Research.
Munnell, A. H., Golub-Sass, A., Haverstick, K., Soto, M., & Wiles, G. (2008, January). *Why have some states introduced defined contribution plans?* Center for Retirement Research at Boston College, 3.
Munnell, A. H., & Quinby, L. (2012). *Legal constraints on changes in state and local pensions*. Center for Retirement Research at Boston College - State and Local Issue in Brief, 25. https://crr.bc.edu/wp-content/uploads/2012/08/slp_25.pdf
National Association of State Retirement Administrators (NASRA). (2023). *Public fund survey*. https://www.nasra.org/publicfundsurvey
Novy-Marx, R., & Rauh, J. (2011). Public pension promises: How big are they and what are they worth? *The Journal of Finance*, *66*(4), 1211–1249. https://doi.org/10.1111/j.1540-6261.2011.01664.x
Peng, J. (2004). Public pension funds and operating budgets: A tale of three states. *Public Budgeting & Finance*, *24*(2), 59–73.
Peng, J. (2008). State public pension management over the business cycle. *Journal of Public Budgeting, Accounting & Financial Management*, *20*(1), 1–21. https://doi.org/10.1108/JPBAFM-20-01-2008-B001
Pennacchi, G., & Rastad, M. (2011). Portfolio allocation for public pension funds. *Journal of Pension Economics & Finance*, *10*(2), 221–245. https://doi.org/10.1017/S1474747211000102
Pew Charitable Trusts. (2013). *Kentucky's successful public pension reform*. https://www.pewtrusts.org/-/media/legacy/uploadedfiles/pcs_assets/2013/20130927kentuckypensionreformbriefpdf.pdf
Randazzo, A., & Alexander, S. (2020). *Calm amid the chaos: Wisconsin's pension system and the 2008 financial crisis*. Equable. https://equable.org/wisconsin-pension-system-and-the-2008-financial-crisis/
Schneider, M. (2005). The status of U.S. public pension plans: A review with policy considerations. *Review of Public Personnel Administration*, *25*(2), 107–137. https://doi.org/10.1177/0734371X04271062
Schneider, M., & Damanpour, F. (2001). Determinants of public pension plan investment return. The role of fund value maximization and public choice theory. *Public Management Review*, *3*(4), 551–573. https://doi.org/10.1080/14616670110070604
Smith, C. (2023, December 15). Political spending by public-sector unions is deep blue. *Governing*.
St. Clair, T. (2013). The impact of budget stabilization funds on state pension contributions. *Public Budgeting & Finance*, *33*(3), 55–74. https://doi.org/10.1111/j.1540-5850.2013.12014.x
St. Clair, T., & Martinez-Guzman, J. P. (2018). Contribution volatility and public pension reform. *Journal of Pension Economics and Finance*, *17*(4), 513–533. https://doi.org/10.1017/S1474747217000129
Stalebrink, O. J., & Donatella, P. (2021). Public pension governance and opportunistic accounting choice: A politico-economic approach. *The American Review of Public Administration*, *51*(3), 227–245. https://doi.org/10.1177/0275074020954397
Thom, M. (2013). All of the above: How fiscal, political, and workforce traits affect pension funding. *State and Local Government Review*, *45*(3), 163–171. https://doi.org/10.1177/0160323X13499733
Thom, M. (2017). The drivers of public sector pension reform across the U.S. states. *The American Review of Public Administration*, 47(4), 431–442. https://doi.org/10.1177/0275074015589342

Tompor, S. (2018, July 18). Even 5 years later, retirees feel the effects of Detroit's bankruptcy. *Detroit Free Press*. https://www.freep.com/story/money/personal-finance/susan-tompor/2018/07/18/detroit-bankruptcy-retirees-pension/759446002/

U.S. Department of Labor Bureau of Labor Statistics. (2024, January 23). *Union members – 2023*. News Release. USDL-24-0096. https://www.bls.gov/news.release/pdf/union2.pdf

Useem, M., & Mitchell, O. S. (2000). Holders of the purse strings: Governance and performance of public retirement systems. *Social Science Quarterly*, *81*(2), 489–506. http://www.jstor.org/stable/42863971

Wang, Q., & Peng, J. (2018). Political embeddedness of public pension governance: An event history analysis of discount rate changes. *Public Admin Review*, *78*(5), 785–794. https://doi.org/10.1111/puar.12968

Yang, T. S., & Mitchell, O. S. (2005). *Public pension governance, funding, and performance: A longitudinal appraisal*. Wharton Pension Research Council Working Papers. https://repository.upenn.edu/handle/20.500.14332/43742

5

INVESTMENT POLICIES AND STRATEGIES FOR PUBLIC PENSION FUNDS

Introduction

In the logic model framework, we identify investments as one of the four important categories of pension decisions. Investment performance is critical to achieving all the main goals of pension management. A sound investment strategy can enhance the efficiency of asset management and generate revenues to ensure pension benefit security, reduce pension costs for both employers and employees, and maintain the solvency and funding sustainability of pension plans. Pension investment performance is highly sensitive to changes in capital market conditions, and many stakeholders, including the pension board, administrators, and professional advisors, are involved in the investment decision-making process. This chapter discusses the authority of pension boards and their decision-making processes in the investment area.

In most public pension plans, it is the pension board's responsibility to review and adopt investment policies that guide the pension fund investment process, although some plans assign this responsibility to a separate entity such as an investment council. The board or the investment council is also responsible for appointing key administrative staff and advisors to manage the day-to-day operations of pension funds. They also regularly review investment performance and approve changes in asset allocation. Some investment policies impose restrictions on the asset classes in which pension assets can be invested. Many plans follow a "prudent person rule," which means that pension assets should be managed in an appropriate way that a prudent person would do with their own assets. Following

DOI: 10.4324/9781032671185-5

a plan's investment policy, fund managers make asset allocation decisions and report their decisions and performance to the board. Performance reports and suggested changes from fund managers are important discussion and action items at the board's regular meetings.

In this chapter, we explain the main decision-making areas in the management of a pension fund's investment activities. In each area, we explain the decisions that are made, how those decisions affect the performance of pension funds, and the challenges public pension plans face in making those decisions.

Investment policy

A pension plan's investment policy is a formal, written document that serves as a long-term guide to govern the investment process. The investment policy is reviewed and adopted by the governing board of trustees. The investment policy also serves as a communication tool to disclose the investment goals and priorities to stakeholders of the pension plan. Pew (2023) finds that most public plans make investment policies publicly available on their website, but the disclosure practices vary significantly. An investment policy usually includes several main items: the investment objectives, the asset allocation strategy, risk management, the role of fund managers, and the process of reviewing fund performance. We describe these elements below and also present an example of an investment policy.

The investment objectives generally relate to the extent to which pension funds will pursue high yields or prefer more security. Investment objectives are often summarized in three primary aspects: safety, liquidity, and return. Safety is about how the plan mitigates fiscal risks such as credit risk and interest risk. Liquidity is about having sufficient funds available to pay operating expenses and benefits. Return is about the rate of return goal the investment portfolio seeks to achieve, considering the safety and liquidity needs.

Regarding the asset allocation strategy, many plans have specified a list of asset classes in which they will invest. The main asset classes include public equities (domestic stocks and international stocks), fixed income (government and corporate bonds), alternative investments (private equities, hedge funds, infrastructure, etc.), and cash equivalents. These asset classes will be discussed in the next section.

Modern portfolio theory (Markowitz, 1952) emphasizes the importance of diversification in an investment portfolio over various asset classes in order to reduce investment risk while aiming to achieve higher returns. Diversification strategies are also usually included in a pension plan's investment policy. Many policies include a table that shows the target percentage of assets to be invested in each asset class and how the portfolios should be rebalanced to meet these investment allocation goals. Diversification and allocation goals are reviewed and adjusted periodically by the pension board or investment council.

Many investment policies also include a statement of the "prudent person rule," which does not restrict assets from certain asset classes but requires that pension funds should be managed in a "prudent" way. Another common element of investment policies is the role and responsibilities of fund managers, as well as ethics codes including conflict-of-interest rules. Codes of ethics and conflict of interest policies require that officers and employees engaged in investment activities must adhere to relevant laws, disclosing any significant interests or information pertinent to these activities. Additionally, decision-makers are required to avoid any actions that could conflict with their responsibilities in the investment process.

Investment policies also include performance objectives for fund managers, along with a section outlining the criteria and process for evaluating their performance. These objectives frequently involve comparisons to specified benchmark return targets, such as the S&P 500 index. Investment policies also specify how often fund managers must report on fund performance to the board and the details that need to be included in these reports.

Below, we will use the Investment Policy Statement of the State of Connecticut Retirement Plans and Trust Funds ("CRPTF") as an example to show the main components of an investment policy. Information is collected from the State of Connecticut Treasurer's Office (2022).

CRPTF consists of 18 pension funds that are managed by the Treasurer of the State of Connecticut. As the sole trustee of the funds, the treasurer established the investment policy, which was also approved by the state's Investment Advisory Council. Below is a statement of the investment and return objectives in CRPTF's investment policy.

The key objective for the CRPTF is to:

- Earn a minimum assumed investment rate of return over market cycles by investing in a global portfolio of assets with different risk and return characteristics
- Affirmatively manage risk through deliberate exposures, use of leverage and management of liquidity across the CRPTF
- Meet or exceed its respective benchmark net of fees within each asset class such that each Trust Fund meets or exceeds its policy benchmark over a market cycle
- Maintain adequate liquidity to prevent the CRPTF from being a forced seller during market downturns

- Rebalance the portfolio to take advantage of market volatility, taking the opportunity to trim assets that have appreciated above the target policy allocation and purchased assets that have fallen below the policy target allocation

(*State of Connecticut Treasurer's Office, 2022, p. 7*)

CRPTF's asset allocation strategy is reviewed and approved by the state's investment council. In the 2022 investment statement, there are several broad allowable asset classes: domestic equity, developed market equity, emerging market equity, core fixed income, noncore fixed income, absolute return, private equity, private credit, real estate, infrastructure and natural resources, and cash equivalents. Table 5.1 shows the CRPTF's target allocation for each asset class.

Like most pension systems, CRPTF selects investment managers through a competitive bidding process and develops a set of investment guidelines for each investment manager, which are incorporated in their contracts with the fund. Investment performance is regularly assessed against asset class performance benchmarks and the investment guidelines. Monthly and quarterly performance reports for each asset class, each investment manager, and total fund performance are then submitted to the trustee and the Investment Advisory Council for review.

TABLE 5.1 Asset Allocation Targets (CRPTF)

Asset classes	*Target (%)*
Domestic equity	22
Developed market equity	11
Emerging market equity	4
Core fixed income	13
Noncore fixed income	2
Private equity	15
Private credit	10
Absolute return	5
Real estate	10
Infrastructure and natural resources	7
Cash equivalents	1
Total	100

Source: Investment Policy Statement for CRPTF, approved by the Investment Advisory Council in 2022.

Note: According to CRPTF's investment policy, investments in these asset classes will be rebalanced within an upper bound and lower bound around these targets.

Asset classes and allocation strategy

In the United States, public pension funds are allocated in a highly diversified investment portfolio. This portfolio includes four major asset classes such as equities (stocks), fixed-income investments (bonds), alternative investments, and cash equivalents (money market funds). Each of these major asset classes can be further categorized into sub-asset classes according to different characteristics. For example, equities include U.S. domestic stocks and international stocks; fixed-income investments include U.S. corporate bonds, international corporate bonds, and government bonds; alternative investments include commodities, real estate, infrastructure, private equity, derivatives, and hedge funds; and cash equivalents include cash, certificates of deposit, and U.S. treasury bills.

An asset class is a group of assets with similar characteristics such as return, risk, and liquidity. High returns are often associated with high risks and/or low liquidity. Although there is general agreement on the major asset classes, the specific class names and categorizations can vary in different lists. For example, real estate can be considered a major asset class or a sub-asset class within alternative investments. U.S. stocks can also be further subcategorized as large-cap, mid-cap, or small-cap, while international stocks can include stocks in developed countries and emerging markets. Table 5.2 shows a list of major asset classes used by U.S. public pension funds. Note that the allowable asset classes and categorization may vary in other lists.

Equities consist of stocks from publicly traded companies. Returns from this asset class include capital gains from stock trading and dividends. Equities are often considered high-return and high-risk. Equities can be further categorized by region (U.S. domestic, non-U.S. developed countries, or emerging markets), by sector (energy, technology, healthcare, etc.), or by the size of the company (large-cap, mid-cap, or small-cap), based on different risk and return expectations. For example, investments in small-cap (small companies) are often riskier but have higher return expectations than investments in large-cap (large companies). Because of a public pension fund's long-term investment horizon, equities are often the largest asset class in a pension fund's portfolio.

Fixed-income investments consist of bonds issued by companies or other entities. Returns from this asset class include capital gains from trading bonds and coupon payments from the bonds. Fixed-income investments are often considered lower risk than equities, although some bonds can also have high risk and high return. Fixed-income investments can be categorized by types of issuers (companies or governments), region (United States or international), credit ratings of the issuers, and maturity

TABLE 5.2 List of Asset Classes Used by U.S. Public Pension Funds

Asset classes	*Sub-asset classes*	*Definition*
Equities (stocks)	U.S. stocks	Stocks of publicly traded companies in the U.S. are often segmented by their market capitalization: large-cap (large-sized companies), mid-cap (medium-sized companies), and small-cap (small-sized companies)
	International stocks	Stocks of publicly traded companies outside the United States, including developed countries such as OECD countries and emerging markets such as Brazil, Russia, China, India, and South Africa (BRICS)
Fixed income (bonds)	U.S. corporate bonds	Bonds issued by companies in the United States
	U.S. government bonds	Bonds issued by a federal, state, or local government in the United States
	International bonds	Bonds issued by entities outside of the United States
Alternative investments	Commodities	Precious metals (gold, silver, etc.), energy (oil, natural gas, etc.), agricultural crops (corn, soybeans, etc.), industrial metals (copper, etc.)
	Real estate	Residential or commercial properties, Real Estate Investment Trusts (REITs)
	Private equity	Investments in companies that are not publicly traded
	Hedge funds	Pooled investment funds that are actively traded using specific strategies
	Infrastructure	Investments in roads, railways, airports, water facilities, etc.
	Derivatives	Options, futures, swaps, forwards, etc.
Cash equivalents	Cash	Cash
	Savings accounts	Accounts held at a bank or financial institution
	Money market funds	Funds that invest in short-term securities
	Certificates of deposits (CDs)	Deposits held at a bank for a fixed period of time
	Treasury bills	Short-term U.S. government securities

Source: Authors' data collection.

(long-term, medium-term, short-term). Bonds issued by governments or companies with good credit ratings are often considered low risk with secure returns, while bonds issued by small companies, especially those with low credit ratings, are high risk. However, some investors are willing to take this risk because of the potential for higher returns. Fixed-income investments are also an important asset class for public pension funds.

Alternative investments include a wide range of various investment vehicles with unique risk, return, and liquidity. Many investment tools that cannot be categorized as traditional stocks, bonds, or cash, are grouped into this alternative category. Commodities include various types of precious metals, energy, agricultural crops, and industrial metals. Investors can also participate in commodity investing through commodity mutual funds. Real estate includes residential and commercial properties. Investments in real estate yield returns from trading and rental income. A popular approach for investing in real estate is through Real Estate Investment Trusts (REITs), in which investors pool their assets to invest in the real estate market. Private equity is a direct investment in companies that are not publicly traded. Hedge funds are pooled investment funds that use sophisticated strategies to gain returns from public markets and minimize the downside risk. Investments in infrastructure, including roads, railways, airports, water, and waste facilities, generate returns through revenue streams such as tolls and user fees from these assets. Finally, financial derivatives are financial instruments whose value is derived from the value of an underlying asset. These instruments include options, futures, swaps, and forwards. Financial derivatives are often considered high-risk and potentially high-return investments.

Cash equivalents include cash, bank savings accounts, money market funds, certificates of deposit, and treasury bills. These assets are characterized by their high liquidity and low risk, typically yielding low returns. Pension funds maintain cash and cash equivalents to meet the liquidity needs, such as making benefit payments.

Figure 5.1 shows the asset allocation in the five major asset classes by major U.S. public pension plans from 2005 to 2021. We can observe some major changes in asset allocation over this period. Equities remain the largest asset class in public pension fund portfolios. However, the portion of pension funds invested in equities decreased from a high of 60% in 2006 to a low of below 45% in 2021. This change appears to have occurred during the Great Recession. The alternative investments class exhibited the most significant changes during this period. In 2006, alternative assets accounted for less than 10% of public pension assets. Since then, there has been a consistent increase in investments in alternatives, reaching highs of more than 25% after 2019. In contrast to alternative

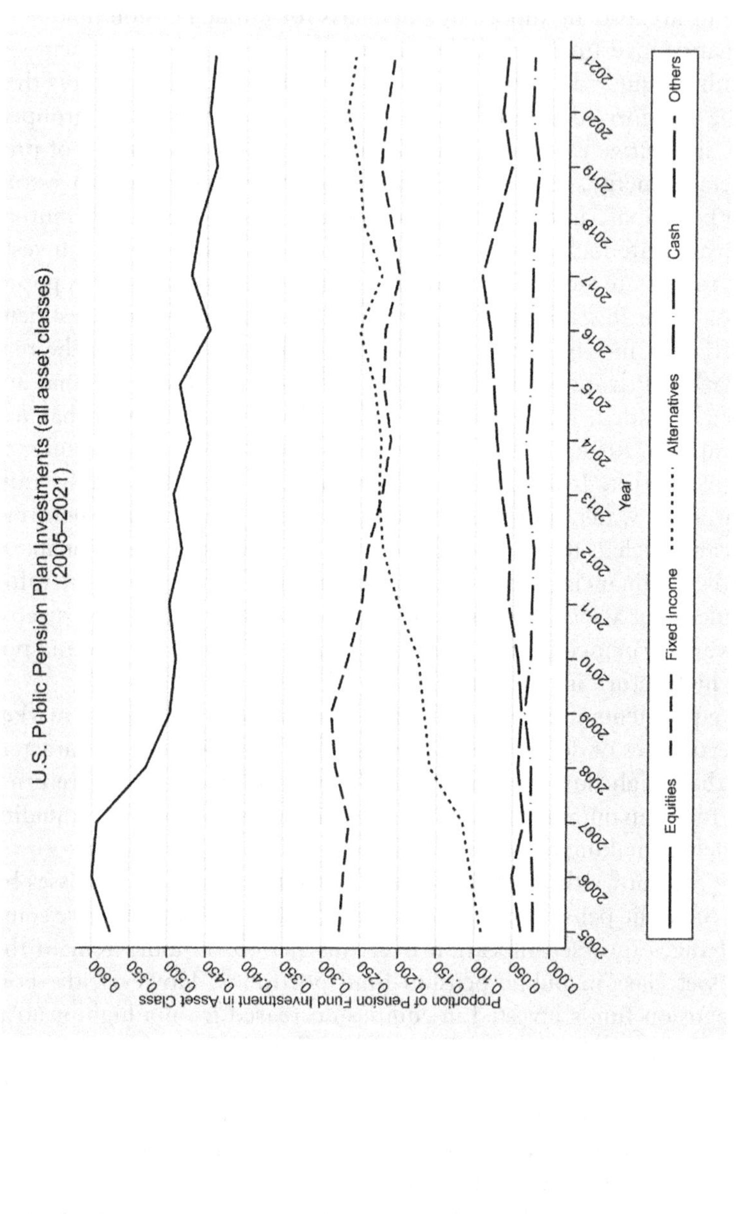

FIGURE 5.1 U.S. Public Pension Plan Investments in All Asset Classes

Source: Authors' calculation based on Pensions and Investments Public 100: Top DB Plans

investments, fixed-income investments gradually declined during this period, falling from above 25% in the early 2000s to around 20% in 2021. Cash and other investments remain small and stable during this period.

Since alternative investments exhibit the most significant change in Figure 5.1, we further examine the subclasses within this asset class based on available data. The Pension & Investments data set categorizes alternative investments into five subclasses: real estate, private equity, hedge funds, commodities, and infrastructure. Figure 5.2 presents the proportion of pension assets invested in these subclasses over the period from 2005 to 2021.

Figure 5.2 reveals that the largest sub-asset class within alternative investments is private equity, which consists of investments in companies that are not publicly traded. The proportion of public pension assets invested in private equity increased from 4% to nearly 11% by 2021. The proportion invested in real estate has remained stable, ranging between 5 and 8%, making it one of the top two subclasses in alternative investments. Another significant subclass is hedge funds, which account for between 1 and 5% of public pension investments. Investments in commodities and infrastructure are low and stable. All the subclasses within alternative investments exhibited growth during this period, collectively contributing to the overall 15% increase in the proportion of public pension funds invested in alternatives.

Investment risk

Asset classes with high returns often come with high risks. Investment risk refers to the uncertainty associated with the fluctuations in investment returns. Due to the volatility of capital markets, returns in some years may be lower than expected or even negative (i.e., investment losses). Many experts agree that investment risk is the most significant financial risk for public pension plans, due to the large amount of pension assets allocated in risky investments.

As illustrated in Figures 5.1 and 5.2, equities, known for their significant investment risk, constitute the largest asset class. Moreover, pension funds are increasingly investing in even riskier asset classes, such as private equity. The pursuit of higher risks by pension funds is driven by the objective to achieve higher returns. Because public pensions typically have large asset size and a long investment horizon, they can afford to invest in riskier assets with the hope that the long-term returns will compensate for the investment risks undertaken. If these expected high returns are achieved, pension funds can have sufficient funding to make generous benefit payments without imposing fiscal strains on governments. However, this is

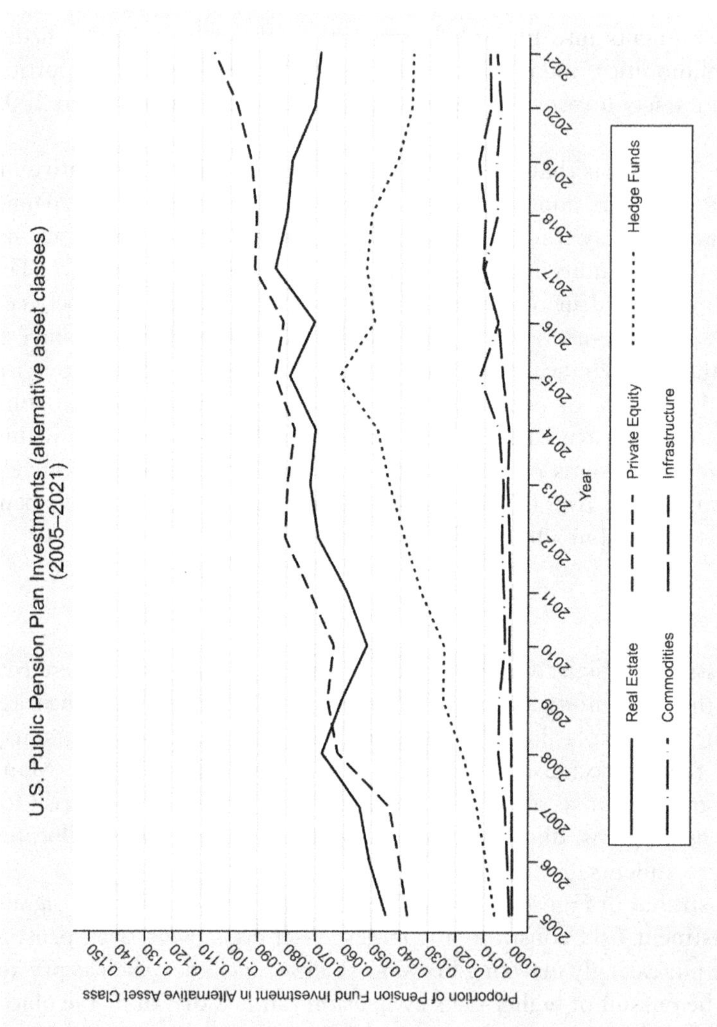

FIGURE 5.2 U.S. Public Pension Plan Investments in Alternative Asset Classes

Source: Authors' calculation based on Pensions and Investments Public 100: Top DB Plans

not always the case, as many funds struggle to meet the expected rate of returns, even in the long run.

When analyzing a pension plan's investment portfolio, several measurements are often used to quantify an investment portfolio's expected returns and volatility (i.e., investment risk).

Expected return is calculated as the average of all possible annual returns over a long period of time. Geometric mean is often used more often than arithmetic mean,[1] due to the geometric mean's ability to accurately capture the effect of compounding, where investment gains are reinvested to generate additional earnings. In public pension plan management, the expected rate of return of the pension fund is reported in a plan's actuarial valuation report and annual financial report. It is worth noting that some scholars (Andonov et al., 2017) attribute the pursuit of risky investments by U.S. public pension plans to the motivation to justify a high assumed rate of return.

Investment risk is often measured by the standard deviation (SD) of investment returns, which is a volatility measure that shows the potential variation in returns within a single year. In a normal distribution, 68% of possible outcomes fall within 1 SD of the mean, and 95% fall within 2 SDs. For instance, if a portfolio has an expected return of 7% and an SD of returns of 6%, there is a 68% chance that the portfolio will realize a return between 1 and 13% in any given year (although actual returns are different from expected return).

When evaluating different asset classes, higher returns are generally associated with higher investment risks. This means that an asset portfolio with higher long-term investment returns typically exhibits higher volatility, at least in the short term. Asset classes differ in terms of their expected returns and the SDs of these returns, with higher expected returns often accompanied by higher SDs.

Investment consultants for pension funds use the so-called capital market assumptions (CMAs) to show the expected returns and SDs for various asset classes based on their analysis of the historical patterns and economic outlooks. Table 5.3 shows the CMAs based on a survey of 35 investment advisors for multiemployer pension plans (Horizon, 2023).

The Horizon (2023) survey also shows that investment consultants have a wide range of CMAs. When different CMAs are used, the expected return on the investment portfolio is also different. Pension plans should be mindful of the models used for these assumptions because different models may lead to different perceived risk and investment decisions. Forecasting the capital market is based on available information and useful models, but the results could be very wrong if the information is limited or if the models were wrong. Also, the further into the future a forecast goes,

TABLE 5.3 2023 Survey of Capital Market Assumptions for Multiemployer Pension Plans

Asset class	*Sub-asset class*	*Expected returns in 10-year Horizon (%)*	*Standard deviations (%)*
Equity	U.S. equity – large-cap	6.90	16.64
	U.S. equity – small/mid-cap	7.38	20.51
	Non-U.S. equity – developed	7.49	18.26
	Non-U.S. equity – emerging	8.21	23.87
Fixed income	U.S. corporate bonds – core	4.71	5.85
	U.S. corporate bonds – long duration	4.80	10.91
	U.S. corporate bonds – high yield	6.43	10.01
	Non-U.S. debt – developed	3.42	7.31
	Non-U.S. debt – emerging	6.29	10.93
	Treasury Inflation-Protected Securities (TIPS)	4.07	6.17
Alternative investments	Real estate	5.95	16.72
	Hedge funds	5.96	8.06
	Commodities	4.96	18.02
	Infrastructure	7.00	17.10
	Private equity	9.46	22.57
	Private debt	8.16	11.73
Cash equivalents	U.S. treasuries	3.38	1.09

Source: Horizon Actuarial Services (2023).

the more likely the results will be different from the actual results. Asset valuation models should be adjusted based on new data or new model development.

Risk management

Risk management is about the process of identifying, assessing, and mitigating various risks. To identify risk, plan managers should understand what the primary risk is and who bears the risk. Most experts agree that when pension funds heavily invest in risky assets, investment risk is a major financial risk for pension funds (see Boyd et al., 2021). The higher the investment in risky asset classes, the higher the risk for the pension fund. In a typical defined benefit plan, retirees receive predetermined pension benefits upon retirement, and the investment risk is borne by the employer.

When investment returns are lower than expected, employers have to increase their contributions to cover the unfunded liabilities.

As mentioned above, investment risk is quantified using the SD of expected investment returns. To better understand and communicate risk, probability-based measures are also used in combination with simulations to estimate the probability of pension assets reaching certain values. For example, pension plan administrators may want to know the probability that the plan's funded ratio will fall below 60% within ten years. To answer this question, a simulation can be conducted to estimate asset growth, taking into account the pension assets' expected returns and volatility. A related approach to assess risk is to show the worst-case scenario values (Huang & Lalani, 2015). For example, how much would the required employer contributions increase if investment returns were in the lowest percentile of earnings? These probability or worst-case risk measures can help pension policy makers understand the level of investment risks they take. They can then better communicate the risk to the plan stakeholders.

After identifying and assessing risks, plan managers can develop strategies to mitigate the risks if they are deemed too high. Specifically, investment risk can be reduced by diversification of the investment portfolio. Pension plans can also share investment risks with plan members. For example, in some plans, cost-of-living adjustments or employee contribution rates are contingent on investment return performance in a specific year (Boyd et al., 2021; Brainard & Brown, 2018). Risk-sharing pension plans and financial risks in defined contribution plans will be further discussed in Chapter 9.

Investment performance

Investment performance refers to the actual returns on an investment portfolio, but these returns can be calculated in different ways. Investment performance in the short term can be very volatile, especially for pension funds that are invested in high-risk, high-return asset classes. Fund managers usually report the one-, three-, five-, and ten-year investment returns. Investment returns over the long term should be used to measure pension funds' investment performance because pension benefits are paid over the long term.

A popular way to evaluate investment performance is by comparing the portfolio's performance to a benchmarking portfolio with similar asset classes and investment risk. The reason to use this comparison with the benchmark performance is because portfolios vary in their different risk-return combinations, due to differing risk-preference levels across pension plans. Therefore, it is only appropriate to compare pension portfolio performance to those with similar risk levels. It is also common to benchmark individual asset classes in the portfolio to specific indexes (possibly with

TABLE 5.4 Asset Class Performance Benchmarks for CRPTF

Asset class	*Benchmark*
Global equity	MSCI All Country World IMI Net Index
Core fixed income	Blend: Bloomberg Barclays U.S. Aggregate Bond and Bloomberg Barclays U.S. Treasuries Index
Noncore fixed income	Bloomberg Barclays U.S. High Yield 2% Issuer Cap Index
Private equity	Russell 3000 + 250 basis points
Private credit	S&P/LSTA Leveraged Loan Index + 150 basis points
Absolute return	Blend: Dynamic-weighted strategy (HFRX)
Real estate	Open End Diversified Core Equity (NFI-ODCE Index)
Infrastructure and natural resources	CPI + 400 basis points
Cash equivalents	U.S. 3-Month T-Bill Index

Source: Investment Policy Statement for CRPTF, approved by the Investment Advisory Council in 2022.

some adjustments); for example, U.S. stocks might be compared to the S&P 500 index. Table 5.4 shows the benchmarks used by CRPTF (mentioned above) to assess investment performance in each asset class.

One important item that will affect investment performance is the investment fees. Investment fees are paid to the fund managers to cover the investment expenses and are usually a certain percentage, such as 0.5 or 1.0% of the assets managed by the fund managers. More complicated investments, such as private equities or actively managed funds, have higher fees. Fund managers and pension boards evaluate the net investment returns of pension funds, which are gross investment returns minus investment fees, to assess the investment performance.

Divestments, ETIs, and ESG investments

Public pension funds might favor certain investments or avoid others for social, economic, or political reasons. The reasoning behind this is that, since public pension funds are funded by public money and employees' contributions, they should not be invested in activities harmful to the public interest but rather directed toward those activities that are beneficial to the society as a whole. There is debate, however, about whether this approach conflicts with the investment goal to maximize returns with reasonable risk, or whether all these goals can be achieved concurrently.

The practice of avoiding certain investments is called divestment. Some public pension funds in the United States have divested from businesses in certain countries or regions for national interests. Some pension funds have also divested from businesses that cause air or water pollution in the environment. For example, several states, including New York, Maine, California, and Colorado, have divested state pension funds from companies that cause pollution (Ellfeldt, 2024). Another popular practice is to target certain investments for economic development purposes, which is called economically targeted investments (ETIs). ETIs could be used to support local businesses and/or businesses led by underrepresented minority groups. For example, to promote economic development in New York City, the city's pension funds invest 2% of their assets toward ETI (New York City Comptroller, 2024).

Current research findings show concerns on the negative effect of divestments or ETIs on pension fund performance (Nofsinger, 1998; Patterson, 1994). It is also unclear whether divestments and ETIs have achieved the social and economic goals they were expected to achieve (Vu, 2024).

Environmental, social, and governance (ESG) investing has gained more popularity in recent years across all areas of investment. The rationale for considering ESG factors is that businesses and other capital market participants increasingly face environmental and social uncertainties. Considering the risks such as climate risk and social risk can help investors assess the resilience of investment options and will be beneficial for the security and performance of investments. Proponents of ESG investing argue that integrating ESG considerations in financial analysis can increase returns and promote socially beneficial outcomes (Aubry et al., 2020). However, whether ESG investing has made a difference in investment performance is still not clear. A recent Center for Retirement Research report (Aubry et al., 2020) shows that at least $3 trillion of public pension assets have been invested with ESG criteria considered in investment decisions. Additionally, among 176 state and local plans studied, around 63% have either a social investment mandate or an ESG policy (Aubry et al., 2020).

A simulation of pension fund investment

To illustrate the asset growth and risk of pension fund investments, this section presents a simulation of pension investments to forecast future returns. Simulations are often used to forecast pension asset growth. Our simulation is based on a simplified pension plan with a hypothetical asset allocation, using the CMAs presented in Horizon (2023).

The simulation follows several steps. First, based on CMAs and the plan's asset allocation, we calculate the expected return and SD of the asset portfolio. Second, we construct a normal distribution using expected

TABLE 5.5 Plan Asset Allocation and Capital Market Assumptions

(1) Asset class	*(2) Sub-asset class*	*(3) Hypothetical portfolio (%)*	*(4) Expected returns (%)*	*(5) Standard deviations (%)*
Equity	U.S. equity – large-cap	15.00	6.90	16.64
	U.S. equity – small/ mid-cap	10.00	7.38	20.51
	Non-U.S. equity – developed	10.00	7.49	18.26
	Non-U.S. equity – emerging	10.00	8.21	23.87
Fixed income	U.S. corporate bonds – core	5.00	4.71	5.85
	U.S. corporate bonds – long duration	5.00	4.80	10.91
	U.S. corporate bonds – high yield	5.00	6.43	10.01
	Non-U.S. debt – developed	2.50	3.42	7.31
	Non-U.S. debt – emerging	2.50	6.29	10.93
	Treasury Inflation-Protected Securities (TIPS)	5.00	4.07	6.17
Alternative investments	Real estate	7.50	5.95	16.72
	Hedge funds	5.00	5.96	8.06
	Commodities	2.50	4.96	18.02
	Infrastructure	2.50	7.00	17.10
	Private equity	5.00	9.46	22.57
	Private debt	2.50	8.16	11.73
Cash equivalents	U.S. treasuries	5.00	3.38	1.09

Source: Horizon Actuarial Services (2023).

return and SD and conduct a stochastic simulation of the returns in the next ten years. Third, we simulate the growth of $100 in this hypothetical portfolio over ten years and calculate the annual return rate.

In Table 5.5, the asset allocation, shown in Column 3, follows the most recent patterns shown in Figures 5.1 and 5.2, which is the average asset allocation in public pension plans. In Columns 4 and 5, the expected returns and SDs of asset classes follow the average values in the "ten-year Horizon geometric mean" and "standard deviation" in Horizon (2023), which are also shown in Table 5.3.

To calculate the returns and volatility of a portfolio, we also need the correlation coefficients between the asset classes. Table 5.6 displays the

TABLE 5.6 Capital Market Assumptions – Asset Class Correlation Matrix

		1	2	3	4	5	6	7	8	9	10	11	12	13	14	15	16	17
U.S. equity – large-cap	1	1.00	0.89	0.81	0.68	0.26	0.25	0.64	0.17	0.50	−0.06	0.14	0.56	0.68	0.33	0.64	0.73	0.51
U.S. equity – small/mid-cap	2	0.89	1.00	0.77	0.66	0.22	0.21	0.65	0.13	0.47	−0.07	0.11	0.55	0.69	0.34	0.60	0.71	0.52
Non-U.S. equity – developed	3	0.81	0.77	1.00	0.76	0.24	0.24	0.61	0.27	0.53	−0.05	0.15	0.50	0.68	0.40	0.60	0.66	0.49
Non-U.S. equity – emerging	4	0.68	0.66	0.76	1.00	0.24	0.21	0.60	0.22	0.60	−0.04	0.18	0.42	0.64	0.40	0.54	0.60	0.46
U.S. corporate bonds – core	5	0.26	0.22	0.24	0.24	1.00	0.86	0.47	0.60	0.55	0.16	0.64	0.25	0.24	0.07	0.29	0.16	0.14
U.S. corporate bonds – long duration	6	0.25	0.21	0.24	0.21	0.86	1.00	0.39	0.57	0.48	0.07	0.57	0.24	0.21	0.02	0.32	0.17	0.16
U.S. corporate bonds – high yield	7	0.64	0.65	0.61	0.60	0.47	0.39	1.00	0.26	0.61	−0.05	0.32	0.45	0.60	0.34	0.54	0.50	0.61
Non-U.S. debt – developed	8	0.17	0.13	0.27	0.22	0.60	0.57	0.26	1.00	0.43	0.16	0.49	0.18	0.14	0.11	0.24	0.12	0.06
Non-U.S. debt – emerging	9	0.50	0.47	0.53	0.60	0.55	0.48	0.61	0.43	1.00	0.05	0.40	0.38	0.48	0.25	0.45	0.39	0.36
U.S. treasuries (cash equivalents)	10	−0.06	−0.07	−0.05	−0.04	0.16	0.07	−0.05	0.16	0.05	1.00	0.16	−0.01	−0.01	−0.02	−0.03	−0.07	−0.07
TIPS (inflation-protected)	11	0.14	0.11	0.15	0.18	0.64	0.57	0.32	0.49	0.40	0.16	1.00	0.19	0.16	0.19	0.21	0.08	0.08
Real estate	12	0.56	0.55	0.50	0.42	0.25	0.24	0.45	0.18	0.38	−0.01	0.19	1.00	0.43	0.25	0.47	0.45	0.35
Hedge funds	13	0.68	0.69	0.68	0.64	0.24	0.21	0.60	0.14	0.48	−0.01	0.16	0.43	1.00	0.38	0.52	0.60	0.54
Commodities	14	0.33	0.34	0.40	0.40	0.07	0.02	0.34	0.11	0.25	−0.02	0.19	0.25	0.38	1.00	0.38	0.30	0.29
Infrastructure	15	0.64	0.60	0.60	0.54	0.29	0.32	0.54	0.24	0.45	−0.03	0.21	0.47	0.52	0.38	1.00	0.55	0.42
Private equity	16	0.73	0.71	0.66	0.60	0.16	0.17	0.50	0.12	0.39	−0.07	0.08	0.45	0.60	0.30	0.55	1.00	0.54
Private debt	17	0.51	0.52	0.49	0.46	0.14	0.16	0.61	0.06	0.36	−0.07	0.08	0.35	0.54	0.29	0.42	0.54	1.00

Source: Horizon Actuarial Services (2023).

correlation matrix, which consists of correlation coefficients between each pair of asset classes. A positive correlation coefficient suggests that the two asset classes tend to move in the same direction, whereas a negative correlation coefficient implies that they tend to move in opposite directions. A larger value indicates a stronger correlation.

Using these assumptions, we can compute the portfolio's expected returns and SD. Initially, we calculate the portfolio's arithmetic mean by multiplying the expected return of each asset class by its allocation weight and summing the resulting products. Then, we convert the arithmetic mean to the geometric mean, which represents the expected return. To determine the portfolio's SD, we multiply the weights, SDs, and the correlation matrix, and then take the square root of the sum. The above calculation shows the portfolio's expected return as 7.11% and its SD as 11.44%.

In the second step, we use the portfolio's expected return and SD to construct a normal distribution, assuming that the rate of return in a given year is a random draw from this normal distribution. Figure 5.3 shows 10,000 random draws from this normal distribution with the center at 7.11%.

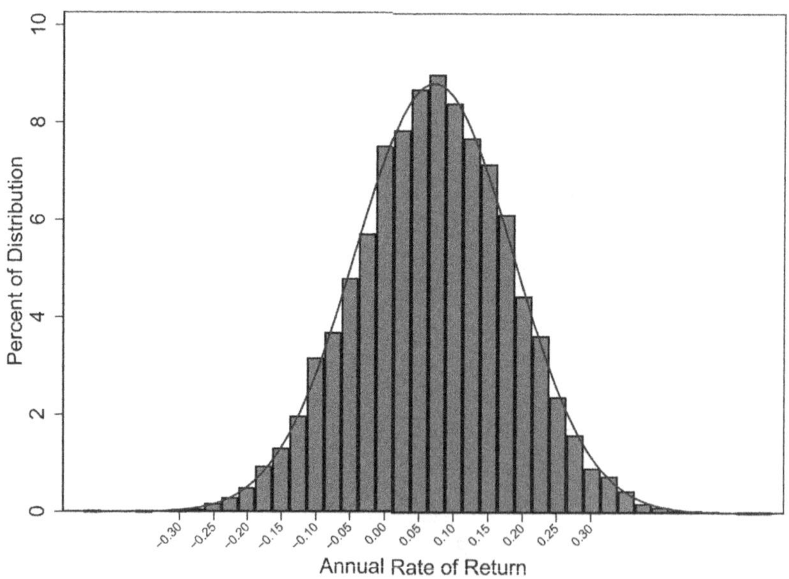

FIGURE 5.3 Distribution of Annual Asset Returns Based on the Hypothetical Portfolio

Source: Authors' simulation

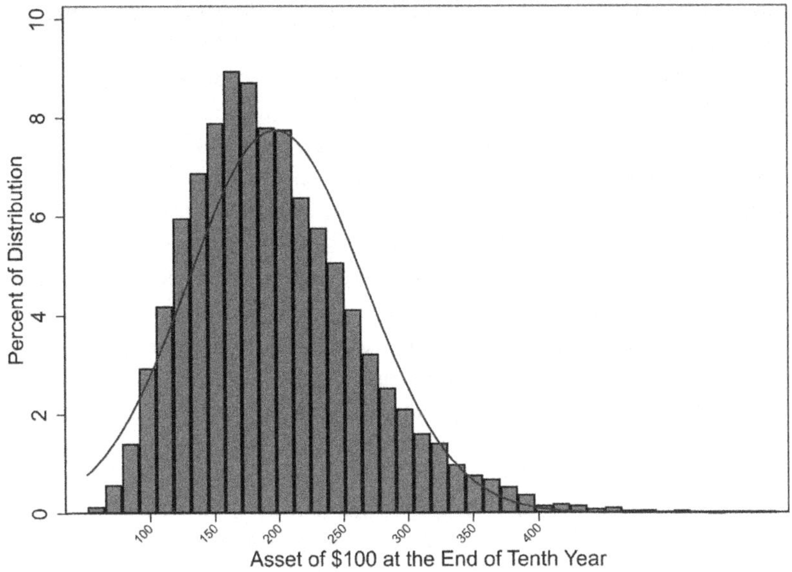

FIGURE 5.4 Distribution of the End-of-Tenth-Year Return

Source: Authors' simulation

We can repeat this random drawing each year for the next ten years and estimate the asset portfolio's growth in that period of time. We assume a portfolio of $100 at the beginning. At the end of the tenth year, the distribution of the possible asset values is shown in Figure 5.4.

We see that the median value is $187.06. In the worst-case scenario (e.g., the 5th percentile), this asset will be $105.61, which is only a 5.61% increase over a ten-year period with an average annual growth rate of 0.55%. In the best-case scenario (e.g., the 95th percentile), this asset will grow to $324.40, which averages a 12.49% annual asset growth rate over ten years. This measure of possible asset growth can be used in combination with liability growth estimation to calculate the level of possible contribution requirements or solvency measurements. If the risk is too high, the plan can adjust asset allocation to reduce investment risk.

Summary

Public pension boards make important policies on pension investments regarding setting investment policy, asset allocation, risk management, performance evaluation, divestments, ETIs, and ESG investments. In this chapter, we describe the key decisions and considerations regarding these investment decisions.

We describe the main components of a public pension plan's investment policy and use the State of "CRPTF" as an example to show how investment policy is used to convey the strategies and goals for pension fund investments. We also discussed the main asset classes and subclasses for public pension plan investments. Data analysis using the Pension & Investments dataset shows that equities are the largest asset class but the proportion of equities in portfolios has declined over time, while investments in alternative asset classes, such as real estate, private equity, hedge funds, commodities, and infrastructure, have steadily increased over time.

We identified risk measures for pension plans and the risk management process of identifying, assessing, and mitigating risks. We also discussed how investment performance is evaluated using benchmarks. In addition, the use of divestment, ETIs, and ESG investments in U.S. public pension plans was addressed. Finally, we constructed a simulation of a prototypical public pension fund to calculate asset growth potential and demonstrate risk in pension fund management.

Note

1 The geometric mean is calculated by multiplying *n* years of returns together and then taking the *n*th root of the product, where *n* is the number of years in the calculation. The arithmetic mean is calculated by summing *n* years of returns together and then dividing the sum by *n*.

References

Andonov, A., Bauer, R., & Cremers, K. J. M. (2017). *Pension fund asset allocation and liability discount Rates*. SSRN. https://papers.ssrn.com/sol3/papers.cfm?abstract_id=2070054 or http://dx.doi.org/10.2139/ssrn.2070054

Aubry, J.-P., Chen, A., Hubbard, P., & Munnell, A. (2020). ESG investing and public pensions: An update. https://crr.bc.edu/wp-content/uploads/2020/10/SLP74.pdf

Boyd, D., Chen, G., & Yin, Y. (2021). *Public pension risk-sharing policies a policymaker's guidebook*. https://www.albany.edu/rockefeller/news/2021-rockefeller-researchers-release-public-pension-risk-sharing-guidebook

Brainard, K., & Brown, A. (2018). *In-depth: Risk sharing in public retirement plans* (p. 64). National Association of State Retirement Administrators. https://www.nasra.org/files/Spotlight/Risk%20Sharing%20in%20Public%20Retirement%20Plans.pdf

Ellfeldt, A. (2024). *Pension funds in liberal states are conservative on climate change*. E&E News by POLITICO. https://www.eenews.net/articles/pension-funds-in-liberal-states-are-conservative-on-climate-change/

Horizon Actuarial Services. (2023). *Survey of capital market assumptions: 2023 Edition*. https://www.horizonactuarial.com/survey-of-capital-market-assumptions

Huang, L., & Lalani, M. (2015). *Corporate pension risk management and corporate finance: Bridging the gap between theory and practice in pension risk management*. Society of Actuaries. https://www.soa.org/49385a/globalassets/assets/files/research/projects/research-2015-corporate-pension-risk-management.pdf

Markowitz, H. (1952). Portfolio selection. *The Journal of Finance*, 7(1), 77–91. https://doi.org/10.2307/2975974

New York City Comptroller. (2024). *Economically targeted investments*. https://comptroller.nyc.gov/services/financial-matters/pension/responsible-investing/economically-targeted-investments/

Nofsinger, J. R. (1998). Why targeted investing does not make sense! *Financial Management*, 27(3), 87–96. https://papers.ssrn.com/sol3/papers.cfm?abstract_id=143709

Patterson, D. J. (1994). Public pension funds and economically targeted investments. *Journal of Public Budgeting, Accounting & Financial Management*, 6(4), 566–598. https://doi.org/10.1108/JPBAFM-06-04-1994-B004

Pew. (2023). *Transparency in investment disclosures helps promote effective public pension administration*. https://www.pewtrusts.org/en/research-and-analysis/issue-briefs/2023/10/transparency-in-investment-disclosures-helps-promote-effective-public-pension-administration

State of Connecticut Treasurer's Office. (2022). *Investment Policy Statement for the Connecticut Retirement Plans and Trust Funds*. https://portal.ct.gov/OTT/Pension-Funds/Investment-Policy/Investment-Policy-Statement

Vu, S. (2024). *Public pension funds should avoid local economically targeted investments*. https://reason.org/commentary/public-pension-funds-should-avoid-local-economically-targeted-investments/

6

ACTUARIAL PROCESSES AND ASSUMPTIONS IN PUBLIC PENSION VALUATIONS

Introduction

Actuarial valuation is a process that involves the use of economic and demographic assumptions, actuarial and financial theories, statistics, and plan characteristics to calculate a pension plan's assets, liabilities, funded status, and required contributions. In public pension plans, this valuation is conducted by in-house actuarial staff or by external actuarial consulting firms hired by the public pension systems. According to the Government Finance Officers Association (GFOA, 2013), "The purpose of an actuarial valuation is 1) to determine the amount of actuarially determined contributions [...] and 2) to measure the plan's funding progress." Actuarial assumptions and valuation results are reported in a plan's financial reports and, in more detail, in its actuarial valuation report. The Actuarial Standards of Practice (ASOP) and Governmental Accounting Standards Board (GASB) Statements play crucial roles in establishing guidelines for actuarial processes and financial reporting.

Although actuarial valuation is conducted by professional actuaries, the pension board of trustees plays a crucial role in selecting actuaries, reviewing valuation and financial reports, and approving changes in actuarial assumptions. While there are general accounting and financial reporting standards for public pension plans, a range of reasonable methods and assumptions is available for use. Given that a pension plan's actuarial assets, liabilities, and required contributions are sensitive to the choice of actuarial methods and assumptions, decisions in the actuarial process may be influenced by a plan's financial condition or even political considerations.

DOI: 10.4324/9781032671185-6

For example, as mentioned in Chapter 4, when the fiscal health of sponsoring governments is in a weakened condition, or when politicians and government officials have political motivations, they may exert influence on public pension systems to delay changes to actuarial assumptions that would increase the required employer contributions.

In the following sections, we will outline the actuarial valuation process, including the inputs used, the results calculated and reported, and the methods of calculation. We will also explain economic assumptions such as discount rate, expected rate of return, and inflation rate, as well as demographic assumptions, including mortality and decremental rates. Additionally, we will cover cost methods, asset smoothing methods, and methods for amortizing unfunded liabilities. To aid the understanding of board members, policymakers, and other stakeholders of public plans who may not have a professional background in finance, accounting, or actuarial science, we will use clear and plain language to explain these processes, methods, and assumptions. A glossary is included at the end of this chapter to explain the terminology that appears in this chapter.

The actuarial process: an overview

How are liabilities and normal costs calculated?

The actuarial process begins with the actuary collecting plan information, such as the number of active employees and retirees, their age and salary distributions, and the plan's benefit rules. The benefit rules include the number of benefit tiers offered, as well as the eligibility criteria and the benefit formula for each tier. Based on workforce data and benefit rules, the actuary can calculate future retirement benefits for current employees, assuming that employees will retire at a certain age and their salaries will increase at a predetermined "salary growth rate" until then. In most defined benefit plans, future benefits are typically calculated as the product of the average final salary before retirement, a benefit factor, and years of service. However, these future benefits do not represent the plan's liabilities because not all current employees will stay in the plan until retirement, and the benefits represent future dollar amounts. To account for the possibility of employees leaving the plan for various reasons and to convert future liabilities to present value, the calculation must also incorporate a discount factor and decremental rates (i.e., death rates, separation rates, disability rates, and early retirement rates). The result of this calculation is the primary component of what is referred to as the "present value of future benefits," or PVFBs.

Besides the normal retirement benefits, which are the benefits received by the employees who remain in the pension plan until reaching the normal retirement age, PVFBs also include other benefits such as vested termination benefits, disability benefits, early retirement benefits, and death benefits. This is because individuals who leave the plan due to voluntary separation, disability, early retirement, or death may also be entitled to certain benefits. The likelihood of individuals becoming eligible for these "ancillary benefits" (which differ from the core retirement benefits), along with the specific amounts according to the benefit rules, is estimated and included in the calculation of the total PVFBs. If all workforce data and assumptions, such as salary growth and decrement rates, are accurate, the PVFBs should be precise enough to cover the plan's obligations for retirement benefits and ancillary benefits for its current employees.

However, PVFBs are still not the plans' actuarial liabilities, because PVFBs need to be allocated over each employee's working years. The portion of an employee's PVFBs allocated to a particular year is known as that year's *normal cost* for the employee. With each additional year of employment, employees accrue more of their PVFBs, aiming to accumulate full PVFBs by retirement. The normal cost can vary depending on the actuarial cost method used for allocating PVFBs annually (this will be discussed later). Regardless of the chosen cost method, PVFBs will be entirely allocated by the end of an employee's tenure.

The normal costs accumulated by all members of the pension plan are the plan's actuarial accrued liability (AAL). For a specific plan member employee, this amount is essentially the sum of the normal costs he or she has accrued over the years participating in the plan. Ideally, a plan should have assets sufficient to cover this employee's AAL, because these liabilities are obligations for pension benefits that they have earned. However, that is not always the case, which will be discussed below.

How are plan assets and funded ratios calculated?

In every working year for a plan member, it is common for public pension plans to require both the employer and the employee to make contributions to the pension fund. Employee contributions often come from automatic deductions from their payroll, such as 5% of their salaries, depending on the plan's contribution policy. Employer contributions are an employer's share to cover the normal cost for an employee's pension benefits accrued in that year, often calculated by the plan's actuary. These contributions accumulate in pension funds as plan assets, which are invested in the capital markets to earn investment returns. If the growth rate of these assets is equal to or higher than the discount rate for the liabilities, the assets can grow to meet AALs when an employee reaches the retirement age. At that point, the assets should be enough to cover the benefits this employee is entitled to receive. As shown in the equation below, in the long run, a pension plan's asset inflows from employee contributions, employer contributions, and investment returns should match its asset outflows, which cover benefit payments as well as administrative and investment expenses.

$$\text{Employee contributions} + \text{Employer contributions} + \text{Investment returns} = \text{Benefit payments} + \text{Administrative and investment expenses}$$

When plan assets are lower than plan liabilities, employers are expected to use their contributions to close the gap. However, since the values of plan assets are affected by the fluctuations in investment returns, the volatility of these asset values can lead to fluctuating employer contributions. As a result, employers may struggle to keep up with the required contributions each year. Therefore, many pension plans "smooth" the value of assets and use the so-called "actuarial value" to calculate required contributions.

Investment gains and losses can be smoothed by spreading them over several years, typically between three and five, to calculate the actuarial value of assets. For example, if there is a 12% loss in one year, this loss could be distributed across the following five years (assuming a five-year smoothing period); similarly, investment gains, such as a 9% increase in the year after a loss, would be recognized over the same duration. Therefore, when asset smoothing is used, the actuarial value differs from the market value, which reflects the current market price of the assets. However, over time, the actuarial value tends to follow the market trends, gradually approximating the market value. This ensures that, in the long run, the actuarial value matches the market value and adequately covers a plan's accrued liabilities.

Because of the concerns that the actuarial value of plan assets may not immediately reflect the current financial condition of the plan, GASB Statement No. 67 requires that plans report the market value of their assets in their annual financial reports (GASB, 2012a). However, GASB standards separate financial reporting from a plan's funding policies. That is, actuarial values incorporating the asset smoothing approach can still be used to calculate the required contributions for funding purposes.

Several factors can lead to a discrepancy between assets and liabilities. For instance, there might be a divergence between the long-term rate of return on assets and the discount rate used for pension liabilities. Recall the previous mention that a discount rate is used to calculate the PVFBs, or in other words, how much future pension liabilities are worth today. A pension plan that uses a higher discount rate to calculate the present value of pension liabilities would have lower liabilities and required contributions.

If a plan uses 8% as the discount rate to calculate the PVFBs, but the assets grow at only 7% over the long term, this difference will result in a shortfall between assets and liabilities. Additionally, if the actual life expectancy of plan members is longer than projected, or if members' salaries escalate more rapidly than expected, their benefits will exceed anticipated amounts, thereby contributing to the mismatch between assets and liabilities.

The shortfall between actuarial assets and AAL is known as the unfunded actuarial accrued liabilities (UAAL). These represent the obligations for benefits that plan members have earned, but the plan does not have adequate assets to cover. The proportion of actuarial assets to actuarial liabilities is referred to as the funded ratio. If this ratio falls below 100%, it indicates that the plan has UAALs. Nonetheless, most observers of public pension plans consider a funding level between 80 and 100% to be adequate (see Chapter 3).

How are the required contributions calculated?

In a pension plan's financial report, the contribution amount that employers are required to pay every year is called the actuarially determined contribution (ADC). The ADC is comprised of two main components: the normal cost and the amortization cost of the UAAL. As discussed above, the plan's normal cost represents the value of benefits accrued (earned) by the plan members in a specific year and tends to remain stable due to the actuarial cost methods for cost allocation. On the other hand, the amortization cost, which is associated with the UAAL, can show volatility influenced by the amortization methods and the values of assets and liabilities.

UAALs are influenced by fluctuations in asset values due to market conditions, or by changes in liabilities resulting from revised actuarial assumptions or benefit rules. When a plan incurs UAALs in a given year, they are often amortized over a number of years, known as the amortization period. In U.S. public pension plans, this period can range from 15 to 30 years. The longer the amortization period, the more time it will take to fully pay off the UAALs. Amortization costs can be further spread into the future if a plan adopts open amortization, where each year's UAALs are re-amortized using the full amortization period. In contrast, closed amortization means that UAALs from a specific year are amortized and fully paid off by a specific year, reducing the remaining amortization period for those UAALs by one year annually.

Many plans are legally obligated to fully pay the ADC every year. Despite the use of asset smoothing and the UAAL amortization, the increase in ADC from one year to the next can still result in contribution volatility, making it challenging for governments to maintain consistent payments.

To mitigate this contribution volatility, some governments establish caps on the increase in the ADC or on the total ADC amount in a given year, aiming to further stabilize annual pension contributions. Additionally, some plans set a minimum contribution amount, such as using the normal cost as the baseline. The process of determining annual contributions, including the assumptions, caps, and floors, is outlined in a plan's contribution policy.

The annual ADC amount is highly influenced by the methods and assumptions chosen in the actuarial process. For instance, during the Great Recession, most pension funds saw significant investment losses. However, due to varying asset smoothing methods, these losses might not have impacted the required contributions until several years after the recession. Among the actuarial assumptions, the discount rate is particularly scrutinized. Because the discount rate is applied to calculate the PVFBs, a higher discount rate results in lower pension liabilities and required contributions. Public pension plans in the United States have previously used the expected rate of return assumption as the discount rate, which is around 8% for most plans. GASB Statements No. 67 and No. 68 require that public pension plans and governments use a blended discount rate to report their pension liabilities. In most plans, the blended discount rate is lower than the expected rate of return, which has led to an increase in reported pension expenses for many governments.

To better explain the terminologies mentioned above in calculating pension liabilities, assets, and required contributions, we include a glossary at the end of this chapter. In the next section, we explain these methods and assumptions in detail and summarize how they are used by U.S. public pension plans. We also present a simulation of a hypothetical public pension plan to show how the liabilities, assets, and required contributions are calculated.

A summary of actuarial methods and assumptions used by U.S. public plans

The discussion above on the actuarial process for determining the values of pension plan liabilities, assets, and required contributions shows that these values are sensitive to the choice of actuarial methods and assumptions. As indicated above, plan sponsors are concerned about the fiscal positions of the pension plans they sponsor and the required contributions they must pay annually, leading to potential fiscal or political influence on the setting of these methods and assumptions.

These influences are possible due to the variety of methods and assumptions used across different public pension plans. Although professional associations like the Society of Actuaries (SOA) and the GASB have established standards for actuarial practices and financial reporting, actuaries and plans retain some discretion over methods and assumptions that are considered reasonable to use.

In this section, we examine data gathered from 211 U.S. public pension plans for the fiscal year 2020, which includes 119 state-administered plans and 92 locally administered plans. The data were obtained from plans featured in the Public Plans Database (PPD) maintained by the Center for Retirement Research at Boston College. We use this data to show the actuarial methods and assumptions that are used by U.S. public plans and to discuss the best practices recommended by the SOA and the GASB.

Actuarial cost methods

Actuarial cost methods are used to allocate future pension benefits over plan members' working years as the annual normal cost. As shown in Figure 6.1, the most used cost methods are entry age normal (EAN), projected unit credit (PUC), and aggregated (AGG). EAN and PUC are similar

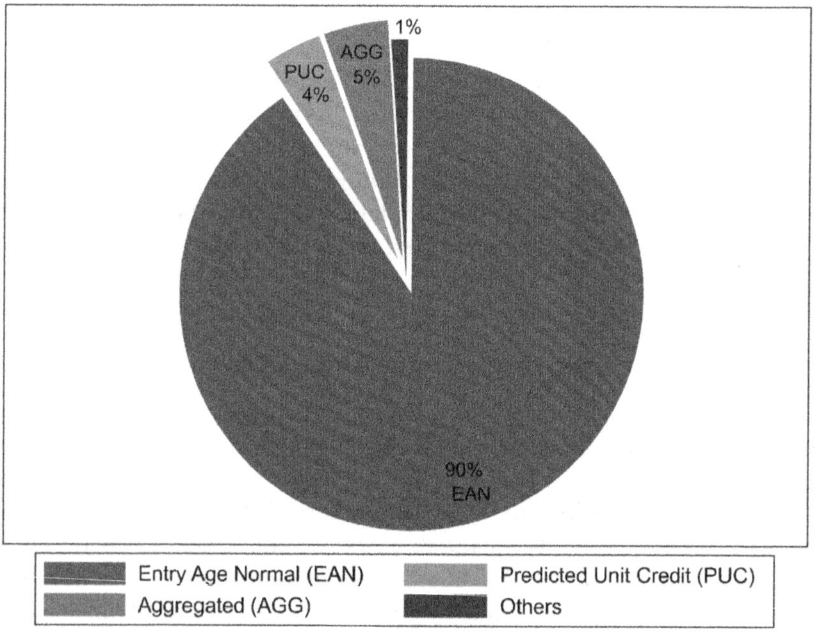

FIGURE 6.1 Actuarial Cost Methods Used by U.S. Public Pension Plans

Source: Authors' calculation based on Public Plans Database (CRR, 2020)

in that they both calculate the projected pension benefits at retirement for individual members and then discount these future benefits to present values. However, they differ in how they allocate PVFB to each year's normal cost and in how they accrue liabilities (i.e., accumulated normal costs in past service years). In PUC, the normal cost is the PVFB divided by total service years. The normal cost will rise because of the discounting effect, but each year's earning service credit remains the same. In EAN, the PVFB is discounted to the employee's entry age and then the entire PVFB is allocated over the employee's working years from entry age to retirement age as a fixed percentage of salary. PUC is straightforward because it only considers the service years and the discounting effect, while EAN must allocate the costs over the employee's working years.[1]

Both EAN and PUC show increasing normal costs over the years; however, EAN shows a smoother increase in normal cost because the PVFB is allocated over the entire service career as a fixed percentage of payroll. PUC also shows an increasing normal cost due to the discounting effect, but with a more rapid increase in the later years of the career. We illustrate the difference in normal costs calculated using EAN and PUC in the next section. Although EAN reports higher liabilities than PUC throughout an individual employee's service career, at retirement age, both methods accrued the same amount of normal costs and liabilities.

The other cost method that is used by public pension plans is the AGG method. In this method, the total cost is calculated for the entire group of employees as a whole, rather than for individual members. The AGG method calculates the difference between the PVFBs for the group and the actuarial value of the plan's assets, then allocates this difference over the group's total earnings. In other words, the unfunded liabilities are incorporated into the normal cost and distributed to the entire group of employees.

For financial reporting and information disclosure purposes, GASB requires public pension plans to report their pension liabilities on an EAN basis. GASB requirements only apply to the reporting of pension costs and liabilities but do not apply to how plans decide on their funding policies. Plans can use other cost methods such as PUC or AGG to calculate required contributions for funding purposes. The use of different cost methods for reporting (to meet GASB standards) and funding (to determine the annual contributions) may result in different numbers of assets and liabilities.

Asset smoothing methods

Asset smoothing is an actuarial technique used by pension plans to recognize their investment gains and losses over several years to reduce the year-to-year volatility in asset values. The asset value without smoothing is called the market value, reflecting the market price of the assets at the point of reporting, while the asset value with smoothing is called the actuarial value. Over time, the actuarial value tends to track and eventually converge with the market value. However, the more years in the smoothing period, the longer it takes for the actuarial value to catch up with the market value. When pension plans experience significant investment losses, extending the smoothing period can delay the increase in required contributions.

GASB Statement No. 67, which sets pension accounting and financial reporting standards for public pension plans, does not allow asset smoothing in the reporting of pension assets. The standard states that

> [...] pension plan investments—whether equity or debt securities, real estate, investment derivative instruments, or other investments—should be reported at their fair value at the end of the pension plan's reporting period. [...] Fair value should be measured by the market price if there is an active market for the investment.
>
> *(GASB, 2012b, pp. 7–8)*

However, because of the separation of reporting and funding, public plans still use asset smoothing to calculate required contributions for funding policies (as noted above, the GASB standards relate to financial reporting; plans continue to use other assumptions to calculate required contributions). The smoothing period varies from three to ten years with most plans using five-year asset smoothing, as shown in Figure 6.2. The longer the smoothing period, the less volatile the required contributions.

UAAL amortization methods

As discussed in the previous section, when a plan's asset value falls below the liability value, UAAL arise. Unfunded liabilities can result from investment losses, benefit increases, or a re-evaluation of pension liabilities. Unfunded liabilities often lead to increased required contributions from the employer. When unfunded liabilities occur, plans can choose to amortize these liabilities over an extended period. The amortization period refers to the number of years over which plans distribute their unfunded liabilities, similar to how home buyers amortize their mortgage. The longer the amortization period, the more time it takes for the plan to pay off the unfunded liabilities. Figure 6.3 shows that most U.S. public pension plans adopt 20–30 years for amortization.

Additionally, plans can choose to either spread the UAAL over the amortization period as a fixed dollar amount each year ("level dollar") or

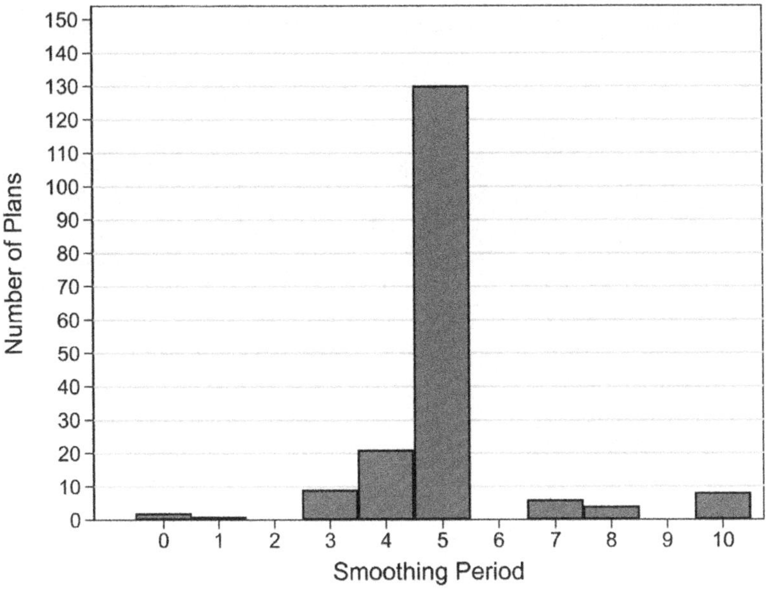

FIGURE 6.2 Distribution of Asset Smoothing Period Used by U.S. Public Plans

Source: Authors' calculation based on Public Plans Database (CRR, 2020)

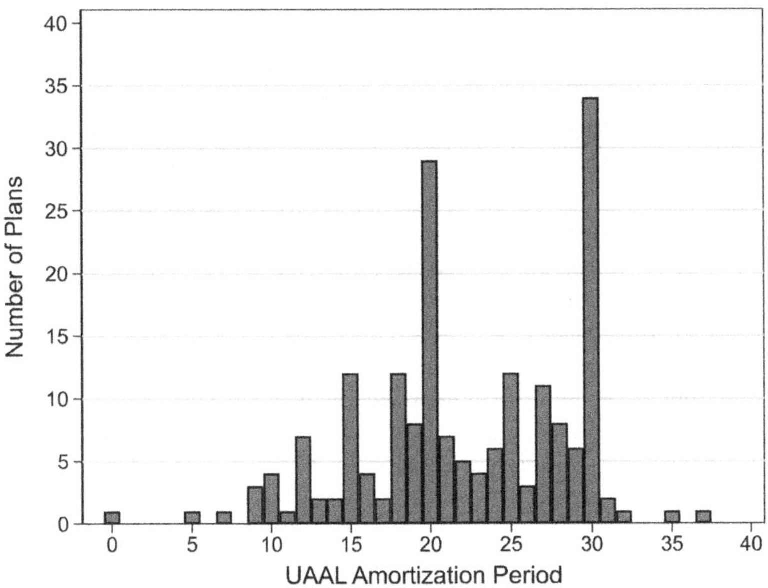

FIGURE 6.3 Distribution of UAAL Amortization Period Used by U.S. Public Plans

Source: Authors' calculation based on Public Plans Database (CRR, 2020)

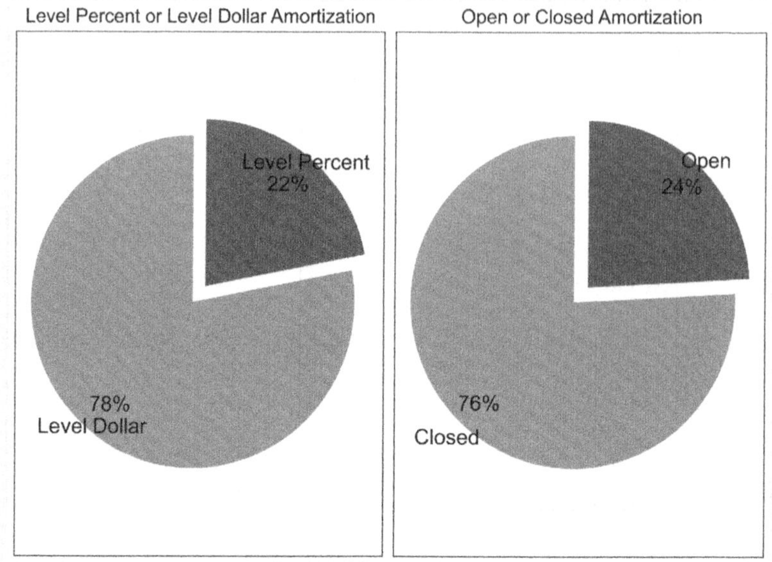

FIGURE 6.4 Amortization Methods Used by U.S. Public Plans

Source: Authors' calculation based on Public Plans Database (CRR, 2020)

to amortize each year as a fixed percentage of payroll ("level percent"). As payroll increases over time, the amortization cost using the level percent of payroll also increases. As shown in Figure 6.4, 78% of plans use the level dollar method of amortization, while 22% use the level percent method.

Plans may also select whether to employ open or closed amortizations. With open amortization, the amortization period is reset to its full length every year. With closed amortization, the unfunded liabilities are set to be eliminated within a specific time frame. That is, the amortization period for the unfunded liabilities is reduced by one year every year. Closed amortization can also be layered. That is, the initial UAAL may be amortized within a specific timeframe, while the new UAALs are also amortized within a new, fixed timeframe (NASRA, 2022). As shown in Figure 6.4, 75% of plans use closed amortization (including layered or non-layered), while 25% use open.

Discount rate and the rate of return assumption

The discount rate is the rate to discount future benefits to present value. A higher discount rate leads to lower liabilities and thus lower required contributions. Historically, U.S. public pension plans have used the expected rate of return assumption (typically around 8%) to discount future liabilities. GASB Statement No. 25, prior to its replacement by the new Statement No. 67, stated that

> the investment return assumption (discount rate) should be based on an estimated long-term investment yield for the plan, with consideration given to the nature and mix of current and expected plan investments and the basis used to determine the actuarial value of assets.

This GASB standard received criticism from financial economists, who argue that liabilities should be discounted based on their risk level, rather than the assets backing these liabilities. Novy-Marx and Rauh (2011) wrote that "Discounting liabilities at an expected rate of return on the assets in the plan runs counter to the entire logic of financial economics: financial streams of payment should be discounted at a rate that reflects their risk." Since pension obligations have the same priority as state general obligation bonds, Novy-Marx and Rauh (2011) suggested alternative risk-free rates such as the yield on a zero-coupon state general obligation bonds or the zero-coupon treasury rate as the discount rate for public pension liabilities.

In 2012, the GASB released Statements No. 67 and 68. GASB Statement No. 67 states that:

> Projected benefit payments are required to be discounted to their actuarial present value using a single rate that reflects (1) a long-term expected rate of return on pension plan investments to the extent that the pension plan's fiduciary net position is projected to be sufficient to pay benefits and pension plan assets are expected to be invested using a strategy to achieve that return and (2) a tax-exempt, high-quality municipal bond rate to the extent that the conditions for use of the long-term expected rate of return are not met.

The discount rate stipulated above is called the "blended rate," as it allows for the use of different discount rates for the funded and unfunded portions of pension liabilities. GASB requires that plans report liabilities using this blended rate in their financial statements. However, for funding purposes, plans may still use the expected rate of return to determine the required contribution amount, resulting in the distinction between the blended discount rate and the expected rate of return.

Figures 6.5 and 6.6 show the difference between the blended rate and the expected rate of return in public pension plans. Figure 6.5 shows that

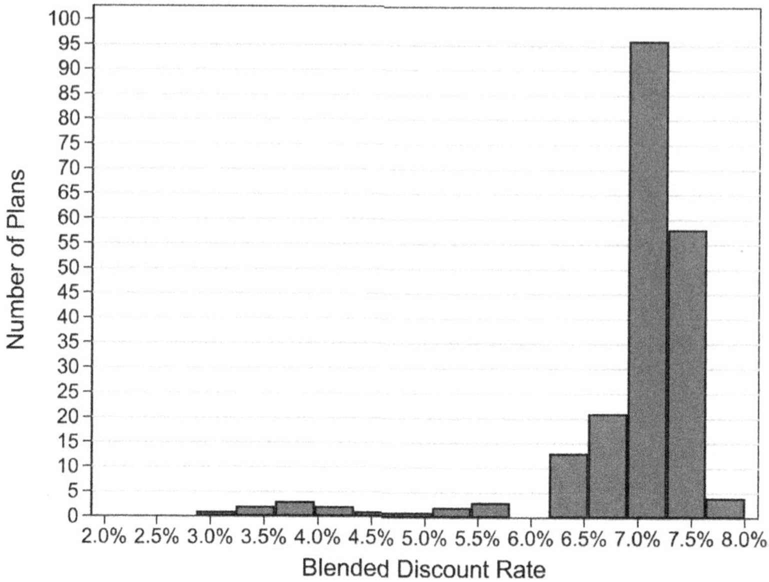

FIGURE 6.5 Distribution of Blended Discount Rate Used by U.S. Public Plans

Source: Authors' calculation based on Public Plans Database (CRR, 2020)

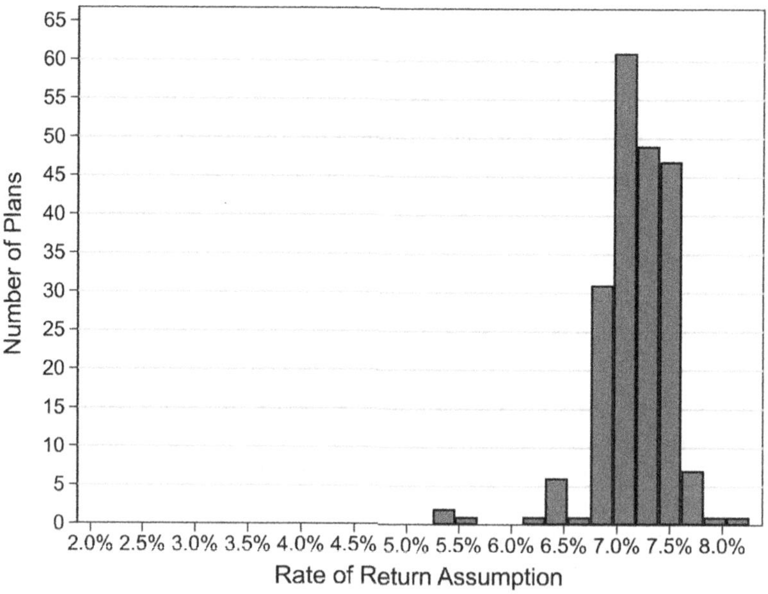

FIGURE 6.6 Distribution of Expected Rate of Return Used by U.S. Public Plans

Source: Authors' calculation based on Public Plan Database (CRR, 2020)

in 2020, the majority of plans used a blended discount rate between 6.5 and 7.5%, while some plans have a blended discount rate as low as 3–4%. Figure 6.6 shows the distribution of the expected rate of return assumption, which is slightly higher than the blended discount rate.

Other assumptions: inflation rate and mortality rates

The other economic and demographic assumptions also bear significant implications for calculating pension liabilities. The inflation rate may influence the expected rate of return assumption, the salary growth assumption, and the cost-of-living adjustment (COLA) assumption, as inflation may be factored into the calculation of these three assumptions. If inflation rates exceed expectations, pension costs and liabilities might surpass anticipated levels, due to higher final salaries and COLAs. The effect of inflation on pension assets is more complex and depends on the plan's investment strategy and how inflation affects the economy. Figure 6.7 shows that most plans adopt an inflation assumption in the range of 2–3%. The implications of high inflation on public pension plans are further discussed in Chapter 11.

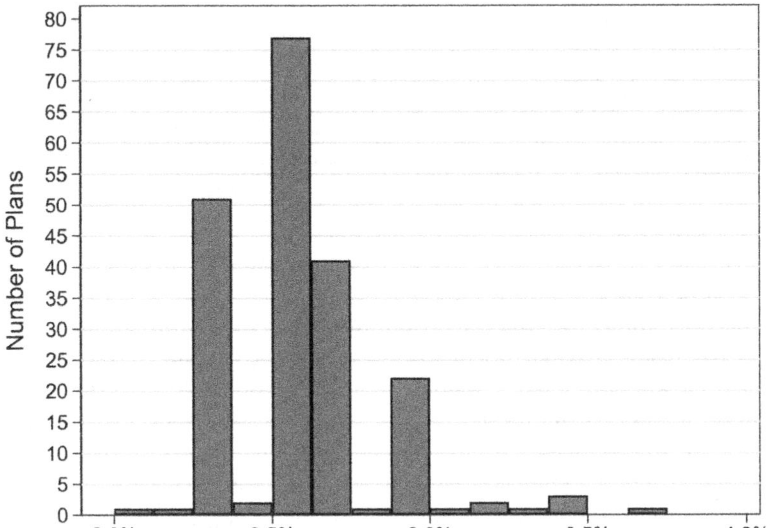

FIGURE 6.7 Distribution of Inflation Rate Assumption Used by U.S. Public Plans

Source: Authors' calculation based on Public Plans Database (CRR, 2020)

Mortality rates are crucial assumptions for calculating pension liabilities because they influence the probability of plan members qualifying for certain pension benefits and also affect beneficiaries' life expectancy assumptions. Plans establish mortality rates based on demographic data. Every several years, plans may conduct an experience study to update the mortality rates. Mortality rates may show improvements over the years due to socioeconomic and healthcare conditions. If actual mortality rates deviate from the rates currently used in the plan, liabilities may increase, and unfunded liabilities may arise. Improvements in mortality rates and their implications will be further discussed in Chapter 11.

A simulation of liabilities, assets, and required contributions

In this section, we use a simulation of a simplified public pension plan to demonstrate the calculation of liabilities, assets, and required contributions, as well as how these values are affected by the choice of actuarial methods and assumptions.

The baseline scenario of the simulation primarily draws from the median values of the 211 plans included in the PPD. The plan is designed with 80 participants, comprising 45 active employees, each representing a distinct age group from 20 to 64 years, and 35 retirees, each from a unique age group spanning from 65 to 99 years. All participants are assumed to begin their employment at age 20 and retire when they reach 65. The salary progression is modeled to reflect a 3.5% annual increment, corresponding to their service duration. This population structure is considered stable, ensuring that each year, a retiring member is replaced by a new recruit at age 20, and with each retiree passing at age 99, a new retiree begins benefit collection. This simplification excludes variations in mortality and separation rates, allowing for a focus on actuarial methods and assumptions.

For one single employee with an entry age of 20 and retirement age of 65, we calculate their normal cost rate and AAL using EAN and PUC. Figure 6.8 illustrates that EAN yields a stable normal cost rate as a percentage of payroll, while PUC shows lower normal costs in the earlier years and higher costs as retirement approaches. Figure 6.9 shows that AAL calculated using EAN is always higher than the AAL calculated using PUC throughout the employee's working years, with the liabilities from both methods converging at retirement.

In order to simulate the plan's assets, funded ratios, and required contributions over the next 30 years, we will have to assume an investment return scenario. To illustrate how amortization period and asset smoothing reduce the contribution volatility, we assume an asset shock scenario with a market decline in years 4 and 5 and recovery in years 6 and 7.

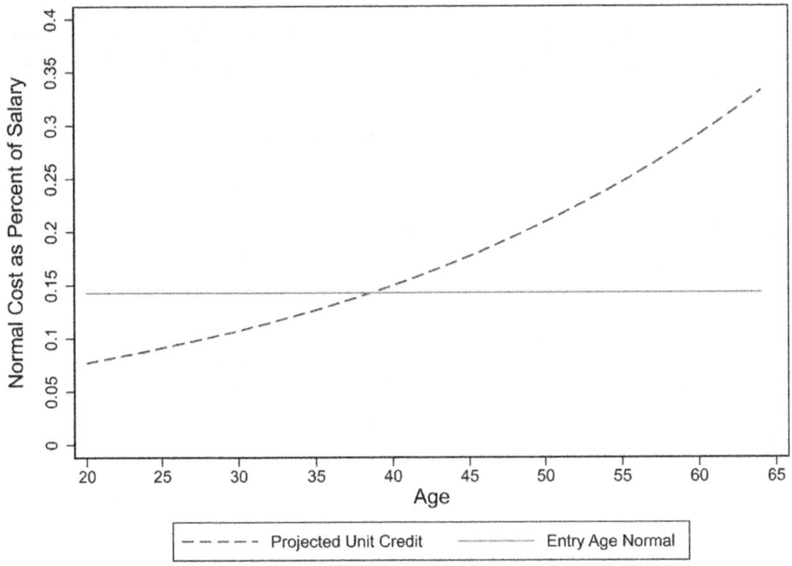

FIGURE 6.8 Simulation of an Individual Employee's Normal Cost

Source: Authors' simulation

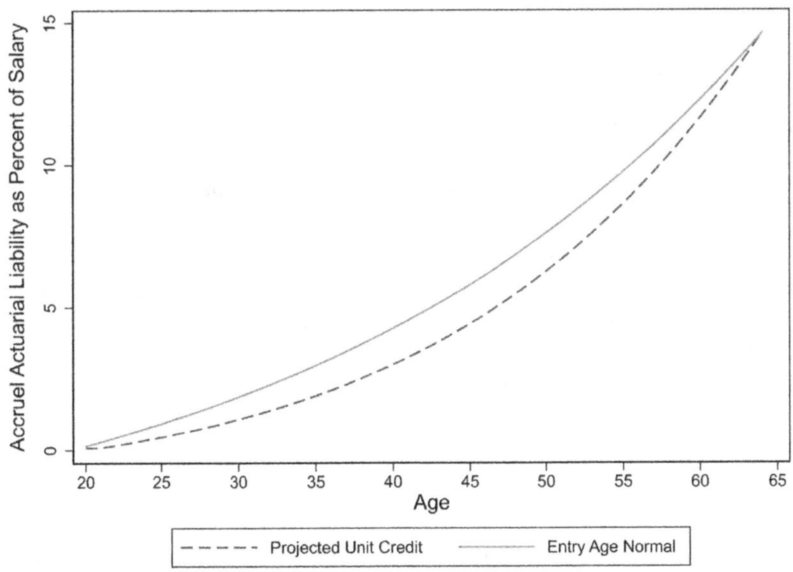

FIGURE 6.9 Simulation of an Individual Employee's Actuarial Accrued Liability

Source: Authors' simulation

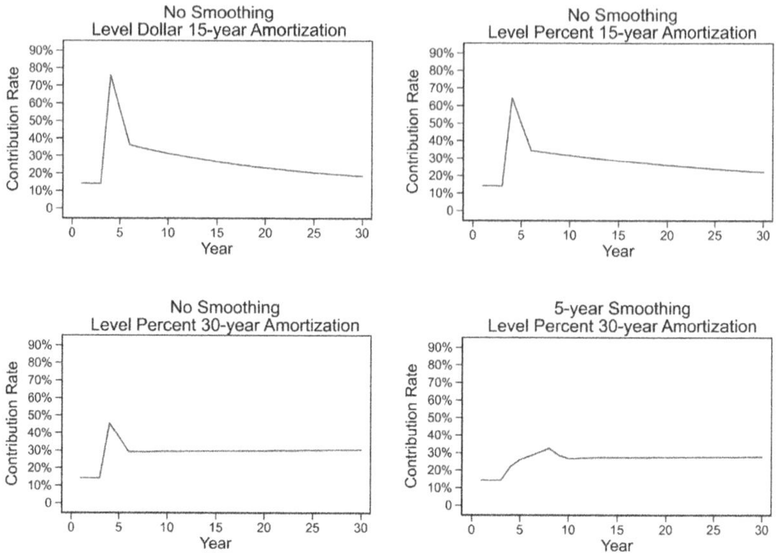

FIGURE 6.10 Required Contribution Rates under Various Funding Policies in an Asset Shock Scenario

Source: Authors' simulation

We assume that in the rest of the years, the investment returns meet the anticipated 7%, aligning with the plan's discount rate.

Figure 6.10 illustrates the contribution rates as a percentage of payroll over 30 years under different funding policies. We observe that, without asset smoothing and amortization, the two-year asset shock increased the required contribution rate to over 70% of payroll, a level nearly impossible for any public plan to sustain. With the use of level percent amortization, longer amortization periods, and asset smoothing over five years, the plan gradually reduces the peak required contribution rate to around 30% of payroll. However, the plan's long-term required contribution rate remains elevated post-asset shock due to open amortization, where unfunded liabilities are continually re-amortized over thirty years.

Figure 6.11 shows the funded ratio of the same plan under the four funding policies in an asset shock scenario corresponding to those shown in Figure 6.10. With asset smoothing, it takes a longer time for the impact of market shocks to be reflected in the funded ratio. Also, with amortization, the plan's funded ratio never returns to 100%. After the asset shock in years 4 and 5, the plan's funded ratio returns to nearly 90% due

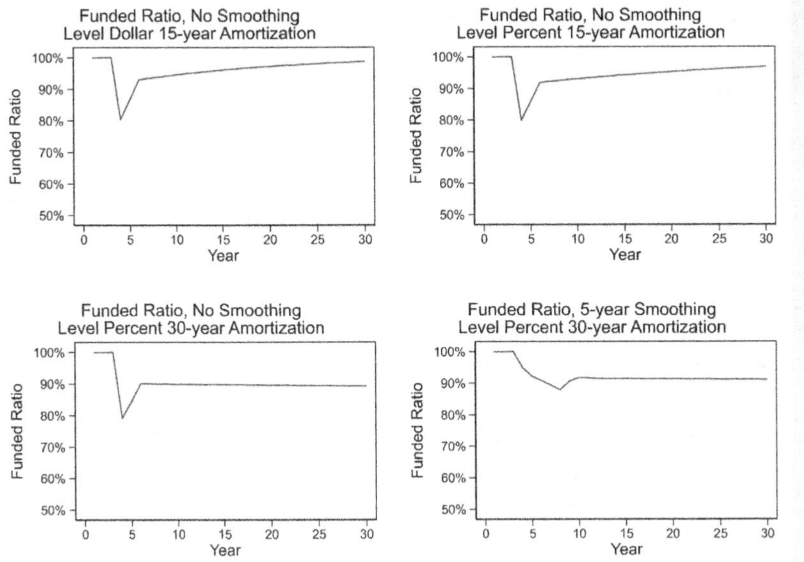

FIGURE 6.11 Funded Ratios under Various Funding Policies in an Asset Shock Scenario

Source: Authors' simulation

to market recovery and contribution increases, but the long-term funded ratio remains at around 90%.

Summary

In this chapter, we explained the actuarial process, assumptions, and methods. We showed how actuarial liabilities, normal costs, assets, funded ratio, and required contributions are calculated and how the calculation can be sensitive to the choice of methods and assumptions. Using data from the PPD, we summarized the methods and assumptions currently used in U.S. public pension plans, including the actuarial cost methods, asset smoothing methods, unfunded liability amortization methods, discount rate, expected rate of return, inflation rate, and mortality rate assumptions. Lastly, we constructed a simulation of pension liability growth to show how one plan member's liability grows from entry to retirement age, and how a plan's funded ratios and required contributions are affected by asset smoothing and unfunded liability amortization methods. This information can help pension plan decision-makers and stakeholders further understand how the actuarial process interacts with management decisions and affects pension plan performance.

Glossary

- Economic assumptions
  - Discount rate: the interest rate to calculate the present value of future pension liabilities. Prior to GASB Statements No. 67 and 68, the discount rate was the same as the ERR; after the implementation of GASB Statements No. 67 and 68, the blended rate should be used as the discount rate.
  - Expected rate of return (ERR): the estimated long-term annual return on pension fund's investments.
  - Inflation rate: the assumed rate of inflation that is often used to project salary increases due to inflation, cost-of-living adjustments, and asset growth due to inflation.
  - Salary growth rate: the expected annual increase in employee salaries, including inflation increases, merit-based increases, and promotion increases.
- Demographic assumptions
  - Mortality rates: the expected rates at which the plan participants die at various ages. For active employees, mortality will cause the member to leave the plan and may incur death benefits; for retirees, depending on the benefit payment rules, mortality may cause the stop of the payment and may also incur death benefits.
  - Separation rates: the expected rates of employees leaving before retirement, which cause the member to leave the plan and may incur vested termination benefits.
  - Disability rates: the expected rates of employees becoming disabled, which may incur disability benefits.
  - Early retirement rates: the expected rates of employees retiring before normal retirement age, which cause the member to leave the plan and may incur early retirement benefits.
- Cost methods
  - Entry age normal (EAN): the cost method that spreads the projected employee benefits over the employee's working years as a level percentage of their salary.
  - Projected unit credits (PUC): the cost method that calculates the normal cost based on the benefits earned in each year of service.

- Aggregated (AGG) cost method: the cost method that calculates the normal cost based on the group as a whole, not individual members.

- Funding policies

  - Present value of future benefit (PVFB): the PVFBs discounted to the present value, accounting for the probability that employees are likely to receive those benefits. These benefits include normal retirement benefits, vested termination benefits, disability benefits, early retirement benefits, and death benefits.
  - Normal cost: the pension cost of benefits an employee earned in a single year. Normal cost may vary depending on cost methods.
  - Actuarial accrued liability (AAL): the accumulated normal costs that an employee has earned to date. AAL may vary depending on cost methods.
  - Asset smoothing: an actuarial method to recognize asset gains and losses over a period of time to reduce the volatility in actuarial value of assets.
  - Actuarial value of assets: the value of assets that is calculated using actuarial methods such as asset smoothing.
  - Market value of assets: the actual current market value of the assets based on market price.
  - Actuarial funded ratio: the ratio of actuarial assets to actuarial liabilities.
  - Unfunded actuarial accrued liability (UAAL): the shortfall between a plan's AAL and its assets.
  - Actuarially determined contributions (ADC): the required contribution calculated by actuary according to the plan's funding policy. ADC includes the normal cost and the amortization payment of UAAL.
  - Amortization of UAAL: the schedule to pay off UAALs over a period of time such as 20–30 years.

Note

1 Another way to explain the difference between EAN and PUC is that PUC accrues the "benefits" in each year (i.e., "benefit accrual" method: for one more working year, the employee earns one service unit into their calculation of pension benefits) and discounts that part of the benefits to present value as the normal cost; EAN accrues the "costs" in each year (i.e., the "cost accrual" method: the total costs are calculated first and allocated from the entry age to retirement age as a fixed percentage of salary, with the normal cost for a year depending on the allocation result for that year).

References

Center for Retirement Research (CRR). (2020). Public Plans Database. https://publicplansdata.org/.

Governmental Accounting Standards Board (GASB). (2012a). *Summary: Statement No. 67. Financial reporting for pension plans.* https://gasb.org/page/pronouncement?pageId=/standards-and-guidance/pronouncements/summary-statement-no-67.html&isStaticPage=true

Governmental Accounting Standards Board (GASB). (2012b). *Statement No. 67 of the Governmental Accounting Standards Board: Financial reporting for pension plans.* https://gasb.org/page/ShowPdf?path=GASBS67.pdf&title=GASBS%2067

Government Finance Officers Association (GFOA). (2013). *The role of the actuarial valuation report in plan funding.* https://www.gfoa.org/materials/the-role-of-the-actuarial-valuation-report-in-plan

National Association of State Retirement Administrators (NASRA). (2022). *Overview of public pension plan amortization policies.* https://www.nasra.org/Files/Papers/NASRA%20Amortization%20Overview.pdf

Novy-Marx, R., & Rauh, J. (2011). Public pension promises: How big are they and what are they worth? *The Journal of Finance*, 66(4), 1211–1249. http://www.jstor.org/stable/29789814

7

UNDERSTANDING BENEFITS DESIGNS AND CONTRIBUTIONS POLICIES FOR PUBLIC PENSION PLANS

Introduction

Pension benefits and contributions are two major decisions for public pension systems. These decisions have large impacts on the sufficiency of the retirement benefits public employees receive upon retirement, and the affordability for the administering governments who have the responsibility to pay for the required employer contributions and hold the fiduciary duties to ensure adequate funding for pension promises. While both sufficiency and affordability are two important goals, these two goals are sometimes in conflict. A higher level of pension benefits can increase benefit sufficiency but can put more financial burden on the government. On the other hand, while lowering pension benefits can make pensions more affordable for the employers, it might reduce the level of benefits for employees, which can make it harder for governments to recruit and retain talent. In addition, different groups of stakeholders have different incentives to advocate for higher or lower pension benefits or increases or decreases in pension contributions. More noteworthy, the benefit and contribution decisions also depend on the legal constraints, including state laws or local statutes. The benefit and contribution decisions require dedicated efforts from the pension systems and the administering governments to balance those goals and the interests of different groups of stakeholders within the state and local legal framework. The following sections will describe factors that influence pension benefits and contributions decisions.

DOI: 10.4324/9781032671185-7

Pension benefit decisions

Public defined-benefit pension systems provide pension benefits for different groups of public employees, including teachers, police officers, firefighters, general employees, judges, and highway patrols. In some states like New York (except for New York City employees), most public employees are enrolled in state-administered pension systems. But in many other states, public employees are enrolled in multiple state and/or local pension plans that are aligned with their occupation. For example, teachers may all be enrolled in teacher retirement plans, state employees in a state plan, municipal general employees in a civilian local plan, and uniformed/public safety officers in their own municipal police and firefighter pension plans. The level of pension benefit generosity varies from one pension system to another, but the amount is typically based on a "defined benefit" (DB) formula that includes three main factors: the final average salary (FAS), the number of years of service (YOS) of the employee, and a benefit multiplier. The three factors are multiplied to derive the pension benefit:

$$\begin{aligned}\textbf{Pension benefit} = {} & \textbf{final average salary (FAS)} \times \\ & \textbf{years of service (YOS)} \times \textbf{benefit multiplier}\end{aligned}$$

FAS is typically the average of the final years of earnings prior to retirement. YOS is the number of years that an employee has worked for a particular employer before their retirement or termination. The benefit multiplier is the percentage of the FAS that will be paid. For instance, for an individual with a FAS of $60,000 who worked in a government for 30 years in a plan with a 2% multiplier, the annual pension benefit will be 60% of the FAS (30 years × 2%), and their pension income will be $36,000 annually ($60,000 × 30 × 2%) or $3,000 per month.

Depending on pension plan design, future pension benefits may be adjusted for inflation through cost-of-living adjustments (COLA). For most public pension plans, employees can estimate their pension benefits using pension calculators available on the plan website or by submitting a request. In the pension calculators, employees can enter basic information, such as the start date, age of retirement, FAS, YOS, tier, etc., to receive the estimated monthly pension payment upon retirement.

The three factors and the possible COLA rate vary depending on pension plan benefit design and can be influenced by state laws, statutes, municipal codes, and labor contracts. Any changes in these factors can affect the benefit levels. In governments with collective bargaining, governments and unions negotiate over labor conditions and compensation, including pension benefits. Decisions related to pension benefits include the requirements for normal (full) retirement eligibility (retirement age, YOS, vesting periods), the level of benefit generosity (benefit multiplier, calculation of pensionable salaries, COLA, the number of final years to calculate average salary), and any early retirement benefits.

Pension benefit formula

Final average salary

FAS is the average of an employee's wage, typically over 36, 48, or 60 consecutive months of service when their earnings were highest, often the last three to five years of employment. The FAS calculation can include regular salary, overtime pay, holiday pay, longevity payments, and merit pay. For most state and local pension plans, the time period and the salary used to calculate FAS are determined by state laws and statutes, and in some cases, those criteria can be influenced by labor negotiations.

Additionally, the time period used for the FAS may vary in a plan for different tiers of employees (which is often dependent on the date of hire) or different employee groups (e.g., civilian versus uniformed, management versus nonmanagement). For instance, in the New York State and Local Retirement System (NYSLRS), the FAS for individuals in tiers 1–5 is based on the average of three consecutive years of earnings, while the FAS for tier 6 is based on the average of five consecutive years; since employee earnings typically increase over time, the five-year average salary would be expected to be lower than the three-year average, leading to a lower FAS for the retirees in tier 6. The FAS in the Texas Employee Retirement System (TXERS) also depends on employment tiers (groups) based on hire dates (see Table 7.1).

Another issue with FAS is pension *spiking*. Pension spiking is an issue when an employee increases their FAS with overtime pay and/or other pay

TABLE 7.1 Employee Groups and FAS (Texas ERS)

Employee groups	*FAS*
Group 1 employees (employed before September 1, 2009)	Average of highest 36 months of salary
Group 2 employees (employed between September 1, 2009 and August 31, 2013)	Average of highest 48 months of salary
Group 3 employees (employed between September 1, 2013 and August 31, 2022)	Average of highest 60 months of salary

Source: https://www.ers.texas.gov/active-employees/retirement/standard-annuity.

to maximize their pension. Since some pension systems include overtime and other pay in pensionable salary, this can lead to excessive amounts of overtime work and other practices such as accrual of unused sick and vacation leave to boost earned income in the final YOS. The issues of pension spiking have been primarily documented among public safety pension plans for police and firefighters (Lewin et al., 2011; Schieber, 2011) but are also seen among other occupations and civilian pension plans for general public employees and teachers (Fitzpatrick, 2017; Mannino & Cooperman, 2013). The prevalence of pension spiking and backlash from the public in response to news of a public employee retiring with six-figure pensions (for instance, the case of the retired fire chief in Omaha, Nebraska, or retired city mayor of Chicago, Illinois) led some governments to impose more restrictions and monitoring mechanisms on allowable pay for the calculation of pensionable salary. For instance, the State of Massachusetts eliminated pension spiking by using only base salary in the calculation of FAS, excluding overtime and other types of pay.

Years of service

YOS or years of credited service are the number of years that an employee works for a particular government employer. Generally speaking, the longer an employee works, the higher the amount of their pension benefits. Service credit hours/days can include paid days, such as sick days, vacation days, and holidays. Unpaid leave or unpaid vacation days are often not counted as creditable service.

Many pension systems allow active plan members to transfer service credits that an employee accumulated with another government agency. For example, eligible active members in Texas can transfer credited service from the Teacher Retirement System (TRS) to the Employee Retirement System (ERS) or vice versa, as long as the employee has at least three years of active service. Additionally, pension plans may allow their employees to purchase service credit for unpaid leaves of absence. Plans may also allow their members to purchase service credit from previous membership in the same DB plan to allow the prior service to count toward their pension calculation.

Benefit multiplier

The pension benefit multiplier is the percentage of pay to which an employee is credited for each year of their service. Similar to FAS, the decisions over pension benefit multipliers can be decided by laws and labor negotiations. Benefit multipliers can vary by a number of factors, including

TABLE 7.2 Benefit Multipliers

Benefit multiplier	*Number of plans*
1.5–1.7%	17
Over 1.7–1.9%	9
Over 1.9–2.1%	17
Over 2.1%	11
Varies	30

Source: 2020–2021 Wisconsin Legislative Council Comparative Study of Major Public Employee Retirement Systems.

retirement age, YOS, and date of employment (employment group/tiers). Pension benefit multipliers usually range between 1.5 and 2.5%. A comparative study conducted by the Wisconsin Legislature found a wide variety of benefit multipliers across major retirement systems, as seen in Table 7.2.

The pension benefit multiplier often increases with age and YOS. This is considered the "pull" effect of pension benefits in the public sector, used by employers to retain employees. But there is also a "push" effect when the marginal increase in the benefit multiplier decreases as an employee stays longer in the system, or after reaching the highest number of YOS for pension calculations. Looking at pension wealth accruals of teacher pension benefits in the Missouri TRS, Koedel et al. (2013) show the system benefits penalize individuals who separate too early and those who stay too long (the push and pull effects). When teachers meet the minimum 25 YOS or the rule of 80 (the total of YOS plus age), their overall pension wealth decreases with each additional year of staying in the system. In the Iowa Public Employee Retirement System (IPERS), for example, the benefit multiplier increases by 2% for every YOS, up to 30 years; the multiplier increases by 1% in each year from years 31 to 35, with no increase after that.

Figure 7.1 shows the benefit factors in the California PERS (CalPERS) system for state miscellaneous and industrial members. The multiplier is 2% at 55 years of age. The benefit factor grows faster for retirees under 55; it continues to grow after this, but at a slower pace.

Eligibility rules for pension benefits

Retirement age and rules of retirement

To be eligible for full retirement benefits, an employee has to meet an age requirement. This can vary for different groups of employees. The earliest

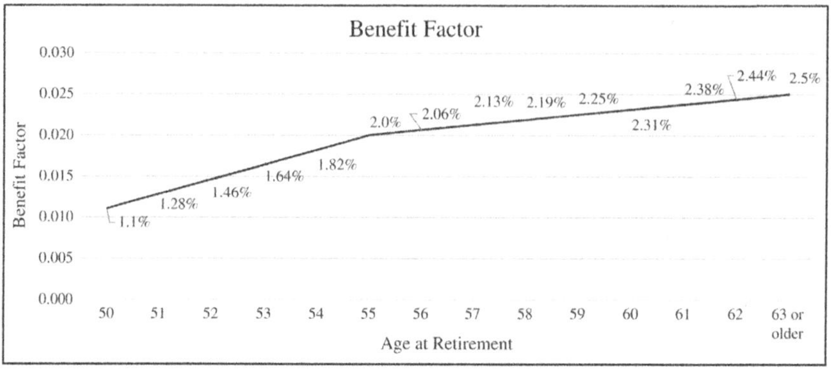

FIGURE 7.1 Benefits Factors for Employees in CalPERS

Source: The authors calculated the benefit factor based on CalPERS – Benefit Factor Chart

age that public pension plans allow their employees to retire with full (normal) pension benefits is often 62, although some plans have a higher minimum age of retirement at age 65 or 67 (as shown in Table 7.3). Public safety personnel often have a lower minimum age requirement due to the physical demands of their jobs. During the period of pension reforms of 2010–2011, many state pension plans raised their minimum age for retirement (see Chapter 8 for more details).

Some pension plans, including teacher pension plans, have adopted "years and out" provisions which allow employees to retire with normal benefits at any age (or combined with a minimum age requirement) after meeting certain YOS requirements. For example, teachers in the State of Missouri pension systems have a 25-year-and-out provision, to allow teachers to retire after 25 YOS. The Wisconsin Legislative Council Comparative Study showed that more than half of the pension funds

TABLE 7.3 Retirement Age and Full Retirement Requirements

Minimum age for normal retirement benefit	*Number of plans*
62 years of age or earlier with 10 or less YOS	25
62 years of age with many years of services	69
65 years of age	15

Source: 2020–2021 Wisconsin Legislative Council Comparative Study of Major Public Employee Retirement Systems.

TABLE 7.4 Years of Services

Years of service and out provision	*Number of plans*
32–35 years of service (age 55 or older)	11
30 years of service (age 55 or older)	23
27–28 years of service (age 55 and older)	3
25 years of service (age 55 and older)	5
20 years of service (age 55 and older)	6
Total	48

Source: 2020–2021 Wisconsin Legislative Council Comparative Study of Major Public Employee Retirement Systems.

in the study (48 out of 87 plans) have the YOS and out provisions (Table 7.4).

Additionally, pension plans apply retirement rules to determine the minimum age and YOS requirements for normal retirement benefits. For example, school employees in the Nebraska Public Retirement System can retire with normal retirement benefits at the age of 65 or if they meet the "Rule of 85." This allows a member who is at least 55 to retire with normal retirement benefits when the total of their age and YOS equals 85. Table 7.5 showed that about a third of state pension funds (28 out of 87 plans) in the study conducted by the Wisconsin Legislative Council have retirement rules of 80, 85, or 90.

Vesting requirement

To be eligible to receive pension benefits, public employees have to meet a minimum years of active employment before their benefits are "vested." The vesting period generally ranges between three and ten years. Among 87 state-wide pension funds selected for the Wisconsin Legislative Study,

TABLE 7.5 Retirement Rules

Retirement rules	*Numbers of plans*
Rule of 90 (or 92)	13
Rule of 85 (or 87 or 88)	11
Rule of 80	4
Total	28

Source: 2020–2021 Wisconsin Legislative Council Comparative Study of Major Public Employee Retirement Systems.

TABLE 7.6 Vesting Requirements

Vesting period	*Number of plans*
Immediate or <1 year	1
3 years	5
4–5 years	42
7–8 years	6
10 years	30
Varying	3
Total	87

Source: 2020–2021 Wisconsin Legislative Council Comparative Study of Major Public Employee Retirement Systems.

about half of the pension funds have four- to five-year vesting periods, and more than a third of them have a ten-year vesting period (Table 7.6).

The longer the vesting period, the more costly it becomes for an employee to leave an employer before meeting the vesting requirement. Thus, a longer vesting requirement can also provide some incentive to nudge an employee to stay in a job longer. If the employee does not meet the vesting requirement, some or all of their accrued pension benefit can be forfeited. If an employee leaves after the vesting requirement is met, they may be able to receive benefits when they eventually retire, and/or may be eligible for service credit transfers within or between pension systems within a state (depending on the state laws). The transfer of credited service offers more flexibility to move to other government agencies, particularly within a state-administered pension system, and greater accommodation to meet the mobility needs of public employees. For example, a teacher in the Texas TRS who has met the three-year employment period can transfer their service credit to the ERS.

Early retirement

Most DB pension plans permit their full-time employees to take early retirement. This allows employees who have not met the full retirement age to retire with reduced benefits. The earlier the retirement, the greater the penalty or benefit reduction. Early retirement benefits are generally based on the normal retirement benefit formula, but a benefit reduction factor is applied. The benefit reduction factor can vary depending on plan requirements, retirement age, and YOS. For example, in the NYSLRS, an employee can elect to retire early, however, depending on the retirement tier an employee belongs to, there will be some percentages of benefit reduction. For example, the percentage of early benefit reduction for employees in tiers 3 and 4 is 27% at age 55 and less than 30 YOS; the percentage is 38.33% for employees in tier 5, and 52% for employees in tier 6.

Adequacy of pension benefits and budget considerations

Social Security coverage

Unlike their private-sector counterparts, not all public employees have Social Security coverage. The Social Security Act of 1935 excluded state and local governments due to concerns over the constitutionality of imposing federal payroll tax authority on state and local governments (Nuschler, 2021). The Social Security Amendment of 1950, though, allowed voluntary participation from state and local governments to elect Social Security coverage for their employees. The Omnibus Reconciliation Act of 1991 required employees of state and local governments that do not offer any pension benefits to participate in Social Security (Crain, 2001). By 1991, over 75% of public-sector employees were covered by the program (Aubry et al., 2022). Today, state and local governments can stay outside of Social Security if their pension benefits are sufficiently generous. Figure 7.2 shows the percentage of pension plans that provide Social Security

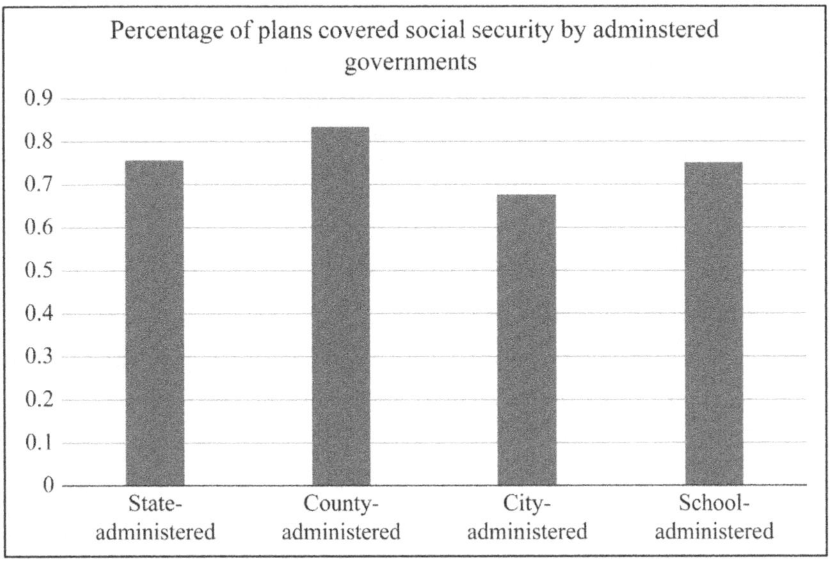

FIGURE 7.2 The Percentage of Pension Plans that Provide Social Security Coverage

Source: Authors calculated based on Boston College – Public Plans Database (2000–2022)

coverage by administering government and plan type. Approximately 70–80% of pension plans provide Social Security benefits to their employees. Among different occupations and plan types (general public employees, teachers, and public safety), public safety plans often have the lowest level of Social Security coverage. The difference in Social Security coverage is noteworthy because it has significant impacts on the financial security of retired members as well as pension benefit design and negotiations. Studies have found that this discrepancy over Social Security coverage can influence the level of pension benefit generosity, with plans that are outside of the Social Security System tending to provide larger pension benefits to offset the effect of not having Social Security coverage (Kelley, 2014).

In addition, to measure whether state and local pension plans comply with the Employment Tax Regulations, the federal government established the Safe Harbor benefit adequacy requirement. For a DB pension plan, the Safe Harbor formula mirrors the DB benefit calculation based on retirement age and sets of benefits factors, including YOS, FAS, and pension benefit multipliers. In defined contribution (DC) plans, the Safe Harbor guideline requires that total employer and employee contributions equal at least 7.5% of annual salary (Aubry et al., 2022). Even though most state and local pension plans are in compliance with Safe Harbor requirements (Aubry et al., 2022), the current high level of unfunded liabilities, low-market investment returns, and pension benefit reduction reforms have raised concerns about whether employees covered by Social Security receive equivalent and sufficient retirement benefits (Abashidze et al., 2021; Quinby et al., 2020). Using simulations, Aubry et al. (2022) found that a significant minority of public pension plans are likely to fall short of providing Social Security-equivalent benefits, and 750,000–1 million noncovered workers might be at risk of receiving pension benefits that fall short of the Social Security benefits level.

Cost-of-living adjustment (COLA)

COLAs are provided by many public pension plans to help plan retirees keep pace with inflation. Similar to Social Security benefits that are adjusted using an annual COLA, state and local pension benefits are designed to help retirees maintain their purchasing power and offset the effect of inflation. The COLA calculation formula can be set by state or local laws and varies across plans. There are several considerations for COLA design:

- *Automatic versus ad hoc*: COLAs may be provided automatically without the need for action or on an ad hoc basis that requires action from the legislature or pension governing body. Approximately 72% of state-administered plans provide some form of automatic COLA and 28% have ad hoc COLA provisions (NASRA, 2022).

- *Fixed rate or inflation-based*: a fixed rate COLA is a constant percentage increase that is not tied to the consumer price index (CPI) inflation measure, while an inflation-based COLA is a percentage increase that is tied to the CPI, but with some limitations. For example, NYSLRS calculates COLAs based on half of the annual rate of inflation, measured at the end of the state fiscal year (March 31), and the annual COLA is between 1 and 3% (OSC, 2024). Similar to the COLA calculation in Social Security benefits, some state and local pension plans also use the CPI-W (urban wage earners and clerical workers) to measure inflation (similar to the Social Security COLA), but others use the CPI-U (based on all urban consumers) or other CPI measures published by the Bureau of Labor Statistics (BLS). Approximately 52% of state-administered pension plans link COLA provisions to inflation, and 34% of them provide a fixed COLA percentage (NASRA, 2022).
- *Performance-based (contingent) COLAs*: the COLA percentage may be tied to investment performance and financial metrics, including the plan funding level and investment rate of return. For example, the COLA could be set between 1 and 3%; the higher level would be used if the plan is fully funded or meets its target investment return, but a lower level would be used if the plan's investment returns do not meet the targets or the plans' funding ratio decreased (Chen et al., 2022). Approximately 14% of state-administered pension plans link COLA rates to investment returns and/or pension funding conditions (NASRA, 2022).
- *Minimum requirement for COLA benefits*: in some plans, retirees do not qualify for COLA increases until they meet certain requirements. For example, COLA eligibility for retirees of general plans might be limited to those who are 62 or older and retired for at least five years, while retirees of uniformed plans may be eligible for a COLA if they are 55 or older and retired for at least ten years. While COLAs are intended to help retirees deal with the rising cost of living, they have contributed significantly to the issue of unfunded pension liabilities (Dabrowski & Klingner, 2016; Rauh, 2015). Due to the significant impacts of COLAs on rising pension costs, some states have adopted or considered changes, such as eliminating or temporarily stopping COLAs until pension funding levels are more sustainable or applying risk-sharing mechanisms or linking COLAs to pension funding levels or pension investment performance (Munnell et al., 2016). According to a NASRA (2022) report, COLA legislative changes affect new hires only in five states (NV, AZ, UT, NE, and MS), both current employees and new

hires in eight states (OR, MT, KS, FL, VA, MD, VT, and CT), and retirees in 17 states (WA, WY, CO, NM, OK, SD, MN, MO, AR, LA, IL, KY, OH, SC, NJ, RI, and ME).

Legal protection for public pension benefits

In many states, pension benefits for public employees are protected by state statutes or state constitutions (Munnell & Quinby, 2012; Thom, 2017). These laws limit the discretion of governments to reduce pension benefits. If the pension benefits are protected under the state constitution, a constitutional amendment is needed to change pension benefits. If the benefits are protected under state statutes, new laws or a constitutional amendment are needed to change benefits. There are two underlying legal arguments for these protections: (1) the property approach, where employees' pensions are considered property and are protected under the 5th and 14th Amendments to the U.S. Constitution from deprivation without due process; and (2) the contract approach, where employees' pension benefits are considered a contractual relationship between employee and employer and, therefore, are protected against substantial impairment under both state and federal constitutions (Monahan, 2010). Changes in pension benefits may also be subject to judicial review for other legal reasons.

Source of legal protections

In seven states, pension benefits are protected by state constitutions (see Table 7.7). In six states, pensions are protected based on statutes enacted

TABLE 7.7 Legal Protections of Pension Benefits

Source of legal protection for pension benefits	*States*
State constitution	AK, AZ, NM, LA, IL, MI, NY
State statute	WY, MO, FL, OH, NJ, ME
Common-law contractual	WA, OR, CA, NV, ID, UT, MT, CO, ND, SD, NE, KS, AR, MS, AL, TN, GA, SC, NC, WV, PA, VT, NH, RI, DE, MD
Common-law contractual and state statute	OK, WI, KY, VA, MA
Other types of protection (court laws, etc.)	MN, IA, TX, IN, CT

Source: Pew Charitable Trusts (2019).

by the legislature. In 26 states, pension benefits are protected under the Contract Clause and court rulings (Pew Charitable Trusts, 2019).

Pension features and aspects

Twenty-two states protect employee accrued benefits from the time they start employment; 13 states protect accrued benefits only after employees meet the vesting requirements or the minimum age and YOS required are met. Three states have some provisions to protect pension benefits only when the employee retires. In two states, accrued benefits are protected only if the employee can prove that they relied on promised benefits to their detriment (Pew Charitable Trusts, 2019).

Deferred retirement option plans (DROP)

Deferred retirement option plans (DROP) refer to a provision of some public DB pension plans that allows members who are eligible for normal retirement to remain on the job for a period of time while also accumulating deferred pension payments. The amount of a DROP participant's monthly retirement benefits is frozen based on the final average compensation prior to the election to enter DROP. The time in the DROP program does not count toward the number of YOS or age used to calculate retirement benefits. During the DROP period, the individual continues to receive a salary; the retirement benefits that would have been paid to the individual are instead deposited into a DROP account. At the end of the DROP period, the individual leaves employment and they receive a lump-sum payment of the accumulated pension benefits, often with interest. Essentially, under DROP, employees who are qualified for normal pension benefits are able to continue working while receiving their pension benefits at the same time, which some have called "double-dipping." DROP options are more common among public safety (police and firefighter) pension plans where the members can be eligible for full retirement at a relatively young age such as 55 years with 20 YOS. The plans have been seen as recruitment and retention tools for many cities to entice their experienced and trained officers to continue working for additional benefits.

The impacts of DROP on public-sector employment and financial sustainability are controversial. On the positive side, research has found that DROP results in a significant increase in labor participation among older workers. Alva et al. (2010) found that employees who elected to join the DROP program in the City of Philadelphia worked an average of 2.1 years more than the age that they would otherwise have retired. In cities like Dallas or Houston, Texas, where they have had difficulties in recruiting uniformed employees, especially police officers, the DROP program has incentivized their experienced officers to continue to work and reduced the urgent issue of lacking qualified and trained officers.

However, there are some concerns related to the DROP program. First, it is more common among public safety employees because they often have lower normal retirement ages (around 55) based on the rationality that the job is physically demanding, and they cannot work at an older age. At the same time, DROP allows those officers to continue to work additional years while still collecting their pensions, which seems to conflict with the rationale for an earlier retirement age.

Second, DROP programs also raise concerns over the cost of public pension systems that offer this feature. At first glance, it might appear that there are no additional financial costs for the sponsoring governments since the systems would have to make the benefit payments to the employees anyway. There are some characteristics of the plan designs that might affect that "cost neutral perspective," though, such as the amount of DROP interest and COLA. While some pension systems do not offer interest on the accumulated DROP account, some offer interest in addition to an annual COLA. For example, the City of Dallas police and firefighter pension systems offer a 4% COLA to DROP deposits and an approximate 7–8% compound interest rate; by 2016, the DROP balances had grown to more than $1.5 billion (DPFP Ad Hoc Committee Report, n.d.). Additionally, the length of DROP participation can affect the costs of the pension plan. The longer employees are allowed to participate in DROP, the higher the cost (GFOA, 2020). For example, the Arizona Public Safety Personnel Retirement System allows members to participate in DROP for up to 84 months; Los Angeles Fire and Police Pensions plan allows members to participate in DROP for up to 60 months (five years). In some systems, there is no specific limit on the duration of DROP participation.

Third, since pension plans are increasingly invested in illiquid assets such as real estate to meet the fund's targeted investment returns, the sudden nature of large DROP lump-sum withdrawals can affect the pension cash flow and the amount of assets that can be used for investment. This issue played a prominent role in the City of Dallas Police and Fire Pension Plan crisis in 2016, which was dubbed the "run to the bank" problem. By 2016, the city had over 3,067 DROP accounts with an average value of $597,000, 517 accounts worth over $1 million, and the highest DROP account had a value of $4.3 million. DROP lump-sum withdrawals worth more than $80 million in 2015 and $500 million in 2016 caused a plummet in the pension funding ratio from 82 to 45.1%, with the risk of the pension system becoming insolvent by 2027 (DPFP Ad Hoc Committee Report, n.d.).

Disability benefits

Many but not all public pension plans provide pension benefits to members who are disabled and/or unable to work. Disability benefits can be coordinated with workers' compensation and Social Security coverage. Duty-related benefits may not require a minimum YOS, but non-duty-related benefits might require five to ten years of credited service, as well as satisfying the definition of disablement (Steffen, 2001). Approximately 90% of public pension plans have some sort of disability benefits provision (Mitchell et al, 2001). Most disability benefits are paid to public safety personnel due to the hazardous nature of the occupations. Some plans allow members to retire with unreduced normal benefits (what they would receive if they worked until full retirement) but may be subject to qualifying age and service conditions. Some disability benefits provide a portion of retirement benefits using lower benefit multiplier factors. For example, members of the NYSLRS can qualify for disability benefits for on-the-job incidents that occurred during the performance of their job duties without minimum service requirements. For other disabilities that may or may not be job-related, a member can only qualify for disability benefits if they meet a minimum of ten YOS, and the benefit is not more than one-third of their FAS.

The financial impacts of disability on public pension plans can vary depending on the provisions, such as the qualifications for the benefits and the level of benefits (normal versus reduced benefits). Since the benefits can be costly and the administrative process of benefit determination (deciding who qualifies for and meets the definition of disablement) tends to be complicated, some pension plans outsource the administrative process to a third party or provide some form of insurance outside the system. One advantage of outsourcing the administrative process is the ability to retain the benefit financing within the system while reducing the fiduciary issues of reviewing/administering individual disability cases (Steffen, 2001).

Survival benefits

Some public pension plans provide continuation of benefits to the survivor of retired members. These options ensure that if a member dies, the named beneficiary can receive a portion of the pension benefits for the remainder of their lifetime. These benefits are often limited to a member's spouse. Members generally have choices regarding survivor benefits. With *single-life allowance*, the member receives full regular pension payments with no continuing benefits to a beneficiary after the member's death. If a member chooses *joint and survivor* (joint-allowance) or *joint and survivor with pop-up*, some benefits will be continued to the living beneficiaries upon a member's death. In the joint and survivor option, a member elects to reduce their pension benefit in order to provide protection to a beneficiary; the reduced payment cannot be changed if the beneficiary dies before the member. For those who choose the joint and survivor with pop-up option, the member's benefit can be restored to the full level if the beneficiary dies before the member. More often, the benefit reduction for the joint allowance with pop-up option is higher to compensate for the costs of providing additional benefits (Steffen, 2001). Some pension systems, such as the NYSLRS, have a *five-to-ten-year certain* provision; if members die within that period following retirement, beneficiaries receive the benefit payment for the remainder of that timeframe.

Replacement rate

One of the main concerns over pension benefits is sufficiency. Retirement income sufficiency is often considered in terms of the replacement rate, which is generally measured as the percentage of preretirement income replaced by retirement benefits (Vanguard, 2022). As mentioned in prior chapters, a replacement rate of roughly 75–80% is commonly considered adequate for retirement income from all sources (Peng, 2008; Young & Lindsay, 2023). Depending on the employees' income preretirement, the replacement rate can vary. Lower income households and households with lower savings rate often need to maintain a higher percentage of preretirement income (i.e., a higher replacement rate) to sustain spending needs (Lobel et al., 2019)

The Pew Charitable Trusts (2020) found that the replacement rate of a public worker who retires at 65 years of age with 35 YOS is about 52% after adjusting for inflation, and if workers also have Social Security coverage, the combined replacement rate is 85%. These statistics provide an assurance that a public pension retiree with both a DB pension and Social Security will have adequate retirement income to ensure a continuation of their preretirement lifestyle. Also, these data underscore the important role of Social Security coverage on public workers' retirement income. For workers not covered by Social Security, their DB pension payments would need to be higher to be commensurate with peers who are also covered by Social Security. Additionally, many state and local governments have transitioned to hybrid or DC plans that may not provide sufficient pension benefits to meet the target replacement rate (Crain et al., 2009). These factors are critical for pension plans to consider to ensure that pension benefits can provide financial security for employees in retirement.

Pension contributions

An overview of public pension revenue sources

The funding for DB pension plans comes from three main sources: employer contributions, employee contributions, and investment returns earned on pension assets. NASRA (2023) reported that from 1993 to 2022, total pension revenues were comprised of 11% from employee contributions, 26% from employer contributions, and 63% from investment earnings. Figure 7.3. shows the revenue trends of state and local public pension plans from 2000 to 2014, and Figures 7.4 and 7.5 show the revenue trends of state and local public pension plans separately from 2015 to 2022, using the U.S. Census Bureau Annual Survey of Public Pension Systems database[1].

Overall, the total pension contributions of state and local public government employers as well as their employees have gradually and consistently increased in the last two decades, although employer contributions have risen at a higher pace than employee contributions. Earnings from investments have been an important source of revenue, but they have a higher level of fluctuation than the contributions from employees and employers. In a good investment year, the earnings can provide more than 70% of pension revenues. However, in economic downturns such as 2001–2003 and 2007–2009, public pension plans witnessed negative returns from

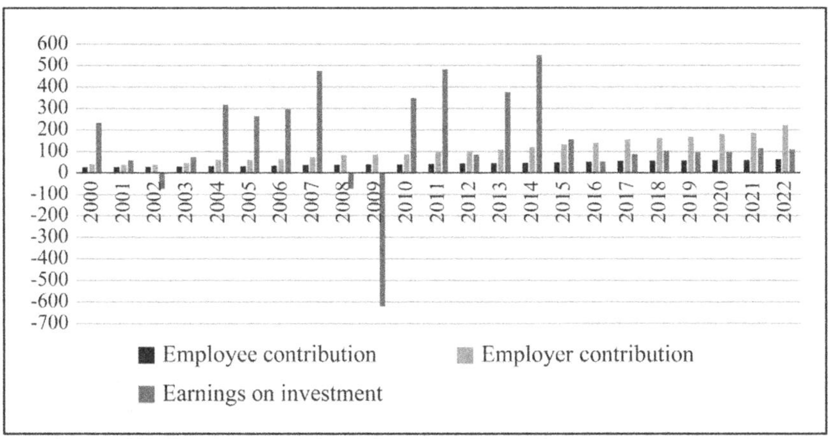

FIGURE 7.3 State and Local Public Pension Revenues (2000–2014) (Presented in Billions of Dollars)

Source: U.S. Census Bureau Annual Survey of Public Pension Systems database

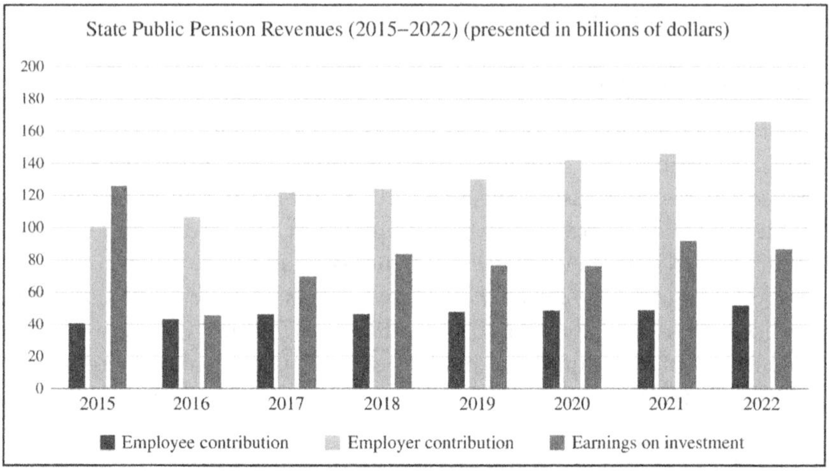

FIGURE 7.4 State Public Pension Revenues (2015–2022)

Source: U.S. Census Bureau Annual Survey of Public Pension Systems database

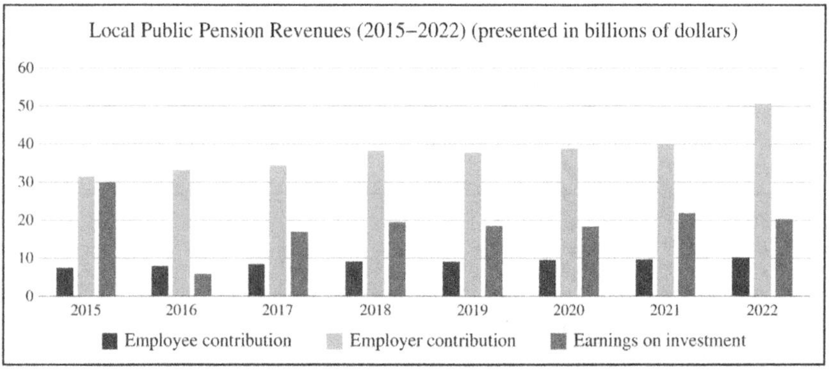

FIGURE 7.5 Local Public Pension Revenues (2015–2022)

Source: U.S. Census Bureau Annual Survey of Public Pension Systems database

their investments. This situation can put pressure on governments to increase their employer contributions to make up for the investment losses and continue to cover pension benefit liabilities. The following sections will provide more detail on how employer contributions are determined and legal constraints on government pension contributions.

Pension contribution policies

While investment earnings fluctuate and depend on the capital markets and the plan's investment strategy, employee and employer contribution policies are set or decided by the governments sponsoring the plan or through collective bargaining agreements. The percentage of employee contributions is often fixed and varies less over time. Employee contribution rates are generally set by legislative bodies, and in some states/local governments, the rates can be negotiated through a collective bargaining process with employee groups. Employer contributions, on the other hand, vary more often and attract more attention due to the implications not only for the funding status of public pension systems but also for the fiscal health of the governments. Employer contributions are determined by the actuarial calculation of pension contributions that are needed to fund pension benefits and the legal limits set by the government's funding policies.

Actuarially determined contribution (ADC)

The actuarially determined contribution (ADC)[2], which is typically reported as an annual total or as a percentage of payroll, is calculated annually and recommended by the system's actuaries. The ADC includes the costs allocated in the current fiscal year (normal cost) plus the amortized payment of unfunded actuarial accrued liabilities (UAAL), which is the difference between pension actuarial accrued liabilities and pension assets.

$$\text{ADC} = \text{Normal Cost} + \text{Amortized payment of UAAL}$$

The contribution costs are influenced by two main factors: the level of benefits and the level of unfunded pension liabilities. The more generous the benefits, the higher the contribution amount. It is important to note that pension assets and liabilities are calculated based on actuarial assumptions. Pension liabilities are the total future benefit payments that the government has promised to employees upon their retirement. Those amounts are discounted to the present value, using the discount rate, to reflect the pension investment returns (see Chapter 6). This information is used by the actuaries to calculate the amount of pension contributions needed to cover the current year's benefits. Since all the information on pension liabilities and pension contributions is calculated based on actuarial assumptions, there are concerns that public pension plans can opportunistically use higher discount rates to purposely reduce their total liabilities and therefore, lower the required contributions (Novy-Marx & Rauh, 2011). Additionally, pension contributions depend on the amount of UAAL and amortization methods. The higher the UAAL, the higher the ADC. Since pension plans are not required to pay all the UAAL at one time but can spread the payment over time, ADC can vary based on how aggressive the amortization methods. Plans with shorter amortization periods are required to pay down a larger portion of UAAL each year and therefore increase the ADC. Most public pension plans amortize their UAAL over many years (e.g., 30–40 years). The decision to use an open or closed amortization strategy can affect pension costs and the level of unfunded liabilities. Open amortization (as unfunded liabilities are "refinanced" each year) makes it hard to fully pay off the unfunded liabilities, while in a closed amortization approach, the amortization period is reduced each year with more commitment and intention to pay off unfunded liabilities by the end of the amortization period.

Furthermore, pension investment returns can also affect the level of ADC. In a DB plan, the investment gains or losses are borne by the plan sponsors. Investment gains give governments more financial resources to fulfill their pension promises. In contrast, investment losses require state and local governments as well as future employees to increase their contributions to fill the gap between assets and liabilities. For example, the bull markets of the 1980s and 1990s increased the funding level of most pension plans, while the economic downturns in the 2000–2002 and 2007–2009 recessions sharply reduced the funding levels of many pension plans (Eaton & Nofsinger, 2008; Norcross & Biggs, 2010; Peng & Wang, 2017; Seligman, 2013). Since DB pension benefits are guaranteed by the plan-sponsor governments regardless of investment returns, decreases in investment earnings impose a greater financial burden on state and local governments to increase their pension contributions to make up for the funding gap.

Government funding policies

It is noteworthy that the ADC is the required contribution recommended by the actuaries, but the full payment is often not legally binding. While the majority of state policies authorize payment of the full ADC, some state policies impose limits on annual increases of the employer contribution rate or only allow payment of a fixed percentage of compensation as specified in statutes in an effort to stabilize the amount of pension contributions paid over time and reduce the budgetary fluctuation of pension costs. In most cases where there are limits on pension contributions paid, the allowed level is often lower than the amount recommended by actuaries, which might contribute to the issue of underfunded liabilities (Brainard & Brown, 2015; Munnell et al., 2008).

NASRA's study of 112 state-sponsored pension plans from 2001 to 2013 found that approximately 34 states are required to pay the full actuarial amount, and about 16 states (32%) are either required to pay a fixed percentage of compensation specified in statute or have set limits on the annual growth of state contributions to the pension plans. For example, employers in state systems in Hawaii, Massachusetts, Maryland (2003–2013), Minnesota, Missouri, Montana, North Dakota, New Mexico, Ohio, Oklahoma, South Dakota, Texas, Virginia (prior to 2012), and Wyoming are required to fund a fixed percentage of compensation specified in statute (Brainard & Brown, 2015). In Florida, the legislature sets the employer contribution rates each year. Figure 7.6 shows the level of ADC required and contributed for the Florida Retirement System from 2001 to 2022. The graph shows that while the state fixed contribution rates can come close to the ADC required, in many years, the fixed rate is lower than the actuarially recommended contribution.

Pension contribution and fiscal implications of pension costs

The financial discipline of paying the full ADC is important for the government to maintain a sustainable pension funding level. Failure to meet those pension contribution obligations can lead to severe consequences

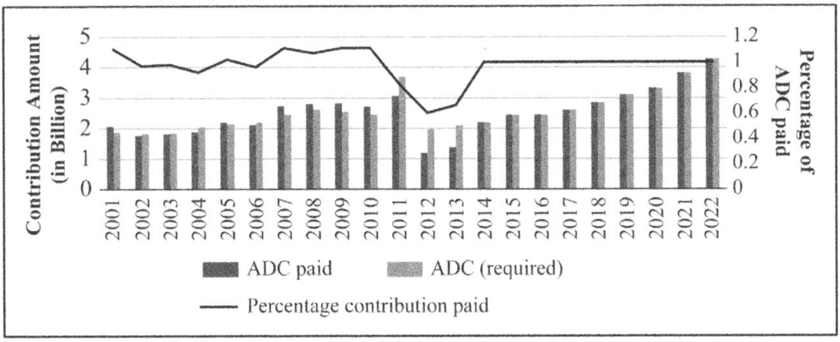

FIGURE 7.6 Annual Contribution in the Florida Retirement System (2001–2022)

Source: Authors' calculation based on the Boston College – Public Plans Database (2001–2022)

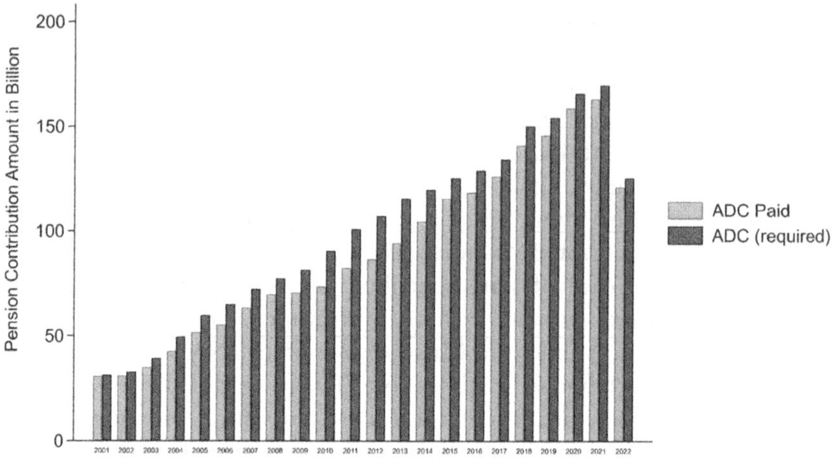

FIGURE 7.7 Average Actuarially Determined Contributions (ADC) and ADC Paid (2001–2022)

Source: The authors' calculation based on the Boston College – Public Plans Database (2001–2022)

of increasing unfunded pension liabilities, reducing the level of assets available for investment, and threatening the financial health of both the pension fund and government. On average, the percentage of ADC paid is approximately 90% in plans in the Public Pension Plan Database, as shown in Figure 7.7.

Besides some concerns about the ADC limits/constraints (as mentioned above) that might have caused the gap between ADC (required) and the paid amount, some scholars have observed that pension contributions have been used as a countercyclical budgetary tool as some state and municipal governments delay or reduce pension contributions below required levels when faced with budget deficits. U.S. GAO reports indicated that many state and local governments have not set aside sufficient funds to cover promised pension benefits and that governments' ability to fully fund their pension system depends on their revenue-raising capacity and the willingness of taxpayers to meet the costs (GAO, 1993, 2008). Peng (2004) showed that pension contributions had been used as a countercyclical budgetary tool as policymakers lower pension contributions below required levels when faced with budget deficits. Since reduced pension contributions do not directly affect current revenue structures or current levels of public service, "borrowing" from pension trust funds during budget shortfalls can be an attractive strategy as long as officials compensate for the underfunding in recovery years (Gorina, 2018; Peng, 2004). The National Conference of State Legislatures (NCSL, 2010) observed that borrowing from pension funds in the form of not making full ADC is often done informally; because this action is less transparent, it can be done at reduced political costs or encounter less political opposition (NCSL, 2010). Giertz's (2003) research of pension funding and state finances from the 1990s to early 2000s indicated that pension assets and state revenues are highly correlated and dependent on the economic cycle. Underfunding issues often occur at the same time as states are under fiscal stress from an economic downturn and declining tax revenues, while funding ratios typically improve during economic expansions (Giertz & Papke, 2007)

St. Clair (2013) offers empirical evidence of the trade-off between state budget stabilization funds and pension contributions in response to fiscal stress. The study found that strict withdrawal rules from budget stabilization funds are inversely associated with the level of pension contribution paid. Scholars have also observed that when confronted with fiscal stress, officials in some state and local governments cut or delay pension contributions to close budget gaps rather than pursuing unpopular tax increases or spending cuts (Bourdeaux, 2018; Munnell et al., 2008; Splinter, 2017).

Overall, pension contribution costs depend on internal decisions that are made by the plans as well as the external economic conditions. In the case of high market returns, there will be relatively less burden on governments to shore up pension funds since the returns from investments can provide enough growth in pension assets. On the other hand, in the case of low market returns, there will be much more burden on governments to shoulder a higher percentage of pension contributions to maintain the plan's funding level (Chen et al., 2022; Rauh, 2010). In terms of internal decisions, changes in pension benefit levels, including the COLA rate, can affect pension total liabilities. Any cost-sharing policy to divide the contribution risk between the employers and the employees can help reduce the financial burden of funding pension plans during a low market return situation, but it might also increase benefit uncertainty for employees.

Besides, it is important for governments to consider how pension costs affect their access to the capital market and how different financing tools can affect the financial health of the government. Some states like Illinois or New Jersey have issued pension obligation bonds (POBs) to increase funding to the state pension systems. This financing tool might help address the short-term issue of pension funding while reducing the pressures on governments to increase their contributions. However, this strategy is not without risk. The success of this funding mechanism depends on a promise that the bond proceeds that are invested through the pension fund yield higher returns than the interest and the cost of issuing the bonds (Munnell et al., 2010). This premise can be influenced by many factors, including the investment market conditions (interest rate, market returns, etc.), the timing of the issuance, and the investment strategies of the plans. Besides, some argue that the issuance of POB does not guarantee the benefits of lowering the total amount of debt for the governments, but more concerning, it changes the nature of the indebtedness. While the payment of unfunded pension liabilities can be somewhat flexible and can be adjusted through internal decisions (i.e., pension reforms, pension amortization, and payment smoothing), POBs are less flexible with more strict annual required payment (Hitchcock & Prunty, 2009; Munnell et al., 2010). Indeed, when facing unfunded pension problems, the pension systems and their administrative governments will need to consider different action plans (either management or financing decisions) to remedy the issues. Those decisions have their own pros and cons that require careful consideration to ensure the affordability and financial sustainability of the pension systems.

Additionally, some pension plans implement cost-sharing policies that provide a longer term approach to pension contribution issues and give plans more flexibility in making adjustments to the employee contribution rate or post-employment benefits based on the rate of investment returns or plan funding levels. These approaches can include: (1) splitting some or all of the total annual costs between the employer and the employees or (2) adjusting the employee contribution in response to investment returns, in which the contribution rate can be raised or lowered if investment assumptions are not met (Pew Charitable Trusts, 2017). Some cost-sharing and risk-sharing mechanisms or policies can be considered by pension plan administrators and boards of trustees to ensure the fairness and sustainability of public pension systems.

Summary

Public pensions, which are still dominantly DB plans, are one of the most important factors to attract and retain public employees. Not only do workers demand pensions, but public organizations also want to provide pensions to incentivize workers. When considering pension benefit designs, employers need to consider different goals of pension benefits, including sufficiency of pension benefits, affordability of pension costs, sustainability of pension funding, efficiency of asset management, and good governance practices. The more generous the benefits, the higher the financial obligations that the governments have to bear to maintain the pension funding level and keep their pension promises. As a best practice, it is critical for pension-sponsoring governments and pension boards to adhere to and strengthen fiscal discipline toward pension contributions while keeping in mind the affordability of pension plans when considering any future commitments to pension benefits. Due to the direct and interconnected effects of both pension benefit and contribution decisions on governments' financial condition, it is critical for the governments and pension boards to consider different scenarios of market returns, economic conditions, and pension accounting in the decision-making process. Furthermore, confronting different choices between balancing the adequacy and attractiveness of public pension benefits, the affordability of pension plans, and the financial sustainability of governments and pension systems, public pension systems have made, and continue to consider, adjustments to pension benefits and contributions (as will be discussed in more detail in the following three chapters). Ideally, during these processes, pension reforms are designed to meet both the needs of the employees and the fiscal goals of governments.

Notes

1 We have to separate the data into two time periods due to the change in sample size in the U.S. Census Bureau Annual Survey of Public Pension Systems. In 2015, the U.S. Census Bureau added more than 2,200 pension systems (largely locally administered plans) to the data. Prior to 2015, the total number of systems was approximately 3,900 systems (230 state-administered and 3,700 locally administered systems). Since 2015, the total number of systems is around 5,300 (290–300 state-administered and 5,000 locally administered systems).

2 ADC (actuarially determined contribution) was often referred to as annual required contribution (ARC) before 2014. The change in ADC was implemented as part of GASB Statements *No. 67 (Financial Reporting for Pension Plans)* and *No. 68 (Accounting and Financial Reporting for Pensions).*

References

Abashidze, N., Clark, R. L., & Craig, L. A. (2021). *Reductions in the generosity of state and local employee pensions: Comparison of plans with and without Social Security coverage.* NBER.

Alva, S., Coe, N. B., & Webb, A. (2010). The impact of a DROP program on the age of retirement and employer pension costs. *SSRN Electronic Journal*. https://doi.org/10.2139/ssrn.1695184

Aubry, J.-P., Liu, S., Munnell, A. H., Quinby, L. D., & Springstead, G. R. (2022). State and local government employees without Social Security coverage: What percentage will earn pension benefits that fall short of Social Security equivalence? *Social Security Bulletin*, *82*(3), 1–20.

Bourdeaux, C. (2018). Loss aversion and strategic choices in cutting budgets. *Public Finance and Management*, *18*(1), 4–38.

Brainard, K., & Brown, A. (2015). *The annual required contribution experience of state retirement plans, FY 01 to FY 13*. National Association of State Retirement Administrators. https://www.nasra.org/files/JointPublications/NASRA_ARC_Spotlight.pdf

Chen, G., Yin, Y., & Boyd, D. (2022). A simulation of risk-sharing policies in U.S. public pension plans. *Municipal Finance Journal*, *43*(1), 67–91.

Crain, R. B. (2001). Regulation and taxation of public plans: A history of increasing federal influence. In O. S. Mitchell and E. C. Hustead (Eds.), *Pensions in the public sector* (pp. 119–131). Pension Research Council Publications.

Crain, R. B., Heller, M., & Yakoboski, P. J. (2009). Chapter 13 Defined contribution pension plans in the public sector: A benchmark analysis. Olivia S. Mitchell and Gary Anderson (Ed.), *The future of public Employee Retirement Systems*, 206–238. Oxford University Press. https://doi.org/10.1093/acprof:oso/9780199573349.003.0013

Dabrowski, T., & Klingner, J. (2016). *What's driving Illinois' $111 billion pension crisis: Retirement ages, COLAs and out-of-sync pension payouts*. Illinois Policy Institute. https://files.illinoispolicy.org/wp-content/uploads/2016/04/Pension-papers_combined_4-8.compressed.pdf

Dallas Police and Fire Pension System (DPFPS) Ad Hoc Committee on Pension. (n.d.). *Pension funding plan*. https://dallascityhall.com/departments/government-affairs/pension-funding-solution/Pages/default.aspx

Eaton, T. V., & Nofsinger, J. R. (2008). Funding levels and gender in public pension plans. *Public Budgeting & Finance*, *28*(3), 108–128. https://doi.org/10.1111/j.1540-5850.2008.00913.x

Fitzpatrick, M. D. (2017). Pension-spiking, free-riding, and the effects of pension reform on teachers' earnings. *Journal of Public Economics*, *148*, 57–74. https://doi.org/10.1016/j.jpubeco.2017.02.007

GFOA. (2020). *Deferred retirement option plans*. https://www.gfoa.org/materials/deferred-retirement-option-plans

Giertz, J. F. (2003). The impact of pension funding on state government finances. *State Tax Notes*, 29(7), 507–513.

Giertz, J. F., & Papke, L. E. (2007). Public pension plans: Myths and realities for state budgets. *National Tax Journal*, *60*(2), 305–323.

Gorina, E. (2018). City revenue structure and unfunded pension liabilities. *State and Local Government Review*, *50*(3), 189–202. https://doi.org/10.1177/0160323X18817806

Government Accountability Office (GAO). (1993). *Underfunded state and local pensions plans* (GAO/HRD-93-9R). https://www.gao.gov/assets/hrd-93-9r.pdf

Government Accountability Office (GAO). (2008). *State and local government pension plans: Current structure and funded status*. https://www.gao.gov/assets/gao-08-983t.pdf

Hitchcock, D. G., & Prunty, R. 2009. *No immediate pension hardship for state and local governments, but plenty of long-term worries*. Standard & Poor's Ratings Direct.

Kelley, D. G. (2014). The political economy of unfunded public pension liabilities. *Public Choice*, *158*(1–2), 21–38. https://doi.org/10.1007/s11127-012-0049-3

Koedel, C., Podgursky, M., & Shi, S. (2013). Teacher pension systems, the composition of the teaching workforce, and teacher quality: Teacher pension systems. *Journal of Policy Analysis and Management*, *32*(3), 574–596. https://doi.org/10.1002/pam.21699

Lewin, D., Kochan, T. A., Cutcher-Gershenfeld, J., Ghilarducci, T., Katz, H. C. C., Keefe, J., Mitchell, D. J. B., Olson, C. A., Rubinstein, S. A., & Weller, C. E. (2011). Getting it right: Empirical evidence and policy implications from research on public-sector unionism and collective bargaining. *SSRN Electronic Journal*. https://doi.org/10.2139/ssrn.1792942

Lobel, H., Jaconetti, C., & Cuff, R. (2019). *The replacement ratio: Making it personal*. Vanguard Research.

Mannino, M. V., & Cooperman, E. S. (2013). Benefit enhancement in public employee defined benefit pension plans: Evidence from three sources. *SSRN Electronic Journal*. https://doi.org/10.2139/ssrn.2206656

Mitchell, O. S., McCarthy, D., Wisniewski, S. C., & Zorn, P. (2001). Developments in state and local pension plans. In O. S. Mitchell & Hustead, E. C. (Eds.), *Pensions in the public sector* (pp. 11–40). Pension Research Council Publications.

Monahan, A. B. (2010). Public pension plan reform: The legal framework. *Education Finance and Policy*, *5*(4), 617–646. https://doi.org/10.1162/EDFP_a_00014

Munnell, A. H., Aubry, J. P., & Cafarelli, M. (2016). COLA cuts in state-local pensions. *Journal of Pension Economics & Finance*, *15*(3), 311–332.

Munnell, A. H., Calabrese, T., Monk, A., & Aubry, J. P. (2010). *Pension obligation bonds: financial crisis exposes risks*. Center for Retirement Research at Boston College.

Munnell, A. H., Haverstick, K., Aubry, J.-P., & Golub-Sass, A. (2008). Why don't some states and localities pay their required pension contributions? Center for Retirement Research at Boston College.

Munnell, A. H., & Quinby, L. D. (2012). Legal constraints in changes in state and local pension. Center for State and Local Government Excellence.

NASRA. (2022). *NASRA issue brief: Cost-of-living adjustments*. National Association of State Retirement Administrators. https://www.nasra.org/colabrief

National Conference of State Legislatures. (2010). *NCSL fiscal brief: State balanced budget provisions*. https://docs.house.gov/meetings/JU/JU00/20170727/106327/HHRG-115-JU00-20170727-SD002.pdf

Norcross, E., & Biggs, A. (2010). *The crisis in public sector pension plans: A blueprint for reform in New Jersey* (Working Paper No.10-31). Mercatus Center - George Mason University.

Novy-Marx, R., & Rauh, J. (2011). Public pension promises: How big are they and what are they worth? *The Journal of Finance*, *66*(4), 1211–1249.

Nuschler, D. (2021). *Social Security coverage of state and local government employees*. Congressional Research Service.

Office of State Controller (OSC). (2024). *New York State & Local Retirement System*. https://www.osc.ny.gov/retirement/retirees/cost-living-adjustment

Peng, J. (2004). Public pension funds and operating budgets: A tale of three states. *Public Budgeting & Finance*, *24*(2), 59–73. https://doi.org/10.1111/j.0275-1100.2004.02402004.x

Peng, J. (2008). *State and local pension fund management*. Routledge.

Peng, J., & Wang, Q. (2017). Affordability of public pension benefit: A historical and empirical analysis of US state and local government pension contributions. *Journal of Pension Economics and Finance*, *16*(1), 21–42. https://doi.org/10.1017/S1474747215000268

Pew Charitable Trusts. (2017). *Cost-sharing features of state defined benefit pension plans*. Retrieved February 5, 2024, from https://www.pewtrusts.org/-/media/assets/2017/05/definedbenefitplansreport.pdf

Pew Charitable Trusts. (2019). *Legal protections for state pension and retiree health benefits: Findings from a 50-state survey of retirement plans*. https://www.pewtrusts.org/en/research-and-analysis/issue-briefs/2019/05/legal-protections-for-state-pension-and-retiree-health-benefits

Pew Charitable Trusts. (2020). *How measuring replacement income can aid assessment of public pension plans*. https://www.pewtrusts.org/-/media/assets/2021/01/how_measuring_replacement_income.pdf

Quinby, L. D., Aubry, J.-P., & Munnell, A. H. (2020). Pensions for state and local government workers not covered by Social Security: Do benefits meet federal standards? *Social Security Bulletin*, *80*(3). https://www.ssa.gov/policy/docs/ssb/v80n3/v80n3p1.html

Rauh, J. (2015). *Why city pension problems have not improved, and a roadmap forward* (No. 15101). https://www.hoover.org/sites/default/files/15101_-_rauh_-_why_city_pension_problems_have_not_improved_and_a_roadmap_forward.pdf

Rauh, J. D. (2010). Are state public pensions sustainable? Why the federal government should worry about state pension liabilities. *National Tax Journal*, *63*(3), 585–601.

Schieber, S. J. (2011). Political economy of public sector retirement plans. *Journal of Pension Economics and Finance*, *10*(2), 269–290. https://doi.org/10.1017/S1474747211000060

Seligman, J. S. (2013). Public sector pensions; Fundings & practice 2001-2010. *National Tax Association Proceedings*, *105*, 14–30.

Splinter, D. (2017). State pension contributions and fiscal stress. *Journal of Pension Economics and Finance*, *16*(1), 65–80. https://doi.org/10.1017/S1474747215000189

St. Clair, T. (2013). The impact of budget stabilization funds on state pension contributions. *Public Budgeting & Finance*, *33*(3), 55–74. https://doi.org/10.1111/j.1540-5850.2013.12014.x

Steffen, K. (2001). State employee pension plans. In O. S. Mitchell & E. C. Hustead (Eds.), *Pensions in the public sector* (pp. 41–65). Pension Research Council Publications.

Thom, M. (2017). The drivers of public sector pension reform across the U.S. states. *The American Review of Public Administration*, *47*(4), 431–442. https://doi.org/10.1177/0275074015589342

Vanguard (2022). *Assessing the retirement readiness of participants*. https://institutional.vanguard.com/content/dam/inst/iig-transformation/insights/pdf/2022/assessing-the-retirement-readiness-of-participants.pdf

Young, R., & Lindsay, T. (2023). *How to determine the amount of income you will need at retirement*. T. Rowe Price Insights on Retirement. Retrieved August 3, 2023, from https://www.troweprice.com/personal-investing/resources/insights/how-to-determine-amount-of-income-you-will-need-at-retirement.html

8

PATHWAYS TO PUBLIC PENSION REFORMS

Current challenges and the path to reform

Since the 2007–2009 economic recession, many state and local governments have adopted significant changes to pension plans to reduce their cost (Brainard & Brown, 2018). Pension reforms impose benefit reductions on employees and increase employee contributions. Some pension reforms also aim to alter the timing of benefit payments, such as increases in retirement age or other full retirement requirements, change pension plan types (i.e., the introduction of defined contribution (DC), cash-balance, or hybrid plans), or make changes in pension governance. Concerns over the financial sustainability of the pension systems and the governments, the high burden of pension contributions on government budgets, and the backlash from taxpayers over the news of pension funding problems have put pressure on governments to initiate and eventually adopt pension reforms. However, the reform process has not been easy. Legal and institutional constraints, as well as the resistance of unions and public employees, have stalled reform initiatives in many states. Using the logic model framework (introduced in Chapter 2), we provide an overview of the determinant factors of the pension reform process in the public sector in Table 8.1.

This chapter focuses on describing how the inputs, including environment, stakeholders, and constraints, influence pension reform decisions. Then, different types of pension reforms, such as changes in pension benefits, contributions, plan types, governance, and cost-sharing mechanisms, are discussed. This chapter mainly focuses on pension reforms and changes to different features of defined benefit pension plans, while

DOI: 10.4324/9781032671185-8

TABLE 8.1 Logic Model for Pension Reform

Inputs			*Outputs*	*Outcomes*
Environment	*Stakeholders*	*Constraints*	*Decisions*	*Performance*
Internal factors • Pension unfunded liabilities • Volatility of pension contribution • Fiscal health of government External factors • Capital markets • Credit ratings • Political pressures • Public opinions • Change in professional standards (GASB67/68)	Elected officials Pension administrators/ pension boards Participating employers (if any) Unions/employees Retirees Taxpayers	State laws on pension benefit protection Court rules on benefits Union contracts	Pension reforms	Impacts of pension reform on public-sector workforce and government financial conditions

Chapter 9 provides a more detailed discussion on DC, cash-balance, hybrid, and risk-sharing pension plans that have been adopted by state and local governments. Using mini case studies, this chapter briefly describes some of the consequences of the reforms. A more in-depth discussion of the impacts of pension reform decisions on pension goals, performance, and outcomes is provided in Chapter 10.

Internal factors

The rise of unfunded pension liabilities

The growth of unfunded pension liabilities has become a hot-button issue for many state and local governments. High levels of pension debt can raise alarms about the financial sustainability of the plan-sponsor governments and damage their credit ratings which can raise their borrowing costs (Martell et al., 2013). The Pew Charitable Trusts (2018) reported that state-run retirement systems had a cumulative $1.4 trillion shortfall between pension liabilities and assets in 2016, and they called the growth of unfunded pension liabilities the most prominent and fastest growing future debt facing governments since 2003.[1] Additionally, from the political standpoint, the continued rise in pension costs and unfunded liabilities caused more public opposition to public pensions and prompted policymakers to take action to address the pension issues. In many states, such as Nebraska, state legislatures held public hearings and established oversight committees to monitor the funding progress and reform actions of local pension plans. With this current fiscal, economic, and political environment, the issue of pension funding shortfalls will continue to attract calls for pension reform.

The rise of unfunded pension liabilities can be attributed to different causes, including lack of financial discipline of the plan-sponsoring governments in paying their required contributions (as discussed in Chapter 7), the fluctuation of pension investment earnings, and the rising pension benefits and pension liabilities. While most private-sector employees are offered DC (i.e., 401(k)) plans which only guarantee the amount of pension contributions, most public-sector employees are covered by defined benefit plans which guarantee a level of promised pension benefits, regardless of the amount of pension contributions or investment returns. Decisions to increase pension benefits can have long-term consequences on pension liabilities, pension contributions, and ultimately the pension funding level.

Benefit increases may be politically or financially motivated. From the political aspect, Anzia and Moe (2017) found that Democratic and Republican politicians alike are in favor of generous pension benefits in normal times but that there is more resistance from Republican politicians to increasing pension benefits during recessions. Research has also shown that local elected officials in politically competitive jurisdictions tend to promise higher pension benefits in their campaigns (Bagchi, 2019). Additionally, since public wages often lag behind the private sector, pension benefits are often seen as a trade-off to fill that gap (Ehrenberg, 1980).

From the fiscal management standpoint, governments have sometimes negotiated with unions on pension benefit increases when facing economic recession or budget stress in exchange for their agreement on temporarily freezing or forgoing scheduled salary raises (Hoang & Ebdon, 2021). While this can provide short-term relief for the operating budget, it can deepen the financial issues for those governments, which may lack the financial capacity to increase their pension contributions in accordance with their actions to increase pension benefits. This can cause a vicious cycle of trading short-term goals of balancing the budget for long-term increases in pension liabilities due to increases in benefits in tandem with contribution shortfalls.

As explained in Chapter 6, the pension normal cost is the amount required to pay for pension benefits that are earned in that year. The normal cost, which does not include unfunded liabilities from benefits earned

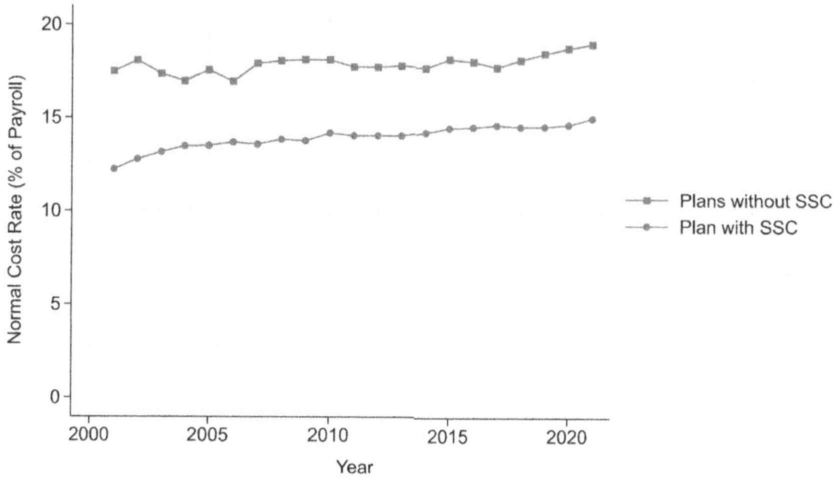

FIGURE 8.1 Normal Cost Rate (% of Payroll) from 2001 to 2021

Source: Authors' calculation based on the Boston College – Public Plans Database (PPD)

in previous years, is one measure of pension cost and benefit generosity (Munnell, 2012). Figure 8.1 shows the trends of pension normal cost rates among plans with and without social security coverage based on the Public Plans Database (PPD) of 210 state and local defined benefit (DB) pension plans. Overall, pension normal cost rates have increased from 2001 to 2021 for public pension plans, even though the changes are relatively incremental. The normal cost increased from 12% of payroll for plans with social security coverage, and around 18% of payroll for plans without social security coverage in 2000, to approximately 15% of payroll for plans with social security coverage, and above 19% of payroll for plans without social security coverage in 2021.

Figure 8.2 presents trends in the normal cost rate as a percentage of payroll for different levels of government, and Figure 8.3 displays the trends for different groups of employees based on the PPD. PPD include 210 state and local pension plans; approximately 56% (118 plans) are state-administered plans, 32% (68 plans) are city-administered plans, 8% (17 plans) are county-administered plans, and 3% (7 plans) are school-administered plans.

The graphs show that county-administered and city-administered pension plans tend to have higher normal cost rates than state-administered and school-administered pension plans. Public safety pension plans (for police officers and firefighters) are more generous than pension plans

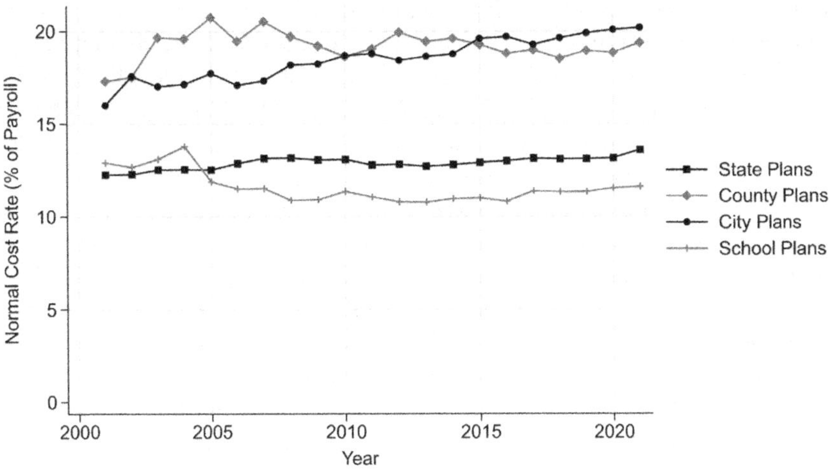

FIGURE 8.2 Normal Cost Rate by Level of Administering Government

Source: Authors' calculation based on the Boston College – Public Plans Database (PPD)

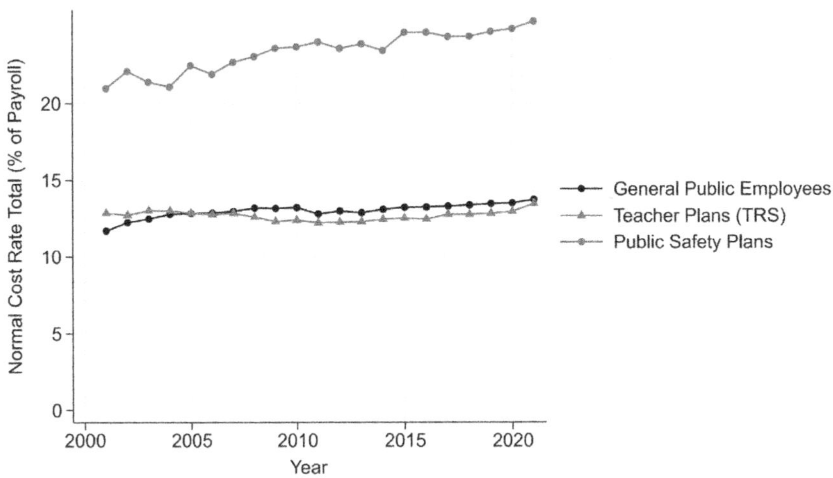

FIGURE 8.3 Normal Cost Rate by Employment Group

Source: Authors calculation based on the Boston College – Public Plans Database (PPD)

for teachers and general public employees for various reasons, such as the influences of municipal unions, political influence, the characteristics of the jobs, and the fact that public safety employees are less likely to be covered by social security (Aubry & Wandrei, 2020; Hoang & Goodman, 2018). Pension generosity increased in the early 2000s, then gradually decreased following the 2007–2009 economic recession.

The adoption of early retirement incentives could be another reason for the increase in pension liabilities. Governments can make payments to those who are close to their retirement age to encourage them to retire early. This may give employers some budgetary relief if they do not fill the vacant positions or pay new hires less than the retired employees. However, these incentives may increase the financial burden on the pension system. For example, the State of Illinois implemented an early retirement incentive program in 2002 that was estimated to cost $622 million in additional unfunded liabilities but ended up costing $2.5 billion because more people took advantage of the program than expected (Luby et al., 2019).

Volatility in pension contributions

Figure 8.4 presents trends in the actuarially determined contribution (ADC) as a percentage of payroll for plans administered by different government types. In the early 2000s, required employer contributions were

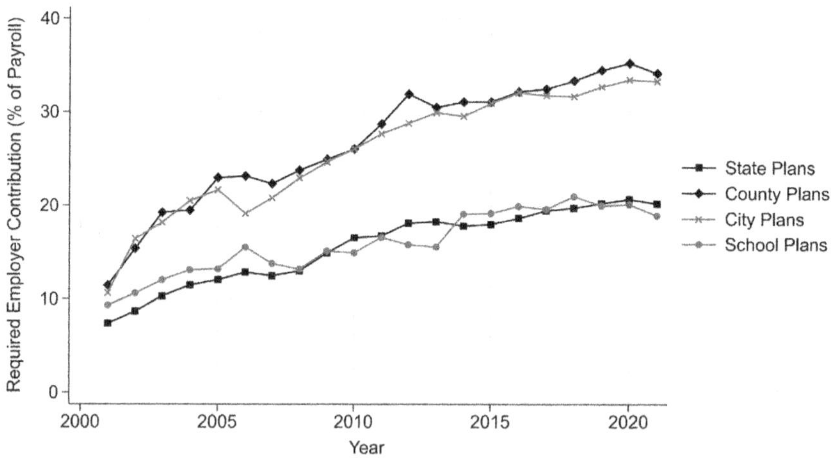

FIGURE 8.4 Required Contribution by Administering Government Type (2001–2021)

Source: Authors' calculation based on the Boston College – Public Plans Database (PPD)

about 10% of payroll, but they have increased since then, especially in county and city-administered plans. The required contributions for state and school plans increased two-fold by 2021 (to around 30%), while they increased more than three-fold for county and city plans (to around 35%).

There are several reasons for the growing level of required contributions. First, increased pension benefits generally require higher contributions. Second, decreases in market returns on investments can increase required contributions, since the employers in defined benefit plans bear all the financial responsibility to fund their pension system. Third, the annual required contribution increases if unfunded pension liabilities from previous years increase, because the required contribution includes the present value of the normal cost (the benefits earned in that year) as well as an amortization payment of the existing unfunded liabilities (see more discussion in Chapter 6). Increases in required contributions have put a significant burden on already-tight government budgets and are considered to be a driving factor of pension reform. St. Clair and Martinez Guzman (2018) illustrated that the level of annual required contributions for states experienced high volatility between 2001 and 2013, and those states with greater fluctuation in required contributions were more likely to reduce pension benefits and increase employee contributions. Hoang (2019) also found states with higher fiscal discipline toward paying their required contribution are less likely to experience benefit reductions or cuts in cost-of-living adjustment (COLA).

Fiscal health of government

A government's financial condition plays an important role in pension management. During times of fiscal austerity or budget deficits, governments have a tendency to adjust their budget allocation and spending. Delaying payments (including payments to the pension fund – i.e., pension contributions) has often occurred during periods of fiscal stress (as discussed above). As budget severity increases, governments might respond by adopting budget cutback packages in a larger scope. On the one hand, the continuing growth of pension costs makes it more likely to be a target of the cutback actions. On the other hand, reforming the pension system or reducing pension benefits is not easy for various reasons (e.g., legal constraints, the legislative process, pushback from public unions, etc.). Governments tend to delay pension reforms when they have other financial resources to support the pension systems. One study found that states are more likely to enact pension reforms, including the transition to DC plans in response to a long-term fiscal outlook signal, such as looming indebtedness, rather than a reaction to a relatively short-term fiscal shortfall (Thom, 2017).

External factors

Market volatility and low investment returns

Investment returns play an important role in the pension funding structure. When the stock market is on the rise, investment returns significantly increase pension assets and funding ratios. However, in a bear market, an investment loss can cause a dramatic decline in pension assets and prompt the need for governments to raise their contribution substantially to fully fund the pension system. Making matters worse, decreases in investment returns often go hand in hand with an economic downturn, which causes declines in government tax revenues while the need for public spending increases, adding to the fiscal strain (Gordon et al., 2012). The decreases in financial markets and investment returns put pressure on governments to pay higher required contributions to maintain a decent funding level or to consider pension reforms to reduce benefits (Chen et al., 2021; Wang & Peng, 2016).

Credit ratings

With concerns over pension solvency looming over governments, rating agencies have started to explicitly account for pensions in their assessment of creditworthiness (Aubry et al., 2017). Credit rating agencies have highlighted the importance of affordability of retirement obligations in assessing long-term sources of credit stress and the necessity of enacting effective measures to increase funding progress (Tax Foundation, 2013). A low pension funding level can lead to a lowered credit rating. This factor puts additional pressure on governments with high levels of unfunded liabilities to initiate pension reforms to restore their funding level.

Political pressures

State and local governments may face political pressure to adopt or consider pension reforms. "Yardstick" comparison by citizens of their governments with their neighboring states/localities can lead to the diffusion of pension reforms from one government to another. Thom (2017) found that policy inertia has a stronger impact than fiscal condition on the likelihood of pension reform adoption. Additionally, studies have documented the relationship among the pension funding situation, housing values, and mobile tax bases. MacKay (2014) found that rising unfunded pension liabilities for the San Diego City Employees' Retirement System were associated with decreases in housing values. Building on the impacts of pension funding issues on fiscal and economic outcomes,

Hoang (2022) identified fiscal competition among states for mobile tax bases as further explanation for the diffusion of pension reforms among states and demonstrated a positive correlation between state population migration patterns and the likelihood of pension reform. In addition to reform diffusion effects, states may put pressure on local governments with low funding levels to initiate pension reforms (Gehl et al., 2013; Hoang & Ebdon, 2021).

Public opinion

Since many private-sector workers and taxpayers have been offered limited pension benefits, the news on the government's low funding ratios, which potentially can lead to increases in taxation, or news on government workers (e.g., a police chief) who retire with six-figure retirement benefits might cause a backlash in the community and put more pressure on the government to solve their pension funding problems.

Changes in accounting standards (GASB Statements No. 67 and 68)

Changes in professional standards, including accounting standards, can affect pension management. The implementation of the Governmental Accounting Standard Board's (GASB) Statements No. 67 and 68 has influenced how pensions select the discount rate used to calculate unfunded liabilities for financial reporting (as discussed in Chapters 6 and 7, a different expected rate of return on investments can be used to determine the actuarially determined required employer contribution). As a result of this accounting standard change, along with a lower market return environment, many pension plans have lowered their discount rates. As shown in Figure 8.5, the average discount rate has declined from about 8% in 2001 to less than 7% in 2022.

Decision-makers and stakeholders

Elected officials

The political environment of state and local governments plays a major role in the pension reform discussion, adoption, and implementation. State pension reform often has a higher chance of adoption when one party controls both legislative chambers and the governorship (McGuinn, 2014). In cities, the mayor may be responsible for labor contract negotiation and pension reforms, but these changes need to be approved by the city council, so collaboration among the elected officials can influence the

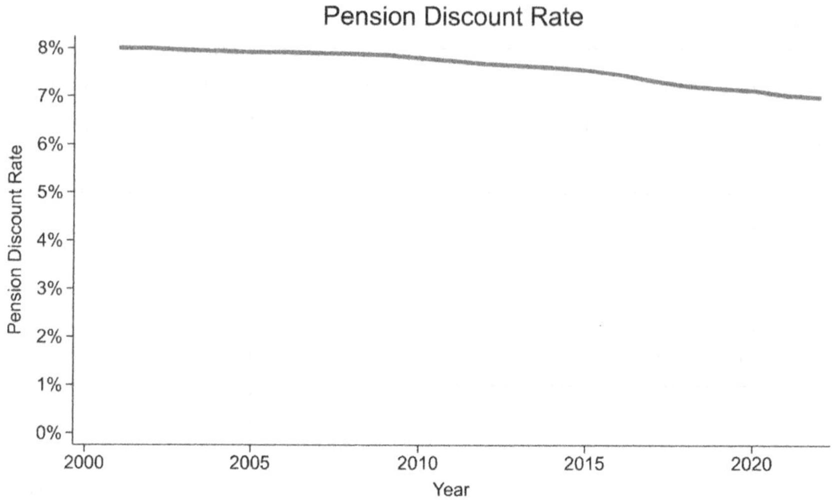

FIGURE 8.5 Pension Discount Rate (2001–2022)

Source: Authors' calculation based on the Boston College – Public Plans Database

success of the pension reform agenda. For example, Gehl et al. (2013) showed that cooperation between the City of Atlanta City Council and the Mayor's office was critical for making changes to pension benefits and contributions.

The role of unions

The presence of unions and union campaign contributions also can influence pension reforms, especially among locally administered pension plans (Hoang & Goodman, 2018). Local governments tend to employ more workers in heavily unionized occupations, such as police officers, firefighters, and teachers. In 2019, the unionization rate for local government employees was 39.4%, compared with the 33.6% average membership rate for all public-sector workers (Bureau of Labor Statistics, 2020). The density of union presence, along with their collective bargaining power, has given municipal unions a stronger influence over pension benefits and pension reforms negotiation (Anzia & Moe, 2015).

Legal constraints and the role of the judiciary

Pension reforms in some states have been challenged in courts by unions and groups of public employees for violating contractual rights (Monahan, 2010). Strong constitutional protections of pension benefits can impose limits on the adoption of reforms as well as reform options (Brown, 2014; Thom, 2017). In states where pension benefits are protected by the State Constitution, the issue of pension reform is likely to be decided by state courts. In the case of Illinois' 2013 pension reform, the Illinois Supreme Court found the legislation unconstitutional as a violation of Article XIII, Section 5 of the State Constitution, which states that "Membership in any pension or retirement system of the State, any unit of local government or school district, or any agency or instrumentality thereof, shall be an enforceable contractual relationship, the benefits of which shall not be diminished or impaired" (Dierks, 2018). On the other hand, the New Mexico Constitution (Article 20, Section 22) states that "the legislature shall not enact any law that increases the benefit paid by the system in any manner or change the funding formular for a retirement plan unless adequate funding is provided." The state Supreme Court sided with the state in allowing future COLA decreases, in the opinion that future COLA is merely a year-to-year expectation that, until paid, does not create a property right under the State Constitution. Once paid, the COLA by State Statute becomes part of the retirement benefit and property right subject to those constitutional protections (NMPERA, 2019).

Pension reforms

State and local governments have adopted different types of pension reforms since the early 2000s, with a large number of governments adopting pension reforms in the years following the economic recession of 2007–2009. For example, as seen in Figure 8.6, the number of states with plan reform was highest between 2009 and 2013 with the greatest number of states (25) adopting reforms in 2011. Since then, states have continued making changes, but the intensity of pension reform has been reduced since its peak in 2010 and 2011. Appendix A provides more details of those pension reforms by type and year.

State and local pension reforms can vary by their design and intensity. Researchers (Gorina & Hoang, 2020; Hoang, 2022; St. Clair & Martinez Guzman, 2018; Thom, 2017) categorize pension reforms differently, depending on their research objectives. We will look at pension reforms based on the impacts of those reforms on major topics of pension benefits, pension contributions, retirement eligibility, and plan type (the introduction of non-DB options). The chapter also provides further discussion of changes in investment practices, board composition and governance, cost-sharing/risk-sharing models, and pension obligation bonds (POBs).

FIGURE 8.6 State Pension Reform (2005–2023)

Source: National Conference of State Legislatures and National Association of State Retirement Administrators' reports

Change in pension benefits

Cut in cost-of-living adjustment (COLA)

COLA in many state and local governments are part of the pension benefit formula to help retirees hedge against inflation or increases in living costs in their retirement years. COLA provisions can be automatic or tied to economic or financial conditions/pension investment returns. Dealing with growing unfunded pension liabilities, many pension plans have adopted changes, including COLA elimination or suspension (often until a healthy funding level is reached), COLA reductions, or delays in automatic COLAs. For instance, Colorado Public Employees' Retirement Association (Colorado PERA) suspended the COLA in 2018 and 2019 and reduced the automatic COLA cap from 2 to 1.5% the year after (Brainard & Brown, 2018).

Decrease in pension benefit multipliers

Another way for governments to reduce pension benefits is to reduce or cap pensionable salary (to avoid pension spiking problems) or reduce the level of the benefit multiplier in the pension formula. The retirement system of Alabama, for example, reduced benefit multipliers for all new hires from 2.0125 to 1.65% for general public employees and teachers, and from 2.875 to 2.375% for police officers (Brainard & Brown, 2018).

Reduction in pension benefits

Instead of going after the benefit formula (such as changing COLA or benefit multipliers), some governments aim to directly cut pension benefits. These reforms are quite challenging and also less common due to a potential backlash from employees and legal constraints limiting governments from amending or altering pension benefits. Benefit reduction provisions are often applied to new hires through the creation of employment tiers (as discussed below) or through increases in penalties for early retirement, as seen in some states (e.g., Connecticut, Hawaii, Maryland, South Carolina, South Dakota, and Texas).

Creation of new employment tiers

Since pension benefits are only protected in some states for people who are already in the system ("grandfathering"), many governments (such as the states of New York, Illinois, and California) have created employment tiers, in which new hires will have less generous pension benefits and higher levels of employee pension contributions. Table 8.2 provides an example of variations across six tiers in the New York State and Local Retirement System.

Change in pension contributions

Increased pension contributions are common reforms to shore up pension assets and funding levels. Contribution increases can apply to both employers and employees.

Increase in employee contributions

Between 2005 and 2023, 42 states increased employee contributions. This often occurred incrementally over time. For instance, in 2017, the Arkansas Teacher Retirement System (TRS) increased the employee contribution from 6 to 7% and the employer contribution from 14 to 15% over a four-year period in 0.25% increments (Brainard & Brown, 2018). Additionally, increases in employee contributions can differ by employee groups (teachers, public safety, judges, general employees, etc.) and by employment status (current employees versus new hires). Pension plans commonly set higher contribution rates for new hires partially due to legal

TABLE 8.2 New York State and Local Retirement System Comparison of Employees' Retirement System (ERS) Benefits by Tiers

	Tier 1	*Tier 2*	*Tier 3*	*Tier 4*	*Tier 5*	*Tier 6*
Applied for members	Before July 1, 1973	July 1, 1973 through July 26, 1976	July 27, 1976 through August 31, 1983	September 1, 1983 through December 31, 2009	January 1, 2010 through March 31, 2012	April 1, 2012 or after
Contributions	No mandatory contribution. Member can elect for voluntary contribution		3% contribution up to 10 years of membership or 10 years of credited service		3% contribution (entire career)	3–6% contribution depending on annual wage
Vesting			After earning 5 years of service credit		After earning 5 years of service credit	After earning 5 years of service credit
Retirement age	Eligible to retire at age 55.	Retire with full benefits at age 62 Reduced benefit between ages 55 and 62.	Full benefits at age 62, or at age 55 with at least 30 years of credited service Reduced benefits at age 55 with less than 30 years of credited service		Full benefits at age 62 Reduced benefits at age 55 Full benefits at age 55 for UCPOs with at least 30 years of creditable service	Full benefits at age 63 Reduced benefits at age 55
Final average earnings calculation			Three highest consecutive years of service		Three highest consecutive years of service	Five highest consecutive years of service

Source: NYSLRS Retirement Benefit by Tiers.

limitations on the ability to change public employees' benefits or due to pressure from current public employees or unions. Approximately 56% of states increased employee contributions for current employees between 2009 and 2021, while 70% increased employee contributions for new hires (new hires are defined as those who are hired on or after 2009). Among those states that increased employee contributions, 44% increased them for both current and new employees (Knapp et al., 2023).

Increase in employer contributions

Twenty-five states increased employer contributions between 2005 and 2023. Similar to employee contribution changes, increases in employer pension contributions are often incremental. For example, the Kansas Public Employee's Retirement System (KPERS) passed a law in 2011 to raise employer contributions by 0.9% in fiscal year 2014, 1.0% for fiscal year 2015, 1.1% for fiscal year 2016, and 1.2% for fiscal year 2017 (Snell, 2010). Laws in some localities (e.g., the City of Omaha) require relatively equal contributions from employees and employers, so both increase at the same time and by about the same rate.

Change in retirement eligibility

Increase in service years or retirement rule

Some state and local governments have increased the years of service (YOS) or the combination of age and service years. This reform increases pension YOS or adjusts the pension rules, so that it takes employees longer to be eligible for normal retirement. From 2005 to 2023, about 29 states increased their YOS requirement or retirement rules. For example, the Mississippi Public Employees' Retirement System increased the service requirement for normal retirement from 30 to 33 years for new hires in 2010. Some systems have changed the pension rule from the rule of 80 (age plus YOS adds to at least 80) to the rule of 85 or 90.

Increase in retirement age

Aligning with some calls for increasing the retirement age for social security benefits, some states and local governments have increased the retirement age to slow down the growth of pension liabilities while extending the period an employee will contribute to the system. For instance, the Illinois TRS increased the eligible retirement age from 60 to 67 for those with 35 YOS and delayed eligibility for a COLA until after age 67 (Brainard & Brown, 2018).

Increase in the final average years of salary (FAS)

Governments have also increased the number of years used to calculate the average salary in the pension benefit formula. This reform is expected to reduce the pension amount because salaries are generally higher in the years closer to retirement. Some common types of reforms are increases from the last three to five years in calculating FAS.

Increase in vesting requirements

"Vesting" refers to the length of service an employee must accrue before qualifying for the benefit. Many governments have increased vesting requirements from three to five years to five to ten years. Employees who leave before vesting lose their rights to the benefits that have accrued in the system, which reduces the plan liabilities.

Changes in plan type – alternative pension design

Some governments have introduced DC, cash-balance, or hybrid plans for new hires. This reform may relieve the plans from accumulated pension benefit obligations and deliver more control for employees over their retirement accounts and investments. In a defined benefit plan, the employer (i.e., the government sponsor) bears the risk and is responsible for an employee's pension benefits upon their retirement, regardless of the outcomes of the investment returns. In a DC plan, employers make matching/employer contributions based on the organization's policies and employment contracts, while employees are responsible for their investment selections before and after retirement; this shifts the risk to the employees. This feature allows employers to better plan their pension contributions (which often fluctuate dramatically in a defined benefit system) and also relieves them from the pressure of ensuring sufficient assets to cover pension liabilities since this duty has been transferred to the employees to manage their individual pension account. However, this transition is not without disadvantages, including some concerns around worker motivation and retention and the cost of administration and sustainability of legacy defined-benefit pension plans (for more detailed analysis on DC, cash-balance, and hybrid plans, see Chapter 9).

Changes in investment practices

In addition to changes in pension benefits and contributions, pension plans also have implemented changes to their investment management and practices to increase investment returns. Over the past few decades, state and local pension plans have gradually shifted from low-risk assets to higher-risk assets. While the majority of pension assets were invested in fixed-income categories such as government bonds during the 1950s–1970s, plans increasingly invested in the stock market in the 1980s–1990s, and over the past decades, more and more pension plans have allocated their assets in alternative investments like hedge funds, private equities, or real estate to boost investment earnings (Aubry & Crawford, 2019a, 2019b; Pew Charitable Trusts, 2022a, 2022b). As of 2022, approximately half of pension assets, on average, were invested in equities (47%), less than a quarter in fixed income (21%), a quarter in alternative assets, including real estate (6.8%) and alternative investments (22.6%) (NASRA, n.d.).

Pooled assets and consolidation

Some pension systems have pooled their assets and/or opted to consolidate their pension systems. The proponents of system consolidation argue that this action can enable pension systems to take advantage of economies of scale in system administration and asset investment, increase workforce mobility within the system, and increase pension oversight(Matkin & Chen, 2015; Munnell et al., 2013). On the other hand, opponents claim that fragmented pension systems improve labor market efficiency by giving jurisdictions the authority to negotiate their own benefits based on the current labor demand/supply for the job. For instance, in some occupations where there is a shortage of labor supply (e.g., correction officials), a higher level of pension benefits can help the county or state in recruitment and retention. Moreover, consolidation is argued to cause some inequity issues or even moral hazard problems; one system member government allowing for "spiking" to increase the pensionable salary spreads the financial burden to the other system members.

Increase in the use of external fund managers and increase in alternative investments

In their quest to increase investment returns, pension plans have moved toward more active investment strategies and higher levels of allocation to riskier assets such as private equity, hedge funds, real estate, etc. Along with this move, more plans have hired external fund management in the hope of maximizing their investment returns (see more details in Chapter 5).

Decrease in pension expected rate of return assumption and decrease in pension discount rate

Over the last decade, public pension boards have voted to lower their rate of return assumption as well as the pension discount rate. This phenomenon may be impacted by the changes in investment markets (low market return environment), changes in accounting standards (as discussed above), and other economic actuarial assumptions.

Changes in board composition and governance

The pension board of trustees plays an important role in pension plan management. Through their management and investment decisions, pension boards can have significant influence over asset allocation, investment returns, and pension funding (Brooks, 2019; Chen et al., 2015; Hoang & Nguyen, 2022). Pension boards can include appointed (politically or non-politically appointed) and elected members, including representatives from employees (plan members), retirees (plan beneficiaries), and the general public. Either due to their professional or personal objectives, board members may have different incentives (e.g., reelection, preference for in-state investment, or benefit-maximizing), which might lead to misaligned goals and possible "opportunistic behaviors" (Anzia & Moe, 2019; Stalebrink & Donatella, 2021) and cause possible conflict with policy changes necessary to ensure sufficient pension contributions, prudent investment, or adequate funding (Andonov et al., 2018; Mitchell & Hsin, 1994).

To strengthen governance structures of pension funds and improve funding and investment outcomes, some studies (Aubry & Crawford, 2019a, 2019b; Government Accountability Office, 2008; Knapp et al., 2023) have suggested practices including:

- Clearly defining fiduciary duties of pension board members;
- Ensuring accountability and transparency;
- Minimizing principle-agent problems related to conflicts of interest;
- Strengthening investment and administrative oversight (maybe considering an investment board in addition to administrative oversight);
- Ensuring stakeholder representation to avoid over- or under-representation (e.g., having at least one ex officio member and only 20–70% active and/or retired participants);
- Ensuring pension system administrators and pension boards have the requisite expertise needed (i.e., finance, actuarial, management, etc.);
- Providing financial and managerial training to keep the board and pension administrators updated on current issues.

Cost-sharing (risk-sharing) model

A number of states with DB pension plans have policies that share the risk of cost increases (and potential gains) between employees and employers. Pension plans deal with three major risks: longevity risk, investment risk, and economic risk (such as inflation risk). Cost-sharing mechanisms can help the plans better control for investment and economic risks by reducing volatility and uncertainty while preserving the ability to pay pension benefits (see more in Chen et al., 2022). A cost-sharing, or risk-sharing, policy distributes unexpected cost increases from short- or long-term deviations from plan expectations between employers and employees. In some cases, cost savings are also shared. A report conducted by Pew Charitable Trusts identified 29 DB plans in 17 states that use cost-sharing mechanisms to manage risk, such as adjustments in employee contributions or postretirement benefits in accordance with investment and economic cycles (Pew Charitable Trusts, 2017).

Cost sharing can be approached from the contribution side by creating a mechanism to split the costs of funding pension systems between the employer and the employees, where they share the costs of pension contribution increases but both sides benefit when contributions go down. For example, total required contribution rates for the Arizona State Retirement System, Nevada Public Employees' Retirement System, and Wisconsin Retirement System are actuarially determined and shared equally by employees and employers. Any increases or decreases to the contribution rate are shared between the employers and employees. In the Maine Public Employees' Retirement System Participating Local District (PLD) Consolidated Retirement Plan, the contribution rates are subject to annual change based on a 55/45% employer/employee split and are capped at 12.5% for employers and 9.0% for employees (Brainard & Brown, 2018). This approach exposes both the employer and the employee to the same financing risk for the plan.

Another approach to cost-sharing is to adjust the employee contribution in response to investment returns. For example, the contribution rate for recently hired employees in Pennsylvania Public School Employees' Retirement System and Pennsylvania State Employees' Retirement System can be raised or lowered by 0.5 percentage points every three years if investment assumptions are not met (Pew Charitable Trusts, 2017). In this case, both employer and employees are bearing part of the investment risk. This strategy helps the pension plan better deal with the fluctuation of the investment market and reduce the fluctuation of their pension contributions when plans do not achieve expected returns.

Cost-sharing policies can also be used to adjust pension benefits (most often COLA), based on pension investment returns or economic conditions. Some plans adopt a contingent or limited COLA which is tied to inflation or investment returns. Massachusetts, for example, limits COLAs for state employees and teachers to the rate of inflation, not to exceed 3% annually, applied to only the first $13,000 of benefits. Retirees with benefits above this threshold bear all inflation risk for that portion of their benefit, as well as all inflation risk when inflation exceeds 3% (Brainard & Brown, 2018). Some plans provide a COLA only if investment performance reaches a certain threshold, such as the plan's actuarial investment return assumption. For example, many retired members of the Maryland State Retirement and Pension System are eligible for an automatic annual COLA of 2.5% as long as the fund's investment return in the previous year was greater than or equal to the system's assumed rate of return (which is presently 7.45%). Other plans set a contingent COLA based on funding level. The South Dakota Retirement System (SDRS) bases the COLA on the actual rate of inflation, with a minimum annual increase of 0.5% and a maximum of 3.5%.

Overall, there are different approaches to cost-sharing and risk-sharing policies. Pension plans should consider the possibility of adopting these reforms, the pension system goals, and the reform impacts before implementing them.

Pension obligation bonds (POBs)

Some U.S. state and local governments have used POBs to address their unfunded pension liabilities. The main principle of this financing tool is that a government issues taxable POBs and invests the proceeds in the pension fund; if the rate of return on the invested proceeds exceeds the interest rate paid on the bonds, the government benefits by reducing/eliminating the unfunded liabilities and therefore reducing the required contributions. This is a short-term solution for pension plans to bring down their unfunded liabilities and increase their funding ratio. Some states, including Illinois and New Jersey, have utilized POBs to lower unfunded pension liabilities. The low-interest rate environment in 2020 and 2021 witnessed a sharp increase in POB issuance including about $7 billion issued by cities and towns in California (Pew Charitable Trusts, 2023).

On the one hand, POBs may seem like a good solution for governments that can afford them, to address their unfunded pension problem without the need to raise taxes or cut spending. On the other hand, POBs are a new debt obligation, and the issuance and default risks of this debt need to be considered carefully. The ability to earn greater investment returns than the interest owed on the debt is strongly affected by the capital markets as well as timing of the investment decision. Additionally, some research has raised concerns about the impacts of POBs on the overall government debt structure (Munnell et al., 2010). Calabrese and Ely (2013) found no positive impacts of POBs on annual budgets in school districts in Oregon and Indiana. Though required, pension contribution payments are somewhat more flexible for the sponsor government because the amount can be smoothed over time or even reduced if other pension reforms were adopted. A bond issuance is inflexible compared to pension-required contributions.

Only a small portion of state and local governments have issued POBs. They may be a promising solution to fund public pension systems for the right government at the right time. However, there is little research confirming the effectiveness of POBs in addressing pension funding problems. Governments that plan to use POBs in the near future need to be cautious about the benefits as well as the risks of this instrument.

Summary

Under fiscal and political pressures, many states and local governments have enacted different types of pension reforms to reduce pension liabilities while increasing pension assets. Over the last two decades, pension reforms have been adopted in almost all 50 states, ranging from changes to pension benefits, contributions, and normal retirement eligibility, to changes in pension governance (pension design, investment strategies, or pension financing). Using our logic model, this chapter has laid out the driving factors of pension reforms while providing detailed descriptions of different reform types. While the growth of pension liabilities (pension benefits), the rising cost of funding public pension systems, and the values of pension assets (investment returns and pension contributions) have a major influence on pension reform adoption, legal constraints (i.e., pension protection laws) and labor union power can create hurdles for passing certain reform laws or limit the scope of pension reforms. Furthermore, external factors, such as political pressures, reactions of credit agencies, and public opinion on pension funding issues, lead to the need for pension reform. Overall, the chapter describes major changes in a wide range of areas, including pension benefits, contributions, retirement eligibility, pension types, investment practices, board governance, cost-sharing models, and POBs. More detailed descriptions of alternative types of pension benefits design (DC, cash-balance, and hybrid plans) are provided in Chapter 9, and the in-depth analysis of pension reform impacts on pension goals is discussed in Chapter 10.

Mini case – state pension reforms in Illinois

The State Retirement System of Illinois (SRS), including the TRS, the State University Retirement System (SURS), the State Employees' Retirement System (SERS), and the General Assembly Retirement System (GARS), experienced low funding levels even prior to the 2007–2009 economic recession. The financial crisis worsened the situation as it significantly reduced the state coffers and heightened the urgency of the pension issues. As of 2015, the aggregate funded ratio had fallen to 41.9% (Dierks, 2018) and the estimated unfunded liabilities of the Illinois plans were $100 billion in 2013 (Brown, 2014).

The Illinois pension system has been criticized for its generous benefit rules. For example, the final average salary is based on 48 months of service, with a full retirement age of 60. The early retirement benefits also contributed to the pension problem in the state. Approximately 69% of TRS, 52% of SERS, 50% of SURS, and 54% of GARS members start collecting their pension benefits in their 50s (Dabrowski & Klinger, 2016). Additionally, retirees at the age of 60 automatically receive a 3% COLA every year.

At the same time, state fiscal problems loomed larger. As of the end of 2013, the state had a $6.3 billion backlog of unpaid bills to various contractors and higher reliance on property tax (Brown, 2014). In addition, half a million people left Illinois between 2000 and 2010, for an estimated economic loss of over $20 billion in net adjusted gross income (Furchtgott-Roth, 2016). By January 2013, Illinois had the lowest credit rating of any state. S&P downgraded Illinois to A–, and Moody's downgraded it to A3.

Under this circumstance, a pension reform bill, which was originally introduced by Illinois Senate President John Cullerton and sponsored by Democratic House Speaker Mike Madigan, passed the General Assembly and was signed by Governor Pat Quinn. The bill: (1) ended automatic 3% annual COLA and curtailed cost-of-living increases for retirees, (2) capped the salary level used to calculate pension benefits, (3) raised the retirement age, (4) and provided a hybrid system with DB and DC plans (optional 401(k) plan). In exchange for the benefit cuts, employee pension contributions would decrease by 1% and the state committed to increased payments into the system by $60–$70 billion (McGuinn, 2014). These reforms were intended to place the fund on a path to solvency by 2042.

However, public-sector unions and employees initiated a lawsuit over the reforms. Article XIII, Section 5 of the Illinois Constitution, often called the pension protection clause, states that membership in any pension or retirement system in the state is a contractual relationship and its benefits shall not be diminished or impaired. The state used the undue economic burden and financial emergency argument to defend its pension reform legislation. At the same time, while credit agencies considered pension reforms in Illinois as a positive signal (a positive outlook was assigned), the legal challenges raised new concerns among credit rating agencies. After the lower court declared pension reforms unconstitutional, the case reached the state Supreme Court. In May 2015, the Illinois Supreme Court again found the reforms to be in violation of Article XIII, Section 5 of the Illinois Constitution, and denied the state's arguments that pension reforms were needed based on the economic emergency. The pension crisis, along with a state budget impasse in fiscal years 2016, 2017, and half of fiscal year 2018, caused major fiscal issues for the state. In 2018, S&P Global Ratings downgraded the state's credit rating to BBB–. This continued a rating decline: from 2011 to 2014, Illinois was downgraded 21 times by three rating agencies (S&P, Moody's, and Fitch) (Dabrowski & Klinger, 2016).

There have not been further attempts to change pension benefits for current public-sector employees. Illinois now operates a two-tier benefit system. Tier 1 employees are those with all the above-mentioned benefits and a 3% automatic COLA. Tier 2 applies to those hired on and after January 1, 2011, with higher contributions and lower pension benefits. The retirement age for tier 2 is 67, and the COLA is tied to the Consumer Price Index for all urban consumers (CPI-U). By virtue of those differences, tier 2 employee contributions are not only used to pay their own benefits but also used to fill in the funding shortfall for tier 1 employees. For the Illinois TRS, there is an optional tier 3 that is a hybrid pension plan with both DB and DC components.

In 2022, Governor J.B. Pritzker signed House Bill 4292 into law and authorized $1 billion in additional general obligation bonds and an extra $500 million payment to the state pension fund. In 2022, Moody's upgraded the rating of State of Illinois debt from Baa2 to Baa1 with a stable outlook, and S&P Global upgraded Illinois' rating on its General Obligation bonds to A– (stable outlook) from BBB+ (stable outlook). As of the end of fiscal year 2023, the state pension system was 50.8% funded, with approximately $210.8 billion in unfunded liabilities (Hill & Carlson, 2023).

The summary of pension reforms process for the SRS of Illinois is presented in Table 8.3.

TABLE 8.3 Pension Reform in the State Retirement System of Illinois

Inputs			*Outputs*	*Outcomes*
Environment	*Stakeholders*	*Constraints*	*Decisions*	*Performance*
Internal factors • Unfunded liabilities • Insufficient contributions • Generous benefits, including automatic COLA • Poor investment returns • Poor fiscal condition External factors • Economic recession • Credit rating • Political pressures • Public opinions	Elected officials (the governor and state legislatures) Judiciary branch Unions (employees)	Legal constraints Illinois Constitution, Article XIII, Section 5	Pension reform initiated in 2013 but was ruled unconstitutional in 2015. Tier 2 is created with higher contributions and lower benefits. For Illinois TRS, teachers are offered an optional Tier 3 (hybrid plan with DB and DC components).	As of 2023, Illinois pension system is only 50.8% funded, with unfunded liabilities of $211 billion. The state authorized additional pension obligation bonds and extra payment to pension systems. Credit rating has gradually improved since the last downgrade to B class, but still at the low level.

Mini case – pension reforms at the local level – the case of the City of Omaha Police and Fire Retirement System (COPFRS)

The City of Omaha administers two local pension plans: one for civilian employees and another for the City's police officers and firefighters. The police and fire unions have maintained a critical role in pension benefit negotiations. Pension benefits and labor contract negotiations have been front-burner issues for the city. The pension reform process conveys the interactive relationships among municipal executive and legislative branches, unions, pension board, personnel board, the state labor court (Nebraska Commission of Industrial Relations or CIR), state legislature, chamber of commerce, and a pension task force.

In 2001, the city's newly elected Mayor Fahey started negotiations with the police and fire unions for new labor agreements. Negotiations became complicated as the city dealt with a large budgetary gap of $7–$10 million during fiscal years 2004–2006. Leveraging this situation, both police and fire members agreed to give up pay raises, and lower starting salaries for new hires, in exchange for future pension benefit enhancements, including lowering the retirement age. The city expected a savings of $1.1 million over two years.

While the city achieved short-term budget savings, the enhanced pension benefits led to an increase in unfunded pension liabilities from $280 million in 2005 to $320.5 million in 2007. Contract negotiations were stalled, and the Great Recession caused a severe loss in the plan's investment returns and asset values. COPFRS was only 39.5% pension funded by the end of 2008. The City Municipal Code requires substantially equal pension contributions between the employer and employees, so the city cannot unilaterally increase their contributions without an increase in employee contributions. Moody's downgraded the city's bond rating from AAA to Aa1 because of high debt levels, lower cash reserves, and pension shortfalls. In 2013, S&P downgraded the city rating to AA, also citing high debt and POBs.

The city and unions could not agree on how to address the issues of pension "spiking," pension benefit calculations, and health insurance costs. In 2008, the labor contract cases went to the Nebraska CIR. The CIR largely ruled in favor of the unions, but the state labor court said that it had no authority to make changes to the pension structure. In 2009, the Mayor, at the end of his two terms, established a pension task force, comprised of members of the Mayor's office, representatives from the business community and Chamber of Commerce, Police and Fire Union presidents, city council and pension board members, and experts in the field of human resource management, finance, accounting, and law, to look at options and recommendations for his successor to address the pension issue.

In 2009, the city's newly elected Mayor Suttle announced his new contracts, which aimed to eliminate pension spiking, reduce pension benefits, and continue wage freezes to close the $6.5 million budget shortfall in fiscal years 2009 and 2010. The new contract was expected to save the city $13.5 million in pension costs per year. By August 2010, the Council voted (4-3) to approve the police contract with benefit cuts (including the elimination of spiking) and higher contributions but did not approve the firefighter contract. In August 2011, the City Council took over the bargaining power and restarted pension reform negotiations. A new firefighter contract was finally adopted in 2012 that eliminated spiking and raised the retirement age and YOS requirement. The city also passed a new restaurant tax to pay for the pension contributions.

During the mayoral race in 2013, police and fire contracts were a hot-button issue. Councilwoman Jean Stothert, who participated in the negotiation for previous contracts, won the election. The City Council then returned negotiating power to the mayor, who got new contracts approved in 2015 (Fire) and 2017 (Police). In 2018, the pension board lowered the investment assumption rate from 8 to 7.75%. In 2019, the state legislature's Retirement Committee held hearings about the seven defined benefit plans in Nebraska with funding issues, including COPFRS. In 2022, S&P Global assigned an AA+ rating with a stable outlook, and Moody's assigned Aa2 with a stable outlook on the City's General Obligation Bonds.

The summary of the pension reform process in COPFRS is presented in Table 8.4.

TABLE 8.4 Pension Reform in City of Omaha Police and Firefighter Retirement System

Inputs			*Outputs*	*Outcomes*
Environment	*Stakeholders*	*Constraints*	*Decisions*	*Performance*
Internal factors • Unfunded liabilities • Budget shortfall • Increases in pension benefit, in exchange for salary freeze External factors • Economic recession • Credit rating • Political pressures from the state politics • Public opinions (general public and business community)	Mayors and City Council Pension board Personnel board State legislature CIR Pension task force (including the chamber of commerce) Unions (employees)	NE CIR (labor court) Municipal code on pension contribution	Establishment of pension task force, including government official and business leader. New labor contracts with police and firefighter, including pension reforms such as benefit cuts, increase in full retirement requirement, and increase in pension contribution. New restaurant tax to pay for pension liabilities.	Pension funding ratio of the plans is close to 64.4% in 2022, with $193 million in unfunded liabilities. Restaurant tax, once unpopular, has helped the city to pay for the pension fund and has become one of the funding sources for the city. Credit rating has improved in comparison to before the reforms.

Note

1 After waves of pension reform to reduce pension benefits and raise pension contributions, state-run retirement systems still had a cumulative $1.25 trillion shortfall in fiscal year 2019, and unfunded pension liabilities are the largest of the three major government long-term obligations, ahead of outstanding debt and unfunded other post-employment benefits (OPEB) (Pew Charitable Trusts, 2022a, 2022b).

References

Andonov, A., Hochberg, Y. V., & Rauh, J. D. (2018). Political representation and governance: Evidence from the investment decisions of public pension funds. *The Journal of Finance*, 73(5), 2041–2086. https://doi.org/10.1111/jofi.12706

Anzia, S. F., & Moe, T. M. (2015). Public sector unions and the costs of government. *The Journal of Politics*, 77(1), 114–127. https://doi.org/10.1086/678311

Anzia, S. F., & Moe, T. M. (2017). Polarization and policy: The politics of public-sector pensions. *Legislative Studies Quarterly*, 42(1), 33–62. https://doi.org/10.1111/lsq.12145

Anzia, S. F., & Moe, T. M. (2019). Interest groups on the inside: The governance of public pension funds. *Perspectives on Politics*, 17(4), 1059–1078. https://doi.org/10.1017/S1537592718003468

Aubry, J.-P., & Crawford, C. V. (2019a). *Impact of public sector assumed returns on investment choice*. Center for Retirement Research at Boston College, No. 63.

Aubry, J.-P., & Crawford, C. V. (2019b). *Does public pension board composition impact returns*. Center for Retirement Research at Boston College, 67.

Aubry, J.-P., Crawford, C. V., & Munnell, A. H. (2017). *How have municipal bond markets reacted to pension reform?* Center for Retirement Research at Boston College.

Aubry, J.-P., & Wandrei, K. (2020). *An introduction to police and fire pensions*. Center for Retirement Research at Boston College.

Bagchi, S. (2019). The effects of political competition on the generosity of public-sector pension plans. *Journal of Economic Behavior & Organization*, 164, 439–468. https://doi.org/10.1016/j.jebo.2019.06.014

Brainard, K., & Brown, A. (2018). *Significant reforms to State Retirement Systems*. National Association of State Retirement Administrators. https://www.nasra.org/reforms

Brooks, J. (2019). Board on the job: Public-pension governance in the United States (US) states. *Journal of Public Policy*, 39(1), 1–34. https://doi.org/10.1017/S0143814X17000241

Brown, J. R. (2014). Reforming public pensions subject to political and legal constraints: The Illinois experience. *National Tax Journal*, 67(4), 941–963. https://doi.org/10.17310/ntj.2014.4.09

Bureau of Labor Statistics. (2020). *Union Members—2019*. https://www.bls.gov/news.release/archives/union2_01222020.pdf

Calabrese, T. D., & Ely, T. L. (2013). Pension obligation bonds and government spending. *Public Budgeting & Finance*, 33(4), 43–65. https://doi.org/10.1111/j.1540-5850.2013.12022.x

Chen, G., Kriz, K., & Ebdon, C. (2015). The effect of board composition on public sector pension funding. *Journal of Public Budgeting, Accounting & Financial Management*, 27(3), 352–376. https://doi.org/10.1108/JPBAFM-27-03-2015-B003

Chen, G., Matkin, D., & Kang, H. (2021). Costs and liabilities of US public pension systems in a low-return environment. *Journal of Pension Economics and Finance*, *20*(2), 169–186. https://doi.org/10.1017/S147474721900043X

Chen, G., Yin, Y., & Boyd, D. (2022). A simulation of risk-sharing policies in U.S. public pension plans. *Municipal Finance Journal*, *43*(1), 67–91.

Dabrowski, T., & Klinger, J. (2016). *What's driving Illinois' $111 billion pension crisis: Retirement ages, COLAs and out-of-sync pension payouts*. Illinois Policy Institute.

Dierks, L. A. (2018). A lesson from Goodfellas: Why current Illinois consideration based pension reform proposals still fail. *Northwestern Journal of Law and Social Policy*, *13*(4), 432–451.

Ehrenberg, R. G. (1980). Retirement system characteristics and compensating wage differentials in the public sector. *Industrial and Labor Relations Review*, *33*(4), 470. https://doi.org/10.2307/2522693

Furchtgott-Roth, D. (2016). *Empowering Illinois' Pension Reform*. Manhattan Institute for Policy Research. https://manhattan.institute/article/empowering-illinois-pension-reform

Gehl, S. B., Willoughby, K. G., & Bell, M. J. (2013). Pension reform in Atlanta: Funding past promises in an uncertain future. *Public Budgeting & Finance*, *33*(3), 3–23. https://doi.org/10.1111/j.1540-5850.2013.12012.x

Gordon, T. M., Rose, H. M., & Fischer, I. (2012). *The state of local government pensions: A preliminary inquiry*. Lincoln Institute of Land Policy Working Paper.

Gorina, E., & Hoang, T. (2020). Pension reforms and public sector turnover. *Journal of Public Administration Research and Theory*, *30*(1), 96–112. https://doi.org/10.1093/jopart/muz009

Government Accountability Office (GAO). (2008). *State and local government pension plans: Current structure and funded status (GAO-08-983T)*. https://www.gao.gov/products/gao-08-983t

Hill, B., & Carlson, J. 2023. *Report: Illinois, Chicago public pension crises worst in U.S.* https://www.illinoispolicy.org/report-illinois-chicago-public-pension-crises-worst-in-u-s/

Hoang, T. (2019). *Managing public retirement systems: Unions, pension reforms, and public sector attractiveness*. The University of Texas at Dallas.

Hoang, T. (2022). Fiscal competition and state pension reforms. *Public Budgeting & Finance*, *42*(3), 41–70. https://doi.org/10.1111/pbaf.12315

Hoang, T., & Ebdon, C. (2021). *Institutional framework and path dependence in pension reform: A case study* (Working Paper).

Hoang, T., & Goodman, D. (2018). Public pensions and collective bargaining rights: Evidence from state and local governments. *Public Administration Review*, *78*(5), 772–784.

Hoang, T., & Nguyen, A. T. (2022). Navigating the public pension landscape: An examination of asset allocations. *Public Finance and Management*, *22*(1), 1–34.

Knapp, D., Asch, B. J., Armour, P., & Okuda-Lim, Z. (2023). *Steps for effectively addressing state and local pension crises: A prototype road map for stakeholders*. RAND Corporation. https://www.rand.org/pubs/research_briefs/RBA2307-1.html

Luby, M. J., Strong, G., & Saustad, D. (2019). Local government long-term liabilities: Pensions, other postemployment benefits, and infrastructure. In M. A. Pagano (Ed.), *The people's money: Pensions, debt, and government services* (pp. 21–48). University of Illinois at Chicago Press.

MacKay, R. C. (2014). Implicit debt capitalization in local housing prices: An example of unfunded pension liabilities. *National Tax Journal*, *67*(1), 77–112. https://doi.org/10.17310/ntj.2014.1.03

Martell, C. R., Kioko, S. N., & Moldogaziev, T. (2013). Impact of unfunded pension obligations on credit quality of state governments. *Public Budgeting & Finance*, *33*(3), 24–54. https://doi.org/10.1111/j.1540-5850.2013.12013.x

Matkin, D., & Chen, G. (2015). The consolidation of state-administered public pension systems in U.S states. *Journal of Public Budgeting, Accounting & Financial Management*, *27*(4), 455–481.

McGuinn, P. (2014). *Pension politics: Public employee retirement system reform in four states*. Brown Center on Education Policy at Brookings.

Mitchell, O. S., & Hsin, P. L. (1994). *Public sector pension governance and performance* (Working Paper 4632). National Bureau of Economic Research. https://doi.org/10.3386/w4632

Monahan, A. B. (2010). Public pension plan reform: The legal framework. *Education Finance and Policy*, *5*(4), 617–646. https://doi.org/10.1162/EDFP_a_00014

Munnell, A. H. (2012). *State and local pensions: What now?* Brookings Institution Press.

Munnell, A. H., Aubry, J.-P., Hurwitz, J., & Cafarelli, M. (2013). *Gauging the burden of public pensions on cities*. Center for Retirement Research at Boston College.

Munnell, A. H., Calabrese, T., Monk, A., & Aubry, J.-P. (2010). *Pension obligation bonds: Financial crisis exposes risks*. Center for Retirement Research at Boston College.

National Association of State Retirement Administrators (NASRA). (n.d.). *Investment*. https://www.nasra.org/investment

New Mexico PERA – Investment and Pension Oversight Committee. (2019). *Cost-of-living adjustment under the PERA Act*. https://www.nmpera.org/assets/uploads/home-banner/IPOC-08052019-Final.pdf

Pew Charitable Trusts. (2017, January 18). *Cost-sharing features of state defined benefit pension plans*. https://www.pewtrusts.org/en/research-and-analysis/reports/2017/01/cost-sharing-features-of-state-defined-benefit-pension-plans

Pew Charitable Trusts. (2018, September 26). *State public pension funds' investment practices and performance: 2016 data update*. https://pew.org/2DjSI73

Pew Charitable Trusts. (2022a, May 3). *State public pension fund returns expected to decline: Review of investment practices and performance for 2018 and 2019*. https://www.pewtrusts.org/en/research-and-analysis/issue-briefs/2022/05/state-public-pension-fund-returns-expected-to-decline

Pew Charitable Trusts. (2022b, July 7). *States' unfunded pension liabilities persist as major long-term challenge*. https://pew.org/3yvxnSE

Pew Charitable Trusts. (2023, July 13). *Government borrowing to lower pension costs carries risks*. https://pew.org/3O0ZPUq

Snell, R. K. (2010). *Pensions and retirement plan enactments in 2010 state legislatures*. National Conference of State Legislatures.

Stalebrink, O. J., & Donatella, P. (2021). Public pension governance and opportunistic accounting choice: A politico-economic approach. *The American Review of Public Administration*, *51*(3), 227–245. https://doi.org/10.1177/0275074020954397

St. Clair, T., & Martinez Guzman, J. P. (2018). Contribution volatility and public pension reform. *Journal of Pension Economics and Finance*, *17*(4), 513–533. https://doi.org/10.1017/S1474747217000129

Tax Foundation. (2013). *Monday map: State Credit Ratings*. https://taxfoundation.org/data/all/state/monday-map-state-credit-ratings-0/

Thom, M. (2017). The drivers of public sector pension reform across the U.S. states. *The American Review of Public Administration*, 47(4), 431–442. https://doi.org/10.1177/0275074015589342

Wang, Q., & Peng, J. (2016). An empirical analysis of state and local public pension plan funded ratio change, 2001-2009. *The American Review of Public Administration*, 46(1), 75–91. https://doi.org/10.1177/0275074014533721

APPENDIX A. FREQUENCY OF PENSION REFORMS BY TYPES (2005–2023)

Pension reform types	*2005*	*2006*	*2007*	*2008*	*2009*	*2010*	*2011*	*2012*	*2013*	*2014*	*2015*	*2016*	*2017*	*2018*	*2019*	*2020*	*2021*	*2022*	*2023*	*Total*
Reduction of benefits	0	0	0	3	6	6	6	4	1	0	0	0	0	1	0	0	0	0	0	27
Reduction of COLA	0	0	0	2	3	7	12	3	4	0	0	0	0	1	0	0	2	1	0	35
Introduction of a non-DB plan (DC or hybrid)	1	1	2	1	1	2	4	4	2	1	1	0	3	0	0	0	1	1	1	26
Increase in employee contribution	0	0	2	2	1	9	11	3	1	1	0	0	1	1	2	2	3	3	1	42
Increase in retirement age	0	0	2	0	3	3	6	3	1	0	1	1	1	0	1	0	0	0	0	22
Increase in service years or the age and year retirement rule	0	0	3	3	3	6	10	4	0	0	0	0	0	0	0	0	0	0	0	29
Increase in final years of service	0	0	2	1	3	6	6	5	5	0	0	0	1	1	0	0	0	0	0	30
Increase in vesting requirement	0	0	1	1	2	4	8	1	1	0	0	0	0	0	0	0	0	0	0	18
Increase in employer contributions	0	0	1	1	1	2	4	1	3	0	0	0	0	0	4	1	2	3	2	25

Note: Pension reform is coded as 1 in the year when a state adopts pension reform and 0 in the year when there is no reform or no changes to pension systems compared with the previous year.

9

DEFINED CONTRIBUTION, CASH-BALANCE, AND HYBRID PLANS IN THE PUBLIC SECTOR

Introduction

While most public-sector employees are covered by defined benefit (DB) pension plans, most private-sector employees in the United States are covered by defined contribution (DC) plans, such as typical 401(k) plans. DC plans have gained increased attention in state and local retirement systems as they explore reforming their traditional DB) plans. The previous chapters primarily focused on DB plans. This chapter focuses on DC, cash-balance (CB), and DB-CD hybrid plans in the public sector.

When a private-sector employee joins a 401(k) plan, they contribute a fixed percentage of their salary before tax into their retirement account and their employer usually also contributes a fixed percentage (such as 6–8%) as a match. Therefore, the contribution amount is "defined." In a DC plan, the pension benefits at retirement depend on the accumulated balance in the individual's pension account. Employee and employer contributions to DC plans are invested in capital markets to gain investment returns. DC plan participants make their own investment choices and bear the investment risk, while the pension plan usually also provides a list of investment options to help participants make reasonable investment decisions.

Because of the fixed amount of employer contributions and the shift of investment responsibilities from the employer to the employee, DC plans can reduce the fiscal burdens and liabilities for the employer. The downside of DC plans, however, is that they might reduce plan participants' pension sufficiency and retirement income security especially when

DOI: 10.4324/9781032671185-9

investment returns are low. Discussions about transitioning public-sector pension plans from DB to DC, or incorporating DC features into public systems, are common. The challenges, however, include the opposition from employee groups and the legacy cost of the current DB plans.

In this chapter, we discuss the features and major types of DC plans, CB plans, DB-DC hybrid plans, and risk-sharing plans, their advantages and disadvantages, the current status of these plans in the public sector, and the challenges of transitioning from DB to other plans.

Features of DC, cash-balance, and hybrid plans

The main difference between DB and DC plans is who (employer or employee) makes the investment decisions and bears the investment risk. In a traditional DB plan, pension assets are pooled into pension funds managed by the retirement system, which receives contributions from both employers and employees. The retirement system makes investment decisions for DB pension funds and bears the investment risk. When DB plan participants reach retirement age, the pension system is responsible for paying the predetermined pension benefits, regardless of the investment performance of the pension funds. Therefore, the investment risk is borne by the employers who sponsor those pension plans.

In a traditional DC plan, plan participants have individual pension accounts. These accounts receive fixed contributions from employers and employees, while the investment choices are made by the employees themselves. If plan participants choose a low-return investment option due to their conservative investment strategy, or if they take high investment risks but experience modest or negative returns because of market volatility, their individual pension account balance would be low, leading to lower pension benefits. In such cases, the risk is borne by the DC plan participants themselves, rather than the employers.

We can envision a spectrum with the traditional DB plan on one end (where employers bear the investment risk) and the traditional DC plan on the other end (with employees bearing the risk), as shown in Figure 9.1.

Between the two ends of the spectrum are plans designed to share some, but not all, of the investment risk and other risks between employers and employees. These plans include contingent benefit DB plans, contingent contribution DB plans, CB plans, and DB-DC hybrid plans.

In a contingent benefit DB plan, some of the benefits are dependent on the investment or funding performance of the pension plan. An example is contingent cost-of-living adjustments (COLAs). In this case, the core pension benefits are still calculated based on the benefit formula, but the postretirement benefits are contingent on the plan's investment returns or

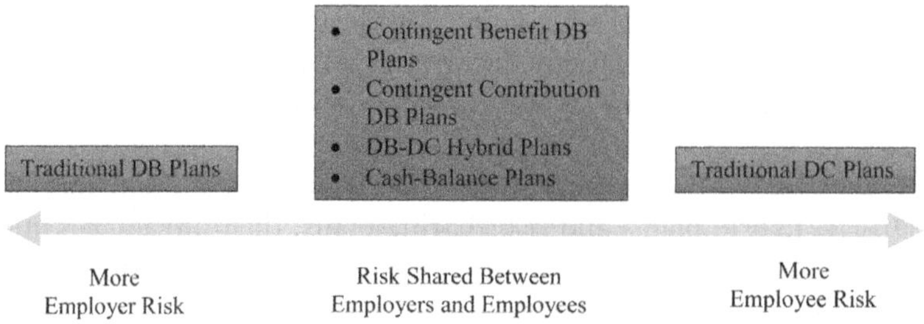

FIGURE 9.1 A Continuum of Risk-Sharing Arrangements in Public Pension Plans

Source: Adapted from Boyd et al. (2021)

funded ratio reaching a certain threshold. Therefore, when investment returns or the funded ratio are low, employees also receive lower COLAs, sharing the investment risk with the employer.

In a contingent contribution DB plan, the employee's contribution amount depends on the investment or funding performance of the pension plan. Asking employees to increase their contribution amount is another way to share risk with employees when the pension plan's investment returns or funding performance does not meet expectations. Contingent employee contributions can involve a 50/50 split of required contributions with employers. When employers face an increased required amount due to poor investment returns, employees are also required to pay an increased amount. Contingent contributions can also involve a variable employee contribution rate, which is adjusted slightly upward when investment returns or funding ratios are low, sharing the risk with the employer.

A CB plan is a special case that also lies in the middle of the spectrum showing the share of investment risk between employers and employees. A CB plan is similar to a DC plan in that employees and employers contribute a fixed percentage of salaries into participants' individual accounts. However, in addition to the fixed contributions, the sponsoring employer also guarantees a certain percentage of asset growth (such as 5%) in individual retirement accounts. In this way, although the final benefits are not guaranteed, employees have a certain level of certainty in their pension benefits. That is, when CB plan participants reach retirement age, they will at least get the accumulated contributions plus the guaranteed annual growth on these contributions. In the CB plan, the employers' required contributions or liabilities are usually lower than in a traditional DB plan, because the guaranteed rate of return (around 5%) is lower than the assumed rate of return (7% or higher) used in a traditional DB plan.

Finally, the DB-DC hybrid plan is a combination of DB and DC components. Employers using a DB-DC hybrid plan might want to encourage participants to enroll in DC plans or slowly transition DB plans to DC plans. They could provide an option with a supplemental DC plan while lowering the DB plan benefits. For example, an employer might provide an option that they will contribute to a DC with 3% of salary employer contribution, while the benefit multiplier for the original DB plan will be lowered. Some pension systems also provide both DB and DC plans and give employees the option to choose one of them when they join the system.

Advantages and disadvantages

Because of the different features of DB and DC plans, they have advantages and disadvantages for employers and employees, as shown in Table 9.1.

DB plans' advantages include sufficient and stable pension benefits for the employees, which also help employers attract and retain high-quality employees. DB plans' investments are pooled and managed by professionals hired by the pension systems, which can be more efficient because more investment options are available, and investment expenses are lower because of the economy of scale.

DB plans' disadvantages include the contribution and investment risks for the employers and the lack of portability for the employees. Because of the pre-funding requirements, DB pension plans hire actuaries to calculate liabilities and required contributions. Investment risk could increase

TABLE 9.1 Advantages and Disadvantages of DB and DC Plans

	Employers	*Employees*
DB plans	Pros – The sufficient and stable pension benefits can help to hire and retain employees Cons – Employers bear investment and contribution risks; Contribution volatility; unfunded liabilities might lower credit ratings	Pros – Stable retirement income; potentially higher benefits Cons – Lack of portability and flexibility; vesting period requirements
DC plans	Pros – Easy to manage; stable and predictable pension expenses Cons – Need to provide financial education and resources to participants; otherwise, pension benefits may be low	Pros – Portable when changing jobs; immediately vested Cons – Need to make investment decisions; potentially lower benefits

contribution volatility because if investment returns are lower than expected, the required contributions from employers will increase. DB plans also have disadvantages for employees who are early in their careers and might change jobs, because DB plans usually have a vesting period, and by design, DB plans accrue benefits faster in the later years of an individual's career. This lack of portability means that when DB plan participants switch to another pension plan, they might lose some or all of the pension benefits or the opportunity to gain more pension benefits.

In contrast, DC plans' advantages include the ease of administration for employers and portability and flexibility for employees. Employers only need to pay a fixed percentage of payroll into individual retirement accounts. The stability of pension expenses is also beneficial for budgeting purposes. The costs of administration are low because minimal investment management is needed. DC plans also provide portability and flexibility to employees. DC plan participants are often immediately vested or will be vested shortly after joining the system. When they switch jobs, they can bring their individual account balance with them, without losing pension benefits. This advantage is attractive to young professionals as they are not sure whether they will stay with the same employer for a long time.

DC plans' disadvantages include potentially lower pension benefits for employees. Because DC plan assets (i.e., individual account balances) are managed by individual participants, their risk preferences and investment knowledge will highly influence the investment decisions they make. When investment decisions are made by individual participants with a lack of investment knowledge and confidence, they often have lower investment returns and thus lower retirement benefits. Although employers are not responsible for the pension benefits participants ultimately will receive in a DC plan, they still have the responsibility to provide basic investment knowledge or investment options to DC plan participants so that they can make more informed decisions. Employers may also provide default investment options that are based on participants' age or financial circumstances. With default options and financial education, DC plan participants may make better investment decisions and get better returns.

Risk-sharing, CB, and DB-DC hybrid plans utilize the advantages of DB and DC plans and try to strike a balance. However, some trade-offs have to be made. For example, with contingent benefits and contingent employee contributions, DB plans' investment and contribution risks for the employers are reduced to some extent, but the benefit sufficiency and stability for employees are also reduced. CB plans have portability and flexibility, and they are relatively easy for employers to manage, but they also provide benefits that are typically lower than traditional DB plans and therefore are less attractive to employees who prefer sufficient and guaranteed pension benefits.

Current status of DC plans in the public sector

A growing number of DC plans have emerged in the public sector in recent years. In 2022, according to the National Compensation Survey (U.S. Bureau of Labor Statistics, 2022), 39% of state and local government employees had access to DC plans (an increase from 29% in 2010); 19% of those with access participated in these DC plans. In comparison, on the DB side, 86% of state and local government employees have access to DB plans and 75% of them participate in DB plans (Zook, 2023).

According to data collected from 22 DC plans in the public sector (Public Plans Database, 2024), the average mandatory employee contribution rate for these public DC plans is 5.19% of compensation, while the average employer fixed rate contribution is 4.81% (there may be additional employer match contributions as well).

There are several different DC plan types, as seen in Table 9.2. The plan type numbers of these employer-sponsored DC plans correspond to the Internal Revenue Code that specifies the tax advantages these plans enjoy. The difference between them relates to the types of organizations that qualify for them and the contribution limits.

TABLE 9.2 Plan Types in PPD Plans (2019)

Plan type	*Eligible employers*	*Annual contribution limit in 2024 ($)*	*Number of PPD plans in 2019*	*Percent of total PPD plans in 2019*
401(a)	Any public or nonprofit employer; mandate participation and contribution	69,000	17	23.61
401(k)	For-profit companies and legacy plans in the public sector	23,000	17	23.61
414(k)	A separate account within a DB plan	N/A	1	1.39
457(b)	Governments or tax-exempt organizations; voluntary	23,000	37	51.39
Total			72	100.00

Source: Public Plans Database (PPD) (2024) Public Defined Contribution Plans.

An analysis of the 72 DC plans included in the Public Plans Database (2024) shows that the majority of these plans are 457(b) plans (51%), followed by 401(a) (24%), 401(k) (24%), and 414(k) (1%) plans. Some governments use multiple plan types. For example, the State of California offers a Savings Plus program that has a 457(b) plan, introduced in 1974, and a 401(k) plan, introduced in 1984 (Savings Plus Program, 2024). Both plans are voluntary retirement saving programs that offer participants investment options for their voluntary contributions as complementary to the CalPERS DB benefits.

401(a) plans may be used in government and nonprofit organizations. The annual contribution limit for these plans is $69,000 in 2024, and employees may be required to contribute. 401(k) plans, on the other hand, are generally for private, for-profit companies, but there are some legacy 401(k) plans in the public sector that are still offered to existing employees (CAPTRUST, 2023). State and local governments were not eligible to adopt 401(k) plans after May 6, 1986 (IRS, 2024a). The 2024 contribution limit for 401(k) plans is $23,000.

A 414(k) plan is a special type of DC plan. Rather than a stand-alone DC plan, the 414(k) plan is a separate account within a DB plan that is treated as a DC component to enhance retirement benefits. The benefits are based on the balance of this separate account. The only 414(k) plan in the above table in the Public Plans Database (2024) is the Public Employee Retirement System of Idaho (PERSI) Choice Plan. PERSI administers two DC plans, the PERSI Choice 401(k) and PERSI Choice 414(k). The 414(k) plan is set up for gain-sharing allocations from the PERSI DB plan. While employees can decide their investment choices in the 414(k) plan, they do not make contributions to this plan (PERSI, 2022).

Tax-exempt organizations (governments and nonprofits) may utilize a 457(b) plan, with allowable contributions of up to $23,000 in 2024 (IRS, 2024b). There are two main differences between the 457(b) and 401(a) plans. Employee participation is voluntary in the 457(b) plan but can be mandatory for 401(a) plans. Also, 457(b) plans have a lower contribution limit than 401(a) plans. Therefore, 457(b) plans are often used as supplemental plans to the primary DB or DC plans in the public sector, while 401(a) plans are often used as primary DC plans.

Another DC plan type, the 403(b) plan may be offered to certain employees of public schools, universities, and tax-exempt organizations under IRC Section 501(c)(3) (IRS, 2024c). This is not included in Table 9.2 because none of the PPD pension plans include this type of DC plan. While similar to 401(a) plans, 403(b) plans differ in terms of contribution limits, investment options, and flexibility regarding participation and contributions (MissionSquare Retirement, n.d.).

Current status of risk-sharing, cash-balance, and hybrid plans in the public sector

At the state level, many retirement systems have introduced DC, CB, or hybrid plans either as their primary or supplemental plans. According to a 2020 report, 18 states have nontraditional plans as their primary retirement plan for employees, including hybrid, CB, and stand-alone DC plans (Aubry & Wandrei, 2020). The reasons for introducing these plans include reducing high pension costs, sharing investment risks with employees, attracting more mobile or younger employees, offering more investment choices for employees for high returns, and avoiding the "moral hazard" problem associated with the tendency that government makes benefit promises without appropriate funding support (Fore, 2001; Munnell et al., 2008, 2014).

At the local level, most small or medium-sized municipalities and counties do not administer their own retirement plans; instead, they join state-administered plans. Localities with their own plans, usually large cities or counties, also see an increasing trend of providing DC plan options. According to a Center for Retirement Research survey (Aubry & Wandrei, 2020), the number of sampled localities that offer nontraditional-DB plans as their primary pension plans for new hires increased from 10.6% in 2001 to 18.9% in 2018. These alternative plans include mostly stand-alone DC plans, followed by hybrid or CB plans (Aubry & Wandrei, 2020).

Contingent employee contribution rates

In traditional DB plans, both employers and employees typically make contributions to the pension plans as a method of sharing pension costs. The employees' contributions are often set at a fixed rate of their pay. To further share contribution risk, some governments have variable employee contribution rates. In these arrangements, employees are expected to increase their contribution rates when investment returns or the funded ratios of the plan fall under certain levels.

Another way to set variable employee contribution rates is to create an automatic 50/50 split of the normal cost or the actuarially determined contribution (ADC) between the employer and the employee. The normal cost can increase due to changes in benefit policies or actuarial assumptions. When the normal cost is shared evenly between the employer and employees, the risk of a normal cost increase is shared. For example, the California Public Employees' Pension Reform Act (PEPRA) was approved in 2012 (CalPERS, 2024), allowing public agencies and school employers to require members in the CalPERS system to pay up to 50% of the total normal cost of their pension benefits. These member contributions are subject to a cap (8% for miscellaneous employees, and 11 or 12% for safety employees) (CalPERS, 2024). If ADC is shared between employers and employees, the investment risk and funding risk are also shared, because investment losses or unfunded liabilities gains or losses are reflected in ADC changes. For example, Wisconsin Act 32 in 2011 required employees in the Wisconsin Retirement System (WRS) to pay 50% of the ADC and prohibited employers from paying the employee share (WRS, 2012).

Contingent cost-of-living adjustments

In the public DB plans, a popular approach to make benefits adjustable is to make the COLAs flexible. Plans often grant COLA adjustments every year to keep up with inflation in order to preserve pension benefits' purchasing power. COLAs are usually tied to the inflation rate. However, when the inflation rate is high, CPI-linked COLAs can be very costly to fund. Therefore, COLAs often have caps and floors and the connection to inflation may be loose. Some governments use contingent COLAs depending on certain benchmarks of investment returns or funded ratios to be reached in one year or over several years.

Among the 90 state pension plans studied by NASRA in 2024 (NASRA, 2024), 16 plans (18%) have variable COLA rates depending on either investment returns or funded ratios. Among these, seven plans have COLAs contingent on investment rate of return, seven have COLAs contingent on funded ratio, and two plans have COLAs depending on both investment returns and funded ratio. For example, since 2011, COLAs in the Maryland State Retirement and Pension System have been tied to CPI and subject to a cap of 2.5% when the investment returns meet or exceed the assumed rate of return (6.8% in 2024). If the assumed rate of return is not met, the cap decreases to 1% (Maryland SRPS, 2024). In the Public Employees' Retirement Association of New Mexico (PERA), as of 2023, COLAs are based on both PERA's funded ratio and investment returns. When the funded ratio is less than 100%, the COLA cap is 3%; when the funded ratio is over 100%, the COLA cap is 5% (PERA of New Mexico, 2023a). In addition, SB72 requires that the COLA rate is the difference between the smoothed investment return rate less the COLA hurdle rate, multiplied by the funded ratio (PERA of New Mexico, 2023b). In the Arizona Public Safety Personnel Retirement System, COLA increases are determined by the CPI, and subject to a cap of 2%. The cap is reduced to 1.5% if the funded ratio drops below 90% and to 1.0% if the funded ratio drops below 80%; the COLA is eliminated when the funded ratio drops below 70% (Arizona PSPRS, 2023; NASRA, 2024).

Cash-balance plans

A CB plan is essentially a DC plan with a guaranteed investment return. The guaranteed returns in a CB plan are usually lower than the expected rate of return in a DB plan. In the years when investment returns exceed the guaranteed returns, those returns can be shared between the employer and employees or can be reserved by the plan for years when investment returns are low. The final pension benefit depends on the accumulated balance in the CB accounts. CB plans have the advantages of a DC plan such as portability and flexibility. Because a certain level of investment return is guaranteed by the plan, the investment risk is shared between the employers and the employees. The investment risk for the employer is lower in the CB plan than it is in a traditional DB plan because the guaranteed CB returns are lower than the DB expected rate of return. CB plans give employees more benefit certainty than a traditional DC plan by explicitly promising a certain level of guaranteed investment returns.

Pew (2014) identified several key plan features for public CB plans. These features include contribution rates, guaranteed investment returns, and rules to distribute dividends (i.e., the returns in excess of the guaranteed return). Table 9.3 provides information for five state-administered CB plans in state retirement systems.

DB-DC hybrid plans

A DB-DC hybrid plan consists of a traditional DB plan and a supplemental DC plan. Depending on the plan design features of the DB component and the DC component, the benefit level and the extent to which risks are shared between the employer and the employees are different. Table 9.4 presents the key features of several DB-DC hybrid plans in state retirement systems, including the benefit multiplier and employee contribution for the DB component and the employee and employer contribution rates in the DC component.

As an example of a DB-DC hybrid plan, the Georgia State Employees' Pension and Savings Plan (ERSGA, 2024) Tier 3 has two components. In the DB component, benefits are calculated using the formula: 1% × years of service × highest average salary over 24 consecutive months. Employees are required to contribute 1.25% of their salary to the DB component. In the DC component, employees are automatically enrolled to contribute 5% of their salary to the DC plan, with employers matching dollar-for-dollar up to 5% of the salary. Employees may voluntarily contribute more than 5% to the DC plan, but the employer match is capped at 5%.

TABLE 9.3 Key Features of Selected Cash-Balance Plans in the Public Sector

	Employee contribution rates	*Employer contribution rates*	*Guaranteed returns*
California State Teachers' Retirement System (CalSTRS), Cash Balance Benefit Program	4%	4%	30-year US Treasury Bonds
Kansas Public Employees Retirement System Tier 3 (KPERS 3) Cash Balance Plan	6%	3–6% (depending on years of service)	4%
Kentucky Retirement Systems (KRS), Hybrid Cash Balance Plan for Tier 3	5% (Nonhazardous Member), 8% (Hazardous Member)	4% (Nonhazardous Member), 7.5% (Hazardous Member)	4% (guaranteed interest rate of 4%, plus additional sharing interest)
Nebraska State Employees' Pension Plan and County Employees Pension Plan	4.5% (county), 4.8% (state)	150% of employees' contributions (county), 156% of employees' contributions (state)	Federal mid-term rate plus 1.5% or the guaranteed minimum annual rate of 5%
Texas County & District Retirement System (TCDRS)	4–7%	At least dollar to dollar up to $2.5 per dollar	7%

Source: Cash-balance plans are selected from Pew (2014); data updated by authors to reflect 2024 information.

Tennessee's hybrid retirement plan offers a DB-DC combination to employees. The employer contributes 4% of compensation to the DB component and 5% of compensation to the DC component (the 401(k) account), while the members are required to contribute 5% of their compensation to the DB component and an optional 2% of their compensation to the DC component (Tennessee Retirement Program, 2023). The DB benefit multiplier was 1% in the hybrid plan. This transition from traditional DB to a hybrid DB-DC plan went into effect in 2014 in an effort to reduce pension costs and liabilities for employers.

TABLE 9.4 Key Features of Selected Hybrid Plans in the Public Sector

Plans	*DB component*		*DC component*	
	Benefit multiplier (%)	*Employee contribution rate (%)*	*Employee contribution rate (%)*	*Employer contribution rate (%)*
Georgia Employees' Retirement System Tier 3	1	1.25	5	Up to 5
Indiana Public Employees' Retirement Fund Hybrid	1.1	None	3	None
Michigan Public School Employees' Retirement System Pension Plus Hybrid Plan	1.5	3–6.4	3	4
Michigan State Police Retirement Plans (Pension Plus)	2	4	2	1
Rhode Island Employees' Retirement System	1	3.75	5	1–1.5
Tennessee Consolidated Retirement System (Hybrid Retirement Plan for State Employees and Teachers)	1	5	2	5
Virginia Retirement System (Hybrid Retirement Plan)	1	4	1	1
Washington Public Employees' Retirement System (PERS) Plan 3	1	None	5–15	None

Source: Adapted from Pew (2015); data updated by authors to reflect 2024 information based on NASRA (2024) and plan documents.

Challenges in the transition from DB to other plans

As governments consider the transition from DB plans to other plans, it is important to recognize several major challenges.

The first challenge is how to deal with legacy liabilities in the traditional DB plans. Most public DB plans have unfunded liabilities. If a DB plan is closed and a DC, CB, or hybrid plan is created for new employees, it is the government's responsibility to provide funding to cover the unfunded liabilities in the legacy DB plan. Most governments would find it difficult to do so. When new members are enrolled in new tiers or new plans with reduced benefits but still contribute to the pension fund, this arrangement may raise concerns about intergenerational equity. Employees joining the new tiers are often paying the same or higher contributions while receiving lower benefits.

The second challenge is the potentially lower investment performance in DC or other plans as compared to pension funds in which DB plans pool assets. Although governments can provide investment options and pool the DC assets to invest in those options, individuals still have the discretion to choose portfolios for their individual pension accounts. When investment decisions are made by individuals without the knowledge or capacity to deal with high-risk investments, they might also be limited in the asset classes they are able to invest in for diversification purposes. The preference for low risk and the lack of diversification opportunities often lead to lower returns, especially in DC plans. Governments are using default investment options and providing financial education to individuals participating in DC plans, but the effectiveness of these tools is still limited.

The third challenge is the impact of the transition to DC or other plans on employees. Public-sector jobs are perceived to be secure with decent income and benefits. DB pension benefits play an important role in this perception. Transitioning to DC or other plans will cause public employment to lose this benefit security feature, which might affect some employees' motivation to join or stay in their positions. DB plans can also be effective in retaining mid-career employees, which are crucial in many public service areas such as education and public safety. DB plan benefits are especially important for teachers, police, and firefighters. Losing or lowering DB benefits (for new employees) in the transition to other plans might affect the public workforce.

The fourth challenge is the trade-off of multiple goals in public pension management. The public sector introduces variable benefits or variable contributions, DB-DC hybrid plans, or CB plans with the goal of improving funding sustainability and cost affordability for the government. But this change will eventually reduce benefit sufficiency for pension plan participants. Research (Boyd et al., 2021) shows that these risk-sharing policies often create trade-offs between the government's goals and pension plan participants' goals. How to balance them is a critical challenge for governments' transition to more sustainable and affordable pension systems.

Looking forward, it is reasonable to expect that governments will take steps to address the unfunded liabilities and fiscal burden in their current DB plans. DB plans with variable benefits or contributions, CB plans, or DB-DC hybrid plans are options for governments to reform their pension systems. The longer governments wait to address their unfunded liabilities, the harder the reform will be. Successful pension reforms need to balance the several goals of pension management, involve the stakeholders, and be carried out within the legal and institutional constraints.

References

Arizona PSPRS. (2023). *Annual comprehensive financial report for the fiscal year ended June 30, 2023*. https://www.psprs.com/uploads/sites/1/PSPRS_FY2023_ACFR.pdf

Aubry, J.-P., & Wandrei, K. (2020). *Have localities shifted away from traditional defined benefit plans?* https://crr.bc.edu/wp-content/uploads/2020/04/SLP70.pdf

Boyd, D., Chen, G., & Ying, Y. (2021). *Public pension risk-sharing policies: A policymaker's guidebook*. https://www.albany.edu/rockefeller/news/2021-rockefeller-researchers-release-public-pension-risk-sharing-guidebook

CalPERS. (2024). *Pension reform impacts*. https://www.calpers.ca.gov/page/employers/policies-and-procedures/pension-reform-impacts

CAPTRUST. (2023). *Navigating the number jumble: A 403(b), 401(k), and 457(b) comparison*. https://www.captrust.com/resources/navigating-the-number-jumble-403b-401k-457b-Comparison/

Employees' Retirement System of Georgia (ERSGA). (2024). *GSEPS: Georgia State Employees' Pension and Savings Plan Tier 3*. https://www.ers.ga.gov/ers-gseps-tier-3

Fore, D. (2001). Going private in the public sector: The transition from defined benefit to defined contribution pension plans. In O. S. Mitchell & E. C. Hustead (Eds.), *Pension in the public sector* (pp. 267–287). University of Pennsylvania Press.

IRS. (2024a). *Government retirement plans toolkit*. https://www.irs.gov/government-entities/federal-state-local-governments/government-retirement-plans-toolkit.

IRS. (2024b). *IRC 457(b) deferred compensation plans*. https://www.irs.gov/retirement-plans/irc-457b-deferred-compensation-plans

IRS. (2024c). *403(b) tax-sheltered annuity plans*. Internal Revenue Service. Retrieved September 23, 2024, from https://www.irs.gov/retirement-plans/irc-403b-tax-sheltered-annuity-plans

Maryland SRPS. (2024). *Cost-of-living adjustments (COLA)*. https://sra.maryland.gov/post/cost-living-adjustments-cola

MissionSquare Retirement. (n.d.). *403(b) vs. 401(a) plans: Benefits & differences*. https://www.missionsq.org/products-and-services/403(b)-defined-contribution-plans/403(b)-vs-401(a)-plans.html

Munnell, A. H., Aubry, J.-P., & Cafarelli, M. (2014, April). *Defined contribution plans in the public sector: An update*. Issues in Brief. Number 37. Center for Retirement Research at Boston College. https://crr.bc.edu/wp-content/uploads/2014/04/SLP_37_508rev.pdf

Munnell, A. H., Golub-Sass, A., Haverstick, K., Soto, M., & Wiles, G. (2008, January). *Why have some states introduced defined contribution plans?* Issues in Brief. Number 3. Center for Retirement Research at Boston College. https://crr.bc.edu/why-have-some-states-introduced-defined-contribution-plans/

NASRA. (2024). *NASRA issue brief: Cost-of-living adjustments*. https://www.nasra.org/files/Issue%20Briefs/NASRACOLA%20Brief.pdf

PERA of New Mexico. (2023a). *2023 PERA member handbook*. https://www.nmpera.org/assets/uploads/forms-kits-handbooks/2023MemberHandbook_Aug2023.pdf

PERA of New Mexico. (2023b). *PERA COLA overview* [Video]. YouTube. https://www.youtube.com/watch?v=Dfx2ZhNB_ic

Pew. (2014). *Public pension cash balance plans: A primer*. https://www.pewtrusts.org/-/media/legacy/uploadedfiles/pcs_assets/2014/cashbalancebriefv7pdf.pdf

Pew. (2015). *Hybrid public pension plans: A primer*. https://www.pewtrusts.org/~/media/assets/2015/04/hybrid-public-pension-plans_brief.pdf

Public Employee Retirement System of Idaho (PERSI). (2022). *Annual Comprehensive Financial Report as of and for fiscal year 2022*. https://www.persi.idaho.gov/docs/news/publications/2022-Annual-Report.pdf

Public Plans Database. (2024). *Public defined contribution plans*. https://publicplansdata.org/public-plans-database/download-full-data-set/

Savings Plus Program. (2024). *Timeline of key events*. https://www.savingsplusnow.com/rsc-web-preauth/about/celebrating-50-years-of-service

Tennessee Retirement Program. (2023). *Hybrid retirement plan for state employees and teachers: Hybrid member guide*. Tennessee Treasury Department. https://treasury.tn.gov/

U.S. Bureau of Labor Statistics (2022). *National Compensation Survey*. https://www.bls.gov/ebs/

WRS. (2012). *Study of the Wisconsin Retirement System in accordance with 2011 Wisconsin Act 32*. https://etf.wi.gov/publications/wrs-studypdf/direct

Zook, D. (2023). *How do retirement plans for private industry and state and local government workers compare?* U.S. Bureau of Labor Statistics. https://www.bls.gov/opub/btn/volume-12/how-do-retirement-plans-for-private-industry-and-state-and-local-government-workers-compare.htm

10

ASSESSING THE IMPACT AND TRADE-OFFS OF PUBLIC PENSION REFORMS

Introduction

Chapter 3 identified five goals for pension systems: sufficiency of pension benefits, affordability of pension costs, sustainability of pension funding, efficiency of asset management, and good governance of pension plans. Balancing these various goals can be challenging for decision-makers, and the focus may shift between goals over time. In addition, priorities may vary across stakeholders. The previous two chapters discussed a variety of pension reforms that state and local governments have implemented. This chapter will address the effects of those reforms relative to the five goals/outcomes.

Table 10.1 summarizes the effects of the reforms across the five goals. A minus sign indicates that the reform has a negative effect on the goal, while a plus sign shows a positive effect of the reform on that goal. In some cases, effects may be mixed or unknown (represented by a question mark). The table includes groups of reform categories, as outlined in Chapter 8. For example, the changes in benefits category in the table encompass four types of changes (cost-of-living cuts, decreases in benefit multipliers, reduced benefits, and new employment tiers). Each reform targets some, but not all, of the goals simultaneously.

The next five sections will discuss the outcomes of the various reforms relative to each of the goals in turn. The chapter ends with conclusions related to what is known (and not known) about the effects of pension reforms.

DOI: 10.4324/9781032671185-10

TABLE 10.1 Effects of Public Pension Reforms

Reform	*Goals*				
	Sufficiency	*Affordability*	*Sustainability*	*Efficiency*	*Good governance*
Change in benefits	–	+	+		
Employee contribution increase		+	+		
Employer contribution increase		–	+		
Change in retirement eligibility	–	+	+		
Change in plan type	–	+	?	?	?
Change in investment practices		?	?	?	
Board composition					?
Cost sharing	+/–	+	+		
Pension obligation bonds		?	?		

Sufficiency of pension benefits

The first goal of pension management relates to the sufficiency of the pension benefits. This refers to the value of the benefits to the plan members. Pension benefit sufficiency is a critical concern of employees. Government officials may also have a personal stake in sufficiency if they are members of the pension system. On the other hand, generous plans are more costly, which limits the flexibility of administering governments to fund public services. However, governments desire a high-quality workforce. If reduced pension benefits make it difficult to recruit and retain good employees, the quantity and/or quality of services provided to the public may be affected.

As seen in Table 10.1, several categories of pension reforms have focused on reducing the sufficiency of the benefits by cutting benefits, changing eligibility requirements, moving toward defined contribution (DC) or other plan types, or cost sharing. An increase in the employer contribution rate does not directly affect pension benefits but may accompany other changes that could result in either increased or decreased overall take-home income. One key point is that changes to benefits often affect only employees hired after a certain date, creating a tiered benefit structure. This may result in differential effects over the short and long term.

A common method of measuring benefit sufficiency is by the replacement rate, which is the ratio of an individual's preretirement income to their retirement income. A 75–80% replacement rate for all forms of retirement income, including Social Security and individual savings, is typically considered to be sufficient (Peng, 2008; Young & Theodore, 2023). Schieber (2011) studied replacement rates of state and local plans. In the lowest quintile, the average replacement rate was 32.4% (not including Social Security), with about 91% of workers covered by Social Security. The replacement rate increased over the remaining quintiles, with an average rate of 65.7% in the highest quintile – only 57.8% of workers in this quintile were covered by Social Security (e.g., almost all public employees in Ohio are not in the Social Security system). If the desirable replacement rate is 80%, then, many retirees will be dependent on their personal savings for a good portion of their retirement funds. Another study, by the Center for State and Local Government Excellence and the National Association of State Retirement Administrators (NASRA, 2014), focused specifically on 24 state plans that changed benefits. This study found an average reduction in benefits of 7.51%. The additional individual savings needed to attain an 85% replacement rate post-reform increased in each state and in some cases was over $100,000.

A number of studies have addressed the effect of pensions on employee recruitment, retention, and quality, with mixed findings. For example, federal employees with high retention and promotion rates value retirement plans (Ippolito, 2002), while public school teachers appear to value wages substantially more than pensions (Fitzpatrick, 2015). In addition, public organizations with more generous pension plans have been found to be better able to recruit and retain high-quality employees from the private sector (Munnell et al., 2015). Reducing pension benefits does appear to negatively affect recruitment, and especially retention. A preliminary study of competitiveness between private and public sectors found that the public sector had more difficulty with recruitment and retention after pension benefit cuts (Quinby et al., 2018). Rhode Island's 2005 pension reforms led to a 2.4 percentage-point increase in separations over the next several years, although the effect on teachers was lower than for other employees (Quinby & Wettstein, 2019). Gorina and Hoang (2020) found that pension reforms that reduced employee benefits across states between 2002 and 2015 increased turnover by 4%, with reforms that explicitly reduced benefits having a larger effect than those that are implicit cuts (increased retirement age, service years, and years of service in benefit calculations).

Some pension reforms have introduced DC, cash-balance, and/or hybrid plans. DC plans are generally considered to be less generous than defined benefit plans: benefits are not guaranteed, the risk is entirely borne by employees, and returns are highly dependent on market conditions and employee investment selections. However, defined benefit plans benefit employees with longer tenures, so the more portable DC plans may be more attractive to potential employees who do not plan on a long career with one organization. Studies to date have generally but not always found that defined benefit plans enhance retention. A private-sector study found that employees with 5–10 years of tenure in organizations with DC plans were 23% more likely to leave their jobs than those with DB plans (Haverstick et al., 2010). A study of Utah's 2011 reforms, where the DB plan was replaced for new employees by a DC and a hybrid plan, found a 30% increase in separation rates following the change (although the authors note that the improving state economy may have played a role) (Clark et al., 2016). A study of the 1987 federal pension reform that created a hybrid plan found a one-third increase in mid-career employees leaving the government (Lewis & Stoycheva, 2016). However, Goldhaber et al. (2015) found that teachers in the State of Washington who voluntarily moved to a hybrid plan were less likely to leave than those who remained in the DB plan.

Overall, it appears that reforms that reduce benefits do tend to negatively affect employee retention, and recruitment and quality to an extent. The effects may vary depending on the structure of the changes, though; for example, direct benefit reductions seem to have a larger effect than those that are more implicit cuts, and the magnitude of the changes can be important. There also may be differences depending on the type of employee, as responses by teachers to benefit cuts and shifts to non-defined benefit plans seem to be less than for other types of employees. In addition, many changes affect only new employees, making it more difficult to study the effects that may take time to manifest.

Affordability of pension costs

Government officials are particularly concerned with having a pension system that is affordable to the government and taxpayers. This is generally related to pension benefit sufficiency; more generous plans will typically be more costly (i.e., less affordable). The higher the costs of the pension system, the greater the opportunity cost for the government, limiting their ability to provide public services and/or requiring higher taxes (e.g., Peng & Wang, 2017). Bond rating agencies also pay close attention to the affordability of pension systems, particularly since the Great Recession when many governments had substantial market losses, resulting in higher unfunded pension liabilities and required contributions. The more creditworthy a government is considered, the lower its debt borrowing costs, which can be considerable cost savings. Governments with more affordable pension systems, then, may be more likely to have higher credit ratings (all else equal).

Table 10.1 shows a negative relationship between the effects of several categories of reforms on benefit sufficiency and on affordability. Reduced pension benefit sufficiency through cutting benefits, changing eligibility requirements, or shifting away from defined benefit plans, has the effect of improving plan affordability by lowering government costs over time. Some systems have also implemented or increased contributions from employees, or other cost-sharing arrangements, which also help to make the system more affordable for the government. The only reform in this table that clearly reduces affordability is where the employer contribution increases, which raises government costs. Changes in investment practices could potentially reduce the employer contribution requirements if they increase investment returns, but a reduced rate of return assumption would have the opposite effect of increasing the requirement contribution.

One measure of affordability is the relationship of the government's long-term liabilities (including required pension contributions, outstanding debt service, and other post-employment benefits) to total government expenditures. FitchRatings considers a carrying cost rate of less than 10% to be worthy of AAA rating, and less than 20% to be AA rating. However, the effect of various reforms on this rate is relatively unknown. Credit ratings themselves are also a reflection of pension affordability. For example, credit rating agencies downgraded the State of Illinois' bond ratings 21 times between 2009 and 2017 due to pension funding issues (Dabowski & Klingner, 2017). Lower credit ratings exacerbate a government's fiscal problems as they result in higher borrowing costs. One study examined the relationship between state pension reforms and general obligation bond ratings between 2004 and 2018 (Hoang, 2023) and found that the adoption of pension reforms by itself does not have a significant effect on credit ratings. However, the type and intensity of the reforms make a difference; those that enhance cash flow, such as employee contributions and reductions in benefit payments, are more likely to lead to credit rating improvements.

Affordability can also be measured by the share of payroll costs that comprise annual required employer pension contributions. According to NASRA's Public Funds Survey (2023c), employer contribution rates have increased steadily over the last 20 years. For plans where employees are covered by Social Security, the median employer contribution rate was 6.0% in 2002 and had increased to 9.5% by 2010, and to 15.1% by 2022. For plans with employees not covered by Social Security, the median employer contribution rate was 10.3% in 2002, 13.5% by 2010, and 22.8%

in 2022. (Note: this sample excludes employee groups with separate plans such as public safety.) There is wide variation across plans, however. Contribution rates in 2022 for plans with Social Security range from 5.4 to 74.6%, while rates for employees without Social Security vary between 9.45 and 61.7%.

Another way to consider affordability is to compare the employer contributions to government revenues. Peng and Wang (2017) studied employer pension contributions relative to state and local government own-source revenues and found that required contributions decreased from about 4% in 1992 to about 3% in 2002, but then increased to close to 6% by 2011. There are large variations across states, however; the mean pension burden between 1992 and 2011 ranged from 1.7% in New Hampshire to 7.5% in Nevada. The variations were related to the employee contribution share, investment returns, the percentage of required contributions paid, the benefit multiplier, and public employees relative to total employment. Another study of a sample of cities found that pension costs as a percent of revenue ranged from 2.7% in the bottom quintile to 12.4% in the highest quintile; the highest was 17.6% in Little Rock, Arkansas (Munnell et al., 2013).

NASRA's Public Funds Survey (2023c) shows an increase in employee rates over time, which is helpful for governments, but not as dramatic as for employers. Median employee rates for plans with employees in Social Security were steady at 5.0% from 2002 to 2011, then started to rise to 6.3% by 2022. For plans with employees not participating in Social Security, the median employee contribution rates were 8.0% from 2002 to 2018, then began rising to a rate of 9.0% in 2022.

Pension obligation bonds (POBs) could potentially have a positive effect on affordability. The proceeds increase the pension assets, thus reducing the government's annual required contributions. Ideally, the interest rate paid by the government for these bonds will be substantially lower than the rate of return on the investments made by the pension system with the bond proceeds. This arbitrage provides additional resources that can be used either for pension funding or other public purposes (Calabrese & Ely, 2013). However, the government is substituting one type of debt (unfunded pension system liability that exists on paper and is based on a series of assumptions) for another (legal debt obligations of the government sponsor that require annual payments to bondholders). There are serious risks involved with POBs, particularly related to market timing. Issuance of POBs, for example, was seen as one factor leading to bankruptcy in the cities of Detroit and Stockton (Niraula, 2018). In another example, the City of Oakland, California, would have saved $250 million as of 2010 if they had made regular pension payments rather than issuing POBs in 1997

(Kilgour 2014). Evidence of POB performance seems to depend on the time period of the study. The Center for Retirement Research at Boston College, for example, found that POBs were a losing proposition for most issuers in a 2009 study, but after several years of an economic recovery, the issuers had an average 1.5% real rate of return by 2014 (Munnell et al., 2014). Researchers have generally concluded that POBs tend to be used by governments that have the most severe fiscal conditions and can least afford the risks posed by these instruments (e.g., Kilgour, 2014; Munnell et al., 2010, 2014).

Transitioning from a defined benefit plan to a DC plan also increases affordability. DC plans require only a specific contribution from the employer, possibly with a share that matches the employee contribution rate. The government has no risk with these plans and has no liabilities for the employees once they retire. Many of the issues with defined benefit plan unfunded liabilities have been related to investment return volatility; market losses or low returns increase the plan liabilities, which results in higher required employer contributions. In the long run, then, DC plans have lower costs for government sponsors. However, there are costs to transition away from defined benefit plans that need to be considered. As current or new employees are enrolled in DC plans, there are fewer remaining employees to pay into the existing defined benefit plan, which can increase the employer costs for that plan over the near term. One study of localities that moved to non-defined benefit plans found, for example, that employer contributions to these plans were generally lower but that the overall pension cost for the government might not be reduced because over two-thirds of employer-defined benefit contributions pay for prior unfunded liabilities rather than normal costs (Aubry & Wandrei, 2020a, 2020b). Another study (Bond et al., 2023) of five states that closed their defined benefit plans to new employees found that plan sponsor costs increased significantly after the change. For example, Michigan's State Employees' Retirement System created a DC plan for employees hired after March 31, 1997. The plan's actuary estimated that in 2021 alone (many years after the reform) the increased cost to the state for this change was $46.6 million.

Many of the pension reforms that have been implemented relate to changing benefits and changing eligibility requirements. These are designed to increase the affordability of the plan for the government. It is important to note, though, that the effects can vary over time. Reducing benefits will have a clear long-term positive effect on employer costs. However, in the short run, many systems have had to increase employer contribution rates to deal with the existing unfunded long-term liabilities, which reduces affordability.

Sustainability of pension funding

One goal of pension management is to be able to sustain the system over the long term. Concerns have arisen about this at varying points in time, especially after the Great Recession when plans lost large portions of their assets in a very short period. Market losses, along with the failure of plans to pay their annual required contributions, can lead to situations where the plan does not have sufficient assets to cover liabilities over time. In theory, defined benefit pension plans should have assets that will fully fund the future liabilities. It is difficult to maintain a 100% funded level consistently, though, due to market fluctuations and variations in actual demographic and economic results versus actuarial assumptions. Because of this, a funded level of 80% or higher is considered to be the standard for sustainability (e.g., Davidyan, 2021).

Most stakeholders are concerned with the sustainability of the system. Retirees, members, employee unions, and pension boards want to know that assets will be sufficient in the future to pay pension benefits. Sponsoring government officials are aware that large unfunded liabilities are likely to result in a need for increased employer contributions in the short and/or long term. Increased contributions may require higher taxes and/or public service cuts which would not be looked on favorably by taxpayers. For example, the City of Omaha's Police and Fire pension system was in crisis with a funded ratio of only 38.6% by the end of 2008. The city implemented a new tax on restaurants in 2011 to increase employer contributions to the system. The tax was politically unpopular with the public and was seen as being at least partially responsible for the mayor losing a reelection attempt in 2013 (Hoang & Ebdon, 2021).

As seen in Table 10.1, most types of pension reforms that have been implemented have a positive effect on sustainability. Cutting benefits in various ways reduces the future liabilities, thereby increasing the funded level. Increases in employer contributions reduce affordability for the government but enhance sustainability because of the positive effect on pension assets. The effects of other types of reforms, including changes in plan type or investment practices, and issuance of POBs, are not as clear.

Funded levels of defined benefit plans vary over time. For plans in the Public Plans Database, the average funded level increased from 79.4% in 1990 to 102.7% in 2000. In 2007, before the Great Recession, the ratio was 86.5% before decreasing over the next several years. In 2018, the ratio was 72.8% (Aubry & Crawford, 2019). The average funded ratio of the plans in the NASRA's Public Funds Survey was 100.8% in 2001, then trended downward to a low of 71.8% in 2013; by 2022, the average funded ratio of these plans was up to 76.1% (NASRA, 2023c). Averages mask a wide variation across plans, however. In 2022, for example, the funded ratio in the 130 plans in the Public Funds Survey ranged from 21.8 to 113.7% (NASRA, 2023c). Overall, many plans are still funded below the benchmark level, even following reforms, but others are well-funded.

It is important to understand that reforms can take years to show significant improvements in the funded ratio. Benefit reductions may affect only new employees, for example, so changes in liabilities will be gradual. Investment practices and policies also affect funded ratios. For example, all 131 plans in the NASRA's Public Funds Survey have lowered their expected rate of return assumption since 2008–2009, which has the effect of increasing the present value of liabilities over time and therefore reducing the funded ratio (NASRA, 2023c). POBs are one measure that can have an immediate positive effect on the funded ratio if the issuing government transfers the proceeds to the pension system for investment. As noted earlier, though, there are risks involved in POBs. One of these is the political risk that the pension fund will now appear to be fully funded or overfunded, leading to pressure to increase pension benefits that may not be sustainable over time (Calabrese & Ely, 2013).

Another way to measure the sustainability of a pension system is by considering the percentage of actuarially determined contribution (ADC) paid. Sustainable systems should pay the full amount of the required contribution. One recent NASRA study (2023b) found that the median employer contributions to statewide pension plans have been at 100% of the ADC for fiscal years 2014–2022. This is a positive result. However, there is a wide variation among plans. For example, in fiscal year 2022, the percentage of ADC paid ranged from 60 to 160%.

Some state and local governments have transitioned to DC, cash-balance, or hybrid plans. There are generally no concerns over the sustainability of DC plans: since there is no guaranteed benefit for members of these plans, they have no liabilities. The effects of the new plans on the sustainability of the existing defined benefit plans may vary. In theory, liabilities of the defined benefit system may not grow over time (depending on the accuracy of actuarial assumptions) as new employees will not be in this system. However, new employees also do not help to pay the outstanding unfunded liabilities for the defined benefit system, and employers are making contributions toward both the old and new systems. As noted in the previous section, studies have found increased costs to some governments with these transitions. Long-term sustainability is also an issue. For example, Bond et al. (2023) found that the funded ratio of the State of Michigan's State Employees' Retirement System decreased from 109% in 1997, when the plan was closed to new employees, to 69% in 2022. This is partially due to the lack of full funding by the state, but also because assets are an increasingly large share of annual benefit payments as covered employees retire, which necessitates selling more assets, sometimes in poor markets where the prices are low.

For the most part, reforms have improved the sustainability of the systems. These effects are often long term in nature, though. It may take many years for a system's funded ratio to improve significantly following reforms. The outcomes will depend on the type of reform, the magnitude, and who is affected by benefit changes (e.g., new versus current employees).

Efficiency of asset management

Pension plans depend on three sources of income: investment returns, employer contributions, and employee contributions. For the plans in the NASRA Public Fund Survey (NASRA, 2023c), investment returns have comprised 63% of revenues over the last 30 years. Wang and Peng (2016) found that investment returns were the primary determinant of changes in funded ratios in the period between 2001 and 2009. If investment returns are lower than expected, fully funding the liabilities will require higher employer/employee contributions and/or benefit reductions. Therefore, managing the investment of pension assets in an efficient manner is a critical goal and an important role of the pension trustees (and/or an investment committee). Because of the importance of investment returns, most stakeholders are concerned with the efficiency goal. Plans are commonly seeking a high rate of return while balancing risks.

The median expected rate of return for the 131 public pension plans in the NASRA Public Fund Survey was 7.0% in 2022. This assumption reflects a decrease over time; the expected rate was 8.0% from 2001 to 2011, before decreasing (NASRA, 2023c). To demonstrate the importance of the rate of return, a 25-basis point reduction in the expected rate of return (e.g., from 7.5 to 7.25%) is estimated to increase plan costs by 2–3% of pay (NASRA, 2023a). Actual rates of return vary significantly over time and are dependent on market forces as well as investment strategy. For example, the median investment return in the NASRA's Public Fund Survey was a gain of 11.7% in 2020 and 13.7% in 2021, followed by a loss of 12.7% in 2022. The median annualized return over these three years was only 4.3% (NASRA, 2023c). Another study examined an extended period of 2001–2016 for the plans in the Public Fund database and found an average annualized return (net of fees) of 5.5% over this period, which included two substantial recessions. The average returns varied across plans, however, ranging from 4.6% in the bottom quartile to 6.3% in the top quartile (Aubry et al, 2018).

As seen in Table 10.1, two groups of reforms relate to the efficiency goal: change in investment practices, and changes in plan type. Asset pooling and/or consolidation is one of the reforms adopted by pension systems. In theory, this allows for economies of scale in administrative and investment costs. Matkin and Chen (2015) found evidence that larger and more concentrated state systems were more likely to have better fiscal health. Bikker (2017) found declining economies of scale for administrative costs in Dutch pension plans, while Dyck and Pomorski (2011) also found that large plans outperformed small plans by 43–50 basis points per year. These studies support the theory of economies of scale, although they do not relate specifically to plans that have actually consolidated or pooled assets.

Other relevant investment practice reforms relate to investment allocations and management. A number of plans have shifted to increased use of external fund managers. If the external managers are more proficient experts than internal managers or board members, investment returns could be higher. These changes may also be related to the increased use of alternative investments. Portfolio diversification may be beneficial to enhance investment returns and to reduce risk, but alternative investments such as private equity and hedge funds are more complex and require different types of expertise than the traditional equity and bond pension assets. Aubry and Wandrei (2020a, 2020b) found that the use of external managers increased by 96% between 2006 and 2018, while average assets increased by only about 50%. The shift to alternative assets is also clear. For example, the average asset allocation for 90 of the funds in the NASRA's Public Fund Survey as of 2022 included 42.2% equities, 20.6% fixed income, 9.1% real estate, 2.4% cash, and 27.4% alternatives (NASRA, 2023c). Not surprisingly, plans with a higher share of alternative investments use more external managers (Aubry & Wandrei, 2020a, 2020b).

Do alternative investments and external managers enhance investment performance? With increased external expertise comes increased fees, which may offset any increases in returns. Dyck and Pomorski (2011) found that a major reason for higher net returns in large pension plans was due to much lower costs with fewer external managers. Aubry and Wandrei (2020a, 2020b) found that the funds with a higher number of external managers pay higher fees; however, no statistically significant relationship was found between the number of external managers and after-fee investment returns. Peng and Wang (2020) note that there is a wide variety of alternative investment usage between pension plans. For example, the use of private equity increased from 2% of plans in 2001 to 12% in 2014, but many plans have no private equity in their portfolio while a few have more than 40% allocated to this area. Over this period, Peng and Wang's analysis found that alternative investments did provide higher returns on average. However, the size of the additional return was small and did not have a lasting effect.

Efficiency of asset management should also be a goal for DC plans, but since governments do not take any risks and do not have liabilities for these plans, this may be less of a concern for the employers (note that cash-balance and hybrid plans have some elements of both DC and defined benefits plans). The government selects the vendor(s) for DC plans and often has a role in determining fund options. However, individual employees make decisions about how the contributions will be allocated across investment options. Performance, then, depends on the employee's risk levels and knowledge. Also, DC plans may have higher administrative and investment fees than defined benefit plans, and the fees vary substantially. A Government Accountability Office study (GAO, 2022), for example, found that record-keeping and administrative service fees ranged from 0.0008 to 2.01% of plan assets, while investment fees ranged from 0.01 to 2.37%. High fees can substantially reduce retirement savings over time, so this is a concern.

Overall, the effect of the reforms discussed in this section on rates of return is not clear. This is largely due to the dependence on market conditions that are highly volatile. Many plans have reduced expected rates of return in recent years, but given historical trends, actual returns over time may not reach even the lowered expectations on average. There does appear to be some benefit from pooling assets, but hiring external managers may not result in enhanced net returns. Plans have increased allocations to alternative assets, although there is wide variation in this usage. There is evidence that alternatives can increase returns, but the effect may be short term in nature.

Good governance of pension plans

The rules and structure related to the governance of pension plans are important in ensuring good management. This goal cannot be easily measured in a quantitative manner, but governance can affect each of the other pension plan goals/outcomes. Good governance includes, for example, practices in following applicable accounting and actuarial standards, due process to control risk and avoid conflicts of interest, documentation, processes for selecting and monitoring investment professionals, regular reporting, and education of employees about benefits and investment. Professional associations such as the Government Finance Officers Association (GFOA) and the NASRA recommend best practices in pension governance. Stakeholders care about governance practices to ensure transparency and accuracy of information, and to ensure that boards are performing their fiduciary duty.

Two of the reform types listed in Table 10.1 may affect plan governance: board composition and change in plan type. Pension boards are comprised of members from various groups. Chen et al. (2015) found that Public Plan Database (PPD) plans were comprised of 50% employee members, 23% political appointees, 18% ex officio, 6% public citizens, and 3% financial experts. Between 2001 and 2009, 24% of these plans changed their board size and/or composition. Differences in political and personal interests and levels of expertise might be expected to lead to different outcomes, but studies of the effects of board composition have had mixed findings. For example, Chen et al. (2015) found that both political appointees and employee members had a significant positive effect on funded ratios, while public members did not. On the other hand, Andonov et al. (2018) found a lower rate of return from state boards with higher levels of ex officio and appointed members. Brooks (2019) found that active employee board members were associated with lower expected rates of return and had higher funded ratios than retired and other members, while Wang and Peng (2018) found that plans with more appointed (political) members were more likely to reduce expected rates of return over a 14-year period than were plans with more elected plan participant board members.

Other factors are also potentially important in board effectiveness. Aubry and Crawford (2019) created a Board Effectiveness Index including the structure of the board (as of 2017, 16% of plans in this database had a separate investment board), board member composition, board size (the average is ten members), financial expertise, and tenure (the average tenure is six years). They found a positive relationship between the effectiveness index and the ten-year investment returns: a one-point increase in the score was associated with a 14-basis point increase in returns.

Various best practices have been identified for managing DC plans, for example, related to provider selection, performance monitoring, investment options, and education and communication with participants. There are limited studies of these plans. A study of local government DC plans in one state found issues with monitoring service providers. Employers were often unaware of fee levels and structures, tended to use local providers, and were unclear on their roles (Chen et al., 2013).

Overall, as discussed in previous sections, efforts have been made to improve the governance of pension plans. Some studies have attempted to determine the effects of governance on various outcomes. We have evidence of a positive effect of best practices related to board effectiveness on investment returns over time. However, studies of the effects of board composition have mixed findings, and we know little specifically about what happens after changes in DB plan governance, and about the management of DC plans.

Conclusion

A variety of pension reform efforts have been discussed and implemented, as described in Chapters 8 and 9. These reforms focus on different pension plan goals, and so have differing effects on the outcomes related to benefit sufficiency, affordability, sustainability, asset management, and overall good governance. Table 10.1 summarizes the effects of various types of reforms as they relate to the five goals we have identified.

Many of the reforms that have changed benefits, retirement eligibility, and plan type, have had the effect of reducing pension sufficiency. These changes appear to have negative effects on employee recruitment, retention, and quality. Affordability is often reduced, at least in the short term, as systems have increased pension contributions to deal with unfunded liabilities. The reforms, for the most part, do appear to have had positive effects on sustainability, although there is a wide range of funded ratios across plans. Effects of reforms on asset management efficiency are not clear, largely due to the importance of market conditions in investment outcomes. Finally, there is some evidence of positive effects from good governance practices, although we have mixed findings related to various board characteristics. Additional research is needed to address outcomes of specific reform efforts, to address short- versus long-term results, to study the extent to which reforms achieved the intended goal, and to examine how the five goals can be better balanced through reforms.

Some governments have transitioned away from defined benefit plans to DC, cash-balance, and/or hybrid plans. These changes relate to all five of the goals. DC plans tend to be less generous than defined benefit plans and may negatively affect employee recruitment and retention. In theory, they enhance affordability and pose no sustainability issues for the government sponsor, although transition costs and long-term sustainability of legacy-defined benefit plans are a concern. DC plans also tend to have high fees, which reduces asset management efficiency, and there is some evidence of lack of adequate oversight of these plans by employers. These concerns may be reduced through cash-balance and hybrid approaches.

One clear theme related to effects of reforms is the existence of trade-offs. Some of the trade-offs are between the various goals/outcomes. For example, many of the reforms have centered around reducing pension generosity to improve affordability and sustainability. Other trade-offs are between short- and long-term effects. For example, a number of reforms have reduced benefits for new employees only; the effects of these efforts may take many years to see an improvement in the funded ratio or sustainability of the system.

The effects of reforms depend on a variety of factors. For example, the magnitude of the reforms can be important. Some plans have made drastic reductions in benefits, for example, while others are more minor. Also, the circumstances of the plan prior to reforms can be important. Severely underfunded plans in crisis will require more extreme changes. As noted above, market conditions are also vitally important in determining pension outcomes and often result in volatile changes in investment returns which can affect all five of the goals.

Throughout this book, we have seen that pensions operate as a system and are not stagnant. Boards and governments make decisions related to reforms based on the status of the plan, its goals, and inputs to the system. These reforms then change the outcomes of the system. The outcomes ultimately lead to changes in system inputs, such as political considerations, laws, public and employee sentiment, and perhaps even the balance sought between the various pension goals. This can then lead to further changes and reforms to the system. The next chapter will further address the system approach to pension management and discuss the conclusions of the book.

References

Andonov, A., Hochberg, Y. V., & Rauh, J. D. (2018). Political representation and governance: Evidence from the investment decisions of public pension funds. *The Journal of Finance*, *73*(5), 2041–2086.

Aubry, J.-P., Chen, A., Munnell, A. H., & Wandrei, K. (2018, July). *What explains differences in public pension returns since 2001?* Center for Retirement Research at Boston College, 67.

Aubry, J.-P., & Crawford, C. V. (2019, August). *Does public pension board composition impact returns?* Center for Retirement Research at Boston College, 67.

Aubry, J.-P., & Wandrei, K. (2020a, April). *Have localities shifted away from traditional defined benefit plans?* Center for Retirement Research at Boston College, 70.

Aubry, J.-P., & Wandrei, K. (2020b, November). *Internal vs. external management for state and local pension plans*. Center for Retirement Research at Boston College, 75.

Bikker, J. A. (2017). Is there an optimal pension fund size? A scale-economy analysis of administrative costs. *The Journal of Risk and Insurance*, *84*(2), 739–769.

Bond, T., Doonan, D., & Ringland, C. (2023, December). *No quick fix: Closing a public pension plan leads to unexpected challenges*. National Institute on Retirement Security.

Brooks, J. (2019). Board on the job: Public-pension governance in the United States. *Journal of Public Policy*, *39*(1), 1–34.

Calabrese, T. D., & Ely, T. L. (2013). Pension obligation bonds and government spending. *Public Budgeting & Finance*, *33*(4), 43–65.

Center for State and Local Government Excellence and National Association of State Retirement Administrators. (2014, April). *Effects of pension plan changes on retirement security*. Retrieved January 26, 2024, from https://www.nasra.

org/files/JointPublications/Effects%20of%20Pension%20Plans%20on%20Retirement%20Income.pdf

Chen, G., Ebdon, C., Kriz, K., & Laforge, O. M. (2013). The management of defined contribution pension plans in local government. *Public Budgeting and Finance*, *33*(3), 75–95.

Chen, G., Kriz, K., & Ebdon, C. (2015). The effect of board composition on public sector pension funding. *Journal of Public Budgeting, Accounting & Financial Management*, 27(3), 352–376.

Clark, R. L., Hanson, E., & Mitchell, O. S. (2016). Lessons for public pensions from Utah's move to pension choice. *Journal of Pension Economics and Finance*, *15*(3), 285–310.

Dabowski, T., & Klingner, J. (2017). *Illinois has the lowest credit rating on record on a U.S. state*. Illinois Policy. https://www.illinoispolicy.org/illinois-now-has-the-lowest-credit-rating-on-record-for-a-u-s-state/#:~:text=Over%20the%20years%2C%20Illinois'%20state,or%20"junk%2C"%20rating

Davidyan, J. Y. (2021). Defined benefit public pension funding determinants and consequences: A review of the literature. *Public Finance and Management*, *20*(2), 214–242.

Dyck, A., & Pomorski, L. (2011). *Is bigger better? Size and performance in pension plan management* (Rotman School of Management Working Paper No. 1690724). University of Toronto. Retrieved February 7, 2024, from https://papers.ssrn.com/sol3/papers.cfm?abstract_id=1690724

FitchRatings. (2021, May 26). *U.S. public finance tax-supported rating criteria: Master criteria*. https://www.fitchratings.com/research/us-public-finance/us-public-finance-tax-supported-rating-criteria-04-05-2021

Fitzpatrick, M. D. (2015). How much are public school teachers willing to pay for their retirement benefits? *American Economic Journal: Economic Policy*, 7(4), 165–188.

Goldhaber, D., Grout, C., & Holden, K. (2015). *Public pension reform and teacher turnover: Evidence from Washington state* (Working Paper 142). National Center for Analysis of Longitudinal Data in Education Research. Retrieved October 2023, from Caldercenter.org

Gorina, E., & Hoang, T. (2020). Pension reforms and public sector turnover. *Journal of Public Administration Research and Theory*, *30*(1), 96–112.

Haverstick, K., Munnell, A. H., Sanzenbacher, G., & Soto, M. (2010). Pension type, tenure, and job mobility. *Journal of Pension Economics and Finance*, *9*(4), 609–625.

Hoang, T. (2023). Public pension reform and credit quality of state governments. *Public Finance Review*, *51*(3), 368–431.

Hoang, T., & Ebdon, C. (2021). *Institutional framework and path dependence in pension reform* (Working Paper).

Ippolito, R. A. (2002). Stayers as 'workers' and 'savers': Toward reconciling the pension-quit literature. *The Journal of Human Resources*, *37*(2), 275–308.

Kilgour, J. G. (2014). Understanding the role of pension obligation bonds: The California experience. *Compensation & Benefits Review*, 46(2), 123–129.

Lewis, G. B., & Stoycheva, R. L. (2016). Does pension plan structure affect turnover patterns? *Journal of Public Administration Research and Theory*, *26*(4), 787–799.

Matkin, D. S., & Chen, G. (2015). The consolidation of state-administered public pension systems in U.S. states. *Journal of Public Budgeting, Accounting & Financial Management*, 27(4), 455–481.

Munnell, A. H., Aubry, J. P., & Cafarelli, M. (2014, July). *An update on pension obligation bonds*. Center for Retirement Research at Boston College, 40.

Munnell, A. H., Aubry, J. P., Hurwitz, J., & Cafarelli, M. (2013, November). *Gauging the burden of public pensions on cities*. Center for Retirement Research at Boston College, 35.

Munnell, A. H., Aubry, J. P., & Sanzenbacher, G. T. (2015). *Recruiting and retaining high-quality state and local workers: Do pensions matter*? (Working Paper 2015-1). Center for Retirement Research at Boston College.

Munnell, A. H., Calabrese, T., Monk, A., & Aubry, J. P. (2010, January). *Pension obligation bond: Financial crisis exposes risks*. Center for Retirement Research at Boston College, 9.

NASRA. (2023a, March). *Public pension plan investment return assumptions*. Issue Brief.

NASRA. (2023b, November). *State and local government contributions to statewide pension plans: FY 22*. Issue Brief.

NASRA. (2023c, November). *Public fund survey summary of findings for FY 2022*. https://www.nasra.org/files/Public%20Fund%20Survey/FY22/PFS_SOF_FY22.pdf

Niraula, A. (2018). *Governments issuing pension obligation bonds risk worsening, not improving, their financial shape*. Reason Foundation. Reason.org/commentary/governments-issuing-pension-obligation-bonds-risk-worsening-not-improving-their-financial-shape/

Peng, J. (2008). *State and local pension fund management*. CRC Press/Taylor & Francis Group.

Peng, J., & Wang, Q. (2017). Affordability of public pension benefit: A historical and empirical analysis of US state and local government pension contributions. *Journal of Pension Economics and Finance*, *16*(1), 21–42.

Peng, J., & Wang, Q. (2020). Alternative investments: Is it a solution to the funding shortage of US public pension plans? *Journal of Pension Economics and Finance*, *19*, 491–510.

Quinby, L. D., Sanzenbacher, G. T., & Aubry, J. P. (2018). *How have pension cuts affected public sector competitiveness?* Center for Retirement Research at Boston College, State and Local Pension Plans No. 59.

Quinby, L. D., & Wettstein, G. (2019, May). *Do benefit cuts encourage public employees to Leave?* Center for Retirement Research at Boston College, State and Local Pension Plans Number 65.

Schieber, S. J. (2011). Political economy of public sector retirement plans. *Journal of Pension Economics and Finance*, *10*(2), 269–290.

United States Government Accountability Office. (2022, March). *Defined contribution plans: 403(b) investment options, fees, and other characteristics varied*. GAO-22-104439. https://www.gao.gov/products/gao-22-104439

Young, R., & Theodore, L. (2023, August 3). *How to determine the amount of income you will need at retirement*. T. Rowe Price insights on retirement. https://www.troweprice.com/personal-investing/resources/insights/how-to-determine-amount-of-income-you-will-need-at-retirement.htm

Wang, Q., & Peng, J. (2016). An empirical analysis of state and local public pension plan funded ratio change, 2001-2009. *The American Review of Public Administration*, 46, 75–91.

Wang, Q., & Peng, J. (2018). Political embeddedness of public pension governance: An event history analysis of discount rate changes. *Public Administration Review*, *78*(5), 785–794.

11

KEY LESSONS AND EMERGING ISSUES IN PUBLIC PENSION MANAGEMENT

Introduction

In this book, we apply a logic model framework to analyze the inputs (environment, stakeholders, and constraints), decisions, and goals of public pension plan management. We also identify the challenges and reforms, as well as the impact of these reforms on both governments and employees. In this concluding chapter, we summarize the lessons learned from the previous chapters and address several emerging issues facing public pension plans today.

Key takeaways

The use of the logic model allowed us to navigate pension plan management from a holistic, system-wide perspective. With this approach, we have identified "lessons learned" that can be useful for effective decision making in pension plan management. This section will discuss these ten key takeaways.

Balancing multiple goals

When managing public pension plans, policymakers and decision-makers must balance multiple key goals to ensure the pension system's overall success. In this book, we have identified five goals for public pension plan management. Effective public pension policies should ensure the sufficiency and security of pension benefits, maintain fiscal affordability of

DOI: 10.4324/9781032671185-11

pension costs, secure long-term sustainability of pension funding, enhance efficiency of asset management, and promote good governance practices. While all these goals are important, policymakers may prioritize them differently depending on the best interests of stakeholders at a given time and within the legal and financial constraints.

Engaging stakeholders

Stakeholder groups often have different, sometimes competing, interests, which can create conflicting goals for the management of public pension plans. The major relevant stakeholders vary between the two types of decision-makers: pension system trustees and administering government officials. On the pension system side, stakeholders include trustees and their constituencies, administrators, and professional advisors. On the government side, stakeholders include employer governments, elected officials, employees and their unions, retirees, and taxpayers. Recognizing these diverse interests and motivations, and actively engaging stakeholders in the decision-making process will help facilitate effective pension policies and implement successful pension system reforms.

Examining the impact of pension reforms

Pensions impose significant fiscal burdens on governments, and as fiscal stress and pension costs grow, these financial pressures are expected to intensify. Many state and local governments have adopted significant changes to pensions to reduce the cost of public pension plans. While much of the current discussion on pension reforms has centered on liabilities and costs, changes to pension systems also have considerable impacts on employees. It is important to consider how these reforms affect both employers and employees, particularly during times when they are already facing fiscal challenges such as high inflation. Exploring the potential effect of pension reforms on employee recruitment, retention, and quality will be helpful for making informed decisions regarding pension policies.

Unpacking the complexity of pension plan management

In this book, we propose a logic model framework for understanding and managing the complexity in public pension plan management. The interplay between various decisions and features of a pension plan can often resemble a "black box." This system approach explains the interaction of various components and highlights the importance of unpacking this "black box." In public plan management, this involves providing decision-makers, such as pension plan board members, with clear information about options, constraints, and consequences, especially when they have difficulty grasping the complexities of pension plan management. By enhancing their understanding, the policies and decisions they make can better align with professional standards and stakeholder interests, ensuring more informed and effective governance.

Considering the fiscal consequences

Key decisions regarding benefits, contributions, investments, and actuarial practices directly influence the funding performance and sustainability of pension systems. Poor funding performance often results from past policies that failed to fully consider their fiscal consequences. Educating decision-makers about the fiscal impact of their choices is crucial. Proposed changes to pension plans should be accompanied by information that clearly outlines their financial implications. This informed approach to governance helps mitigate fiscal risks and ensures that pension reforms support the financial stability and security of retirement systems.

Considering short- and long-term impacts

When considering pension reforms, it is crucial to evaluate both the short-term consequences, such as immediate cost savings or improvements in the funded ratio, and the long-term consequences, including the sustainability of pension systems and retirement security for employees. Regularly assessing these outcomes and establishing a feedback loop for continuous evaluation and adjustment ensures that both immediate and future results align with overall policy objectives and the interests of stakeholders.

Holistic approach to reform

A successful pension reform often involves a holistic approach that goes beyond merely making small adjustments to benefit or contribution policies. A viable path forward requires examining various dimensions of the pension system, including benefits, contributions, investments, and actuarial practices, and designing a comprehensive reform strategy. Many state and local governments have introduced cash-balance (CB) plans, DB (defined benefit)-DC (defined contribution) hybrid plans, or cost-sharing and risk-sharing policies that aim to reduce the volatility and uncertainty of pension costs. Decision-makers must evaluate the interconnections between environments, stakeholders, constraints, and decisions. By addressing these various factors and integrating them into a comprehensive strategy, pension reforms can be designed to meet current challenges while ensuring future fiscal sustainability and benefit adequacy.

Transparency and ethics in decision making

In a public pension plan, administrators, board members, and professionals each have certain decision-making discretions, with their collective input shaping policies and strategies. Professionals such as fund managers, actuaries, and financial advisors often exert significant influence on the decision agenda due to their expertise. However, their personal interests and motivations may introduce bias into the process. To mitigate bias and conflicts of interest, it is important to recognize the distinct roles each party plays, hold them accountable for their decisions, and ensure that decisions are made collectively and with transparency. This approach helps maintain integrity and accountability in the decision-making process.

Understanding the fiscal, political, and regulatory context

Governments must carefully navigate the interplay between government finances and pension plan management, recognizing that a government's fiscal situation and political landscape heavily influence its approach to pension management decisions. Each pension plan operates within a unique context shaped by its environment and specific constraints. There is no one-size-fits-all solution for pension reforms. Every plan requires detailed attention to its circumstances, while professional standards and regulations may evolve over time. By tailoring reforms to the specific fiscal, political, and regulatory context, governments can more effectively fulfill their financial responsibilities while ensuring the sustainability of the pension systems they administer.

Managing risks and uncertainties

Dealing with risks and uncertainties is a critical aspect of pension plan management. In an increasingly complex and volatile environment, factors such as high inflation, demographic changes, or possibility of a recession can significantly impact the outcomes of pension decisions and reforms. Assumptions that underlie pension plan management must be regularly reviewed and adjusted to account for these changes and future uncertainties. By incorporating strategies to mitigate risks and prepare for uncertainties, government can create more resilient retirement plans that are better equipped to withstand future challenges.

Emerging issues in the post-COVID era

When the COVID-19 pandemic erupted in early 2020, its immediate impact quickly reached every aspect of the global community. Governments were at the center of the collective actions to respond to this pandemic. The demand for public resources and the decline in tax revenues created fiscal challenges for governments. In March 2020, due to the rapid and severe disruption of economic and commercial activities, the fear of a pandemic-related recession caused capital markets to collapse, leading to a decline in pension assets. As the federal government provided stimulus packages to businesses, governments, and households, the economy and capital markets quickly recovered. Investment gains and contributions increased quickly afterward, but the economy faced new challenges, such as high inflation rates. The shift to online work, public health concerns, and work-life balance considerations have led public employees to reconsider their decisions to join, stay in, or leave their positions in the public sector. In the post-pandemic era, whether pensions still provide enough motivation to attract employees to work in the public sector remains a question. In this section, we address several emerging issues that face public pension plans in the post-COVID era.

Capital markets and public pensions

At the beginning of the pandemic, the stock market experienced sudden and severe losses due to concerns over the consequences of the pandemic on the economy and society. The S&P 500 index dropped by more than 34% from its peak in February 2020 to its low point in March 2020, causing many public pension plans to worry about their asset values, as they heavily relied on returns from equities to fund their plans. Many governments also struggled to keep up with their required contributions to pension plans, facing significant revenue losses and increased expenditures in response to the pandemic. Some pension systems considered reducing contributions for that year or issuing pension obligation bonds to address the funding gap.

Following the outbreak of the crisis, governments quickly implemented several stimulus packages to support state and local governments, businesses, and households. The economy and capital markets swiftly recovered, reaching new highs by the end of 2020. As state and local governments received funding from the federal government, concerns over revenue losses and fiscal stress began to fade. Although the federal government's COVID aid was not specifically designed to fund public pensions, the fiscal relief allowed these governments to maintain service levels, reduce fiscal stress, and continue funding their pension plans. Despite these changes and the recovery of financial losses from the early COVID years, most public plans still failed to meet their expected rates of return by the end of 2020, resulting in a decline in funded ratios for many plans (Randazzo & Moody, 2020; Sielman, 2020).

In fiscal year 2021, the capital market continued to reach all-time highs as the economy recovered. The funding level of pension plans increased significantly, reaching a new high by the end of the fiscal year due to strong investment returns and contributions from governments. Based on a study of the 100 largest U.S. public pension plans, the average reported funded ratio rose from 70.7% in 2020 to 85.0% in 2021, driven by surging market returns throughout the year (Sielman & Gordon, 2021). Similarly, Randazzo and Moody (2021) noted record-setting investment returns, with an average return of 27.5% in 2021, far exceeding the average assumed return of 7.03%, leading to a 10-percentage point jump in the average funded ratio based on the 164 public pension plans they studied.

In fiscal year 2022, pension plans experienced investment losses as capital markets declined due to high inflation, supply chain disruptions, and the war in Ukraine. These investment losses in 2022 erased nearly half of the gains from 2021, resulting in the average funded ratio decreasing from 83.9% in 2021 to 77.3% in 2022, based on the public pension plans studied in the Equable Report series (Randazzo & Moody, 2023). In 2023, the average funded ratio showed a modest improvement to 78.1% (Randazzo & Moody, 2023). In their report series, Randazzo and Moody (2024) describe the state of public pension plans as "fragile" in the post-COVID era, citing factors such as sizable existing unfunded liabilities and the persistent failure of investment returns to meet long-term return targets.

High inflation rates since 2022

The COVID-19 pandemic and subsequent events since 2020, including federal fiscal policy, job position vacancies, supply chain disruptions, and changes in energy prices, have contributed to the rise of inflation since 2020 (Ball et al., 2022; Bernanke & Blanchard, 2023). In June 2022, the change in the Consumer Price Index (CPI), an indicator of inflation, reached 9.1%, the highest in several decades (BLS, 2024). The Federal Reserve increased interest rates aggressively during 2022 and 2023 in response to this high inflation (Federal Reserve Bank, 2024).

The influence of high inflation on public pension plans has multiple facets, affecting both assets and liabilities, but the effects also vary based on different factors such as the plan's investment, contribution, and benefit policies.

On the asset side, high inflation often increases uncertainty and volatility in stock market returns. Although the relationship between inflation and stock market performance is complex and varies depending on asset classes, the overall increase in uncertainty and volatility can make it challenging for pension funds to make investment decisions. Fixed-income assets, especially bonds with long durations, could be negatively impacted by high inflation due to rising interest expenses, while commodities and real estate might perform well in such an environment. A pension plan with a more diversified and larger asset pool, along with an investment policy designed to manage investment risks, could do better in an economic environment with high uncertainty and volatility.

On the liability side, inflation often leads to increases in active employees' salaries, although the salary growth rate is not necessarily directly tied to the inflation rate. When salaries rise at a rate higher than expected, both the normal costs and future pension liabilities will increase in a DB plan. If the plan's contribution policy sets the employee contributions as a percentage of payroll or variable employee contributions depending on costs and liabilities, the contribution amount from employees will also rise, but this may not be sufficient to offset the increase in normal costs and pension liabilities. If so, the unfunded liabilities and the required employer contribution amount will also increase due to inflation (Strom, 2022).

For pension benefits, the impact of inflation depends on the plan's cost-of-living adjustment (COLA) policy. In plans with automatic COLAs linked to the inflation rate, high inflation will cause pension liabilities, normal costs, and required contributions to rise (Aubry, 2022). However, many of these automatic COLAs have caps that could help mitigate the increase in pension benefits. According to Aubry's (2022) estimate, an 8% inflation rate (such as what the United States experienced in 2022) sustained over two years would increase total retiree liabilities by 1.8–5.7% for most plans that use CPI-linked COLAs. For plans that do not link their COLAs to the inflation rate, or have a COLA cap that cannot keep up with high inflation, the purchasing power of retirees' pension benefits will decrease, substantially affecting retirees' well-being during periods of high inflation. According to a 2022 study (Equable, 2022), the average COLA provided for state and local retirees in 2021 was 1.58%, much lower than the inflation rate during that time (BLS, 2024).

Changes in mortality rates

Due to the high infection rate of the COVID-19 virus, along with the severe illness and death it has caused among vulnerable populations, many worry that the pandemic might change mortality rates and life expectancy, which are used in the calculation of future pension liabilities. Since the outbreak of the COVID-19 pandemic, over 1 million people in the United States have died from this disease (CDC, April 2023). Elderly people, racial and ethnic minorities, and people with underlying medical conditions are more likely to experience severe illness, hospitalization, and death from COVID-19. It is reasonable to expect that the population overall or these specific groups of people will see an increase in their mortality rates as a result of the COVID-19 pandemic. COVID-19 survivors, especially those with pre-existing medical conditions and who have experienced severe illness and "long COVID," might also have a lower life expectancy.

Mortality rates and life expectancy are used to calculate future pension liabilities for those who participate in pension plans. Pension plan actuaries use a mortality table to estimate how many active employees will live to claim normal retirement benefits and how many will claim death benefits. In a DB plan, many retirees choose to receive their pension benefits as an annuity. Mortality rates for retirees each year are used to estimate the value of the life annuity.

Pension actuaries estimate the mortality rates based on experience studies using pension plans' historical data. If mortality rates have increased due to COVID-19, actuaries might update the mortality table to reflect these changes, and as a result, pension liabilities might change. This change might be more obvious for plans with a participant population that is disproportionately affected by COVID-19 due to their nature of work or geographic region.

The question becomes whether COVID-19 has substantially changed the mortality rates and life expectancy, or if that information has already been taken into consideration when plan actuaries estimate mortality rates. Those who are most at risk of dying from COVID-19, such as elderly people and those with underlying medical conditions, also already have high mortality rates.

The current studies on mortality rate changes due to COVID-19 are based on available data that are updated over time. A study in 2022 (Wettstein et al., 2022) shows that COVID-19 deaths were small relative to the size of the population. Also, COVID deaths mostly occurred within the group of people who already have high mortality rates. Because of this "selection effect," survivors after the COVID years see modestly decreased mortality rates in the near future. Another study (Tilstra et al., 2024) used data from the United Nations World Population Prospects to examine the long-term effects of the COVID-19 pandemic on U.S. population structure. The study found that the pandemic has reduced the population in the long term, but this effect is primarily due to net migration loss during the pandemic. Meanwhile, the high mortality rates among the older population have led to only a small reduction in the dependency ratio. As a result, whether pension plans need to update their mortality rates to reflect post-pandemic changes depends on each plan's specific circumstances such as the current mortality rate tables and the age structure of the workforce.

Impact on public workforce

The COVID-19 pandemic has also caused changes in workforce participation. The so-called "Great Resignation" described the phenomenon in 2021 when a wave of public- and private-sector employees quit their job due to various reasons such as concerns over public health risks at the workplace, the high and long-lasting unemployment subsidies during the pandemic, the challenges of work-life balance, and the lack of support for remote work (Fuller & Kerr, 2022). This "Great Resignation" increased turnover rates and caused labor shortages in many sectors including government.

A few studies have empirically examined the impact of the pandemic on labor force participation. These studies have related the degree of impact to socioeconomic characteristics such as age, gender, educational background, race, and ethnicity. Quinby et al. (2021) use the Current Population Survey (CPS), which includes both public- and private-sector workers, to compare the quit and retirement rates during the pandemic (March–December 2020) and before the pandemic. They find that the likelihood of older workers (age 55 and older) leaving their work increased by 7.6 percentage point. Women, those without a college degree, Asian Americans, and those who do not have access to telework options were more likely to leave their job positions than others. The retirement rate only slightly increased from the pre- to the post-pandemic period.

The impact of job separations and retirements on pension liabilities depends on whether these factors were already considered in the separation and retirement rates. A pension plan's liabilities are calculated using separation and mortality rates based on experience studies using the plan's historical data. It is reasonable to assume that if separation rates and retirement rates increase, plans will have to update the separation rates table to reflect the new numbers. As a result, pension liabilities and costs would also change accordingly.

Looking ahead

Besides the pandemic, public pension plans also face other economic and political uncertainties, such as potential future economic recessions and changes in federal tax and regulatory policies affecting state and local governments. What will governments and public services look like in the post-pandemic era? How will public pension plans be affected by these emerging issues? Based on what we discussed in this book, we offer some thoughts and important questions for future studies.

Regarding benefit policies, several issues have gained more attention since the outbreak of COVID-19. The first issue is the role of retirement benefits in recruiting and retaining employees in the public sector. During the pandemic, state and local governments in the United States struggled to fill positions with qualified employees. Public pension benefits were always viewed as an essential component of compensation packages that motivate employees to work for the public sector. The difficulty in recruiting and retaining employees has made it even harder to cut pension benefits, as many systems had been attempting to do before the pandemic. However, with new changes in work style and workforce, will pensions remain important for employees choosing to work in the public sector, or will they prioritize other factors such as work-life balance? If so, could DC, cash-balance, and DB-DC hybrid plans offer more flexibility and help attract employees? When part-time employees are used to promote flexible employment in the public sector, how can governments provide pensions and other benefits to these part-time workers? These are questions that future studies need to address.

Another issue regarding benefits is the purchasing power of pension benefits when the inflation rate increases. Many pension systems will likely re-examine their COLA policies as inflation persists. For pension systems with COLA linked to inflation, the concern is the increased contributions and liabilities due to rising inflation. In contrast, for pension systems without a COLA or with a low COLA, the concern lies in the loss of purchasing power for retirees. Also, DC, cash-balance, and DB-DC hybrid plans face significant disadvantages in preserving purchasing power, particularly for public employees who are not covered by Social Security.

On contribution policies, an important discussion is about how governments can ensure their fiscal discipline in paying pension contributions during a crisis. During the COVID-19 pandemic, state and local governments were able to get fiscal assistance from the federal government, and fortunately, the capital markets quickly recovered from the downturn in early 2020. However, it is likely that pension systems and governments will encounter another recession caused by other external shocks, while the federal government may be unable to provide fiscal assistance due to its own debt issues and political challenges. During a crisis, contributions to pension systems could become difficult as governments focus on responding to the situation and maintaining critical services. What fiscal tools or rules can be used to stabilize governments' contributions to pension plans is an important question to explore in the post-pandemic era.

On investment policies, the issue is on the investment risk public pension plans bear with current investment strategies. Public pension plans increasingly invest in riskier asset classes such as equities and alternative investments, which is partially driven by the fact that these assets see a steady increase in their values over the years. However, how pension systems measure and report fiscal risks to their stakeholders becomes an important question. In recent years, there have been more discussions about using different risk measurement approaches, such as sensitivity tests, stress testing, value at risk (VaR), and stochastic simulations to assess these risks. As governments face more uncertainty in the post-pandemic era, these risk measures would be helpful for decision making in public pension systems.

We should also note that the above discussions are based on available data and analysis as of 2024. As more data become available, our understanding of the impact of the emerging issues and the important considerations for pension systems will also improve. Some important data and trends to observe include the mortality rate changes among public employees, work style changes post-pandemic, capital market returns, and the inflation rates.

In this book, we offer a logic model framework to help pension plan decision-makers and stakeholders navigate the complexities of public pension plan management. In the chapters, we emphasize balancing five key goals: sufficiency of pension benefits, affordability of pension costs, sustainability of pension funding, efficiency of asset management, and good governance practices. We also explain the key decisions related to benefits, contributions, investments, and actuarial practices. Additionally, we explore the legal and financial constraints, the various stakeholders within sponsoring governments and retirement systems, and the broader economic and political environment. Facing growing concerns over the financial liabilities and costs of pension plans, many state and local governments have implemented pension reforms. We examine these reforms and discuss their short- and long-term impacts on both employers and employees. We conclude with ten takeaways for public pension plan decision-makers and stakeholders to consider, along with emerging issues they should monitor in the post-pandemic era. We hope this book offers valuable insights as they build a path forward in managing public pension plans.

References

Aubry, J.-P. (2022). *Public pensions contend with falling markets and rising inflation*. Center for Retirement Research at Boston College. https://crr.bc.edu/wp-content/uploads/2022/08/IB_22-13-2.pdf

Ball, L. M., Leigh, D., & Mishra, P. (2022). *Understanding U.S. Inflation during the COVID era* (Working Paper 30613). National Bureau of Economic Research. https://doi.org/10.3386/w30613

Bernanke, B., & Blanchard, O. (2023). *What caused the U.S. pandemic-era inflation?* Hutchins Center Working Paper # 86. https://www.brookings.edu/wp-content/uploads/2023/06/WP86-Bernanke-Blanchard_6.13.pdf

Bureau of Labor Statistics (BLS). (2024). *12-month percentage change, Consumer Price Index, selected categories*. Retrieved September 1, 2024, from https://www.bls.gov/charts/consumer-price-index/consumer-price-index-by-category-line-chart.htm

Centers for Disease Control and Prevention (CDC). (2023, April). Trends in United States COVID-19 deaths, emergency department (ED) visits, and test positivity by geographic area. https://covid.cdc.gov/covid-data-tracker/

Equable. (2022). *Are public pensions protected from inflation?* https://equable.org/public-pensions-protected-from-inflation/

Federal Reserve Bank. (2024). *Federal funds effective rate*. https://fred.stlouisfed.org/series/FEDFUNDS

Fuller, J., & Kerr, W. (2022). The Great Resignation didn't start with the pandemic. *Harvard Business Review*. https://hbr.org/2022/03/the-great-resignation-didnt-start-with-the-pandemic

Quinby, L. D., Rutledge, M. S., & Wettstein, G. (2021). How has COVID-19 affected the labor force participation of older workers? Center for Retirement Research at Boston College. Retrieved from https://crr.bc.edu/wp-content/uploads/2021/10/wp_2021-13.pdf

Randazzo, A., & Moody, J. (2020). *State of Pensions 2020: Pension trends in the age of Covid-19*. https://equable.org/wp-content/uploads/2020/12/State-of-Pensions-December-Update_12102020.pdf

Randazzo, A., & Moody, J. (2021). *State of Pensions 2021: Pension trends in an era of accelerating volatility*. https://equable.org/wp-content/uploads/2021/12/State-of-Pensions-2021_Dec-Update_Final.pdf

Randazzo, A., & Moody, J. (2023). *The State of Pensions 2022: The era of volatility: Asset shocks, inflation, and war.* https://equable.org/wp-content/uploads/2023/01/State-of-Pensions-2022_Year-End-Update_Jan-2023.pdf

Randazzo, A., & Moody, J. (2024). *The State of Pensions 2023: Market uncertainty, politics, and risk addiction in the age of volatility*. https://equable.org/wp-content/uploads/2024/01/State-of-Pensions-2023_January-Update_Final.pdf

Sielman, R. (2020). *2020 Public Pension Funding Study*. Milliman White Paper. https://www.milliman.com/-/media/milliman/pdfs/2020-articles/ppfs/12-3-20-ppfs_v1.ashx

Sielman, R., & Gordon, R. (2021). *2021 public pension funding study*. Milliman White Paper. https://www.milliman.com/-/media/milliman/pdfs/2021-articles/10-25-21-public-pension-funding-study-2021.ashx

Strom, M. (2022). *The impact of inflation on public pensions*. NCPERS Actuary. https://www.segalco.com/media/3048/ncpers-persist_fall_2022_article_7.pdf

Tilstra, A. M., Polizzi, A., Wagner, S., & Akimova, E. T. (2024). Projecting the long-term effects of the COVID-19 pandemic on U.S. population structure. *Nature Communications*, *15*(1), 2409. https://doi.org/10.1038/s41467-024-46582-4

Wettstein, G., Gok, N., Chen, A., & Munnell, A. H. (2022, August). *Will survivors of the first year of the COVID-19 pandemic have lower mortality?* (CRR WP 2022-10). Center for Retirement Research at Boston College. https://crr.bc.edu/wp-content/uploads/2022/08/wp_2022-10-1.pdf

INDEX

Note: Page numbers in **bold** and *italics* represent tables and figures respectively.

actuarial accrued liability (AAL) 94
actuarial assumptions 7
actuarial cost methods *98*, 98–99
actuarially determined contribution (ADC) 23–24, 30–31, 49, 96–97, 131–132, 146
actuarial practices 29
actuarial process 93–97
Actuarial Standards of Practice (ASOP) 64, 92
actuarial valuation 92–93
adequacy of pension benefits: cost-of-living adjustment 122–124; deferred retirement option plans 125–126; disability benefits 127; legal protection for public pension benefits **124**, 124–125; replacement rate 128; Social Security coverage 121–122, *121*; survival benefits 127–128
ad hoc cost-of-living adjustment 122–123
administering government, factors affecting decisions of 26–27
administrators, pension 27, 61
advisors 61–62
affordability of pension cost 23–24, 40–42, 49, 190–193
aggregated (AGG) method 99
alternative investments 77
alternative pension design 156
amortization methods, UAAL 100–102, *101–102*
amortization period 100
assets: allocation strategy 72, 74; calculation of 94–96; classes 75–79, **76**, *78*, 81; management, efficiency of 24–25, 44–45, 196–198; pooled 157; simulation of 106–109; smoothing 99–100, *101*
automatic cost-of-living adjustment 122–123

"black box" of public pension management 10–12

California PERS (CalPERS) system 117, *118*
capital market assumptions (CMAs) 81, **82**, 85, **86**
capital markets 26, 56–57; during COVID-19 pandemic 208–209
cash-balance plans 181, **182**; current status of 179; features of 173–175
cash equivalents 77
closed amortization 102

codes of ethics 73
conflict of interest policy 73
Connecticut Retirement Plans and Trust Funds (CRPTF) 73–74, **74**
constraints, as input factor for public pension plans management 28, 63–66, **64**; actuarial standards of practice 64; court decisions 66; generally accepted accounting principles 64–65; labor union contracts 65–66; state and local laws 65; state legal protections of pension benefits 65
contingent employee contribution rates 179–180
contracts, union 65–66
contribution rates 108, *108*; contingent employee 179–180
cost-of-living adjustment (COLA) 3, 49, 105, 114–115; automatic *vs.* ad hoc 122–123; benefits, minimum requirement for 123–124; contingent 180; cut in 152; design, considerations for 122–124; fixed rate 123; inflation-based 123; performance-based 123
cost-sharing (risk-sharing) model 159–160
COVID-19 pandemic, issues during: capital markets and public pensions 208–209; inflation rates 209–210; mortality rates 210–212; public workforce 212
credit ratings 27, 59, 148

DB-DC hybrid plans 181–182, **183**; current status of 179; features of 173–175
decision-makers 149–150; *see also* stakeholders
deferred retirement option plans (DROP) 125–126
defined benefit (DB) plans 3, 5, 17, 39, 93, 114, 172; advantages and disadvantages of **175**, 175–176; challenges in transition to other plans 183–184
defined contribution (DC) plans 3–4, 7–8, 41, 172–173; advantages and disadvantages of **175**, 175–176; current status of **177**, 177–178; features of 173–175
disability benefits 127
discount rate 102–105, *104*
divestment 84–85

early retirement 120–121
economically targeted investments (ETIs) 85
elected officials 62–63, 149–150
electoral politics 27, 59–60
eligibility rules, pension benefits: early retirement 120–121; retirement age and rules of retirement 117–119, **118**; vesting requirement 119–120, **120**
employee contributions 153, 155
employer governments 27–28, 62
employer-sponsored pension plans: defined benefit plans 3; defined contribution plans 3–4
entry age normal (EAN) 98–99, 106
environment, as input factor for public pension plans management 26–27, 55–56, **56**; capital markets 56–57; credit ratings 59; electoral politics 59–60; fiscal health of government 58–59; fiscal health of pension system 57; political embeddedness 57–58; political ideology 59
environmental, social, and governance (ESG) goals 45, 85
expected rate of return (ERR) 44, 50, 81, 102–105, *104*
external factors, public pension reforms: changes in accounting standards 149; credit ratings 148; market volatility and low investment returns 148; political pressures 148–149; public opinion 149

final average salary (FAS) 48–49, 114, **115**, 115–116, 156
financial security, and importance of public pension plans 5–6
fiscal health: of government 58–59, 147; of pension system 26, 57
fixed-income investments 75, 77
fixed rate cost-of-living adjustment 123
457(b) DC plan 178
414(k) DC plan 178
401(k) DC plan 178

403(b) DC plan 178
funded ratio 9, 19, 24, 26, 43, 49–50, 57, 108–109, *109*; calculation of 94–96
funding, public pension plans: sustainability of 24, 42–44, 49–50

Generally accepted accounting principles (GAAP) 64–65
goals, public pension plans 38; affordability of pension costs 40–42; balancing **47**, 47–48; efficiency of asset management 44–45; good governance of pension plans 45–46; sufficiency of pension benefits 38–40, **40**; sustainability of pension funding 42–44
governance: changes in 158; pension system 6–8; of public pension plan 25, 44–46, 198–199
government, fiscal health of 26–27
Governmental Accounting Standards Board (GASB) 25, 28, 92; Statement No. 67 95, 100, 103, 149; Statement No. 68 149
Great Recession 26, 42, 56

hedge funds 77

Idaho Public Employees Retirement System 61
Individual Retirement Accounts (IRAs) 4–5
inflation-based cost-of-living adjustment 123
inflation rates 105, *105*; during COVID-19 pandemic 209–210
input factors, public pension plans management 25; constraints 28, 63–66, **64**; environment 26–27, 55–60, **56**; stakeholders 27–28, **60**, 60–63
internal factors, public pension reforms 142–147; fiscal health of government 147; rise of unfunded pension liabilities 142–146, *144*, *145*; volatility in pension contributions *146*, 146–147
investments 29, 71; alternative 77; economically targeted 85; fees 84; fixed-income 75, 77; objectives 72; performance 83–84, **84**; policy 72–74; portfolio 72–73; practices, changes in 156–158; returns 148; risk 79, 81–82, 83; simulation of 85–89, **86**, **87**, *88–89*

judiciary, role of 150–151

labor unions *see* unions
legal protection, for pension benefits **124**, 124–125
liabilities 24, 42; calculation of 93; simulation of 106–109, *107*; unfunded 9, 17, 59, 142–146, *144*, *145*
lifetime take-home income 23
liquidity 72
logic model framework, for public pension management 17–18; existing 18–23, **21**; goals and outcomes 23–25; inputs *see* input factors, public pension plans management; outputs and decisions *see* outputs, of decision making in pension plan management

market volatility 148
Mississippi Public Employees' Retirement System 155
mortality rates 106; during COVID-19 pandemic 210–212
multiplier, pension benefit 116–117, **117**, 152–153

New York City Teachers' Retirement System (NYCTRS) 48, 115; Annual Comprehensive Financial Report (2022) 48–49; employers' contribution rates 49; expected rate of return 50; funded ratio 49–50; governance and policies 50–51; replacement rate 48–49
New York State and Local Retirement System 153, **154**

open amortization 102
other post-employment benefit (OPEB) 42, 43
outputs, of decision making in pension plan management 28; actuarial practices 29; contributions 30–31; investments 28; pension benefits 29–30

pension benefits 8, 29–30, 113; adequacy of *see* adequacy of pension benefits; change in 152–153; decisions 114–115; eligibility rules for *see* eligibility rules, pension benefits; formula 115–117; legal protection for **124**, 124–125; multiplier 116–117, **117**, 152–153; reduction in 153; state legal protections of 65; sufficiency of 23, 38–40, **40**, 48–49, 188–190
pension boards 6–7, 28; changes in 158; decisions 28–30; political embeddedness of 57
pension contributions: actuarially determined contribution 23–24, 30–31, 96–97, 131–132; change in 153, 155; employee 153, 155; and fiscal implications of pension costs 133–136; government funding policies 132–133; policies 131; public pension revenue sources *129–130*, 129–131; volatility in *146*, 146–147
pension cost, affordability of 23–24, 40–42, 49, 190–193
pension crisis 42
pension governance 6–8
pension obligation bonds (POBs) 160–161
pension plan funding, sustainability of 24, 42–44, 49–50, 194–196
pension reforms *see* reforms, public pension
pension spiking 115–116
pension system 10, 28; fiscal health of 26, 57; governance of 6–8
pension trustees: factors influencing decisions of 26
performance-based cost-of-living adjustment 123
political embeddedness 26, 57–58
political ideology 27, 59
political pressures 148–149
portfolio theory 72–73
present value of future benefits (PVFBs) 93, 94, 99
Primary Insurance Amount (PIA) formula 2–3
private equity 77
private savings 4–5
projected unit credit (PUC) 98–99, 106
prudent person rule 25, 45, 65, 71, 73
Public Choice Theory 18
public opinions 149; on public pension costs 42
public pension plan: benefits 8, 29–30; during COVID-19 pandemic 208–209; defined benefit plans 3, 5; funding, sustainability of 24, 42–44; funding ratio of 42; goals of *see* goals, public pension plans; governance of 25, 44–46, 198–199; importance, financial security and 5–6; investment policy 72–74; management of 6–12; reforms *see* reforms, public pension; risk-sharing arrangements in *174*
Public Plans Database (PPD) 41, 57, 98, 144; plan types in **177**
public retirement systems 7; financial sustainability of 9
public-sector employees 5, 37; and defined benefit plans 3
public unions 28
public workforce, impact of COVID-19 pandemic 212

rate of return *see* expected rate of return (ERR)
Real Estate Investment Trusts (REITs) 77
reforms, public pension 9, 141–142, 151, *152*; decision-makers and stakeholders 149–150; determinant factors of **142**; effects of 187, **188**; external factors 148–149; frequency by types 171; holistic approach to 206–207; internal factors 142–147; legal constraints/role of the judiciary 150–151
replacement rate 5, 23, 38–39, 128
retirees 28, 37
retirement: age of 117–119, **118**, 155; early 120–121; eligibility, change in 155–156; rules of 117–119, **118**, **119**
retirement income, sources of: employer-sponsored pension plans 3–4; private savings 4–5; Social Security 2–3
risk management 82–83
Roth IRAs 4

Social Security 30, 39; coverage 121–122, *121*; replacement rate for 5; as retirement income source 2–3
Social Security Act of 1935 121
Social Security Amendment of 1950 121
Society of Actuaries (SOA) 25
stakeholders 27–28, 38, 60–63, **63**, 149–150, 205; advisors 61–62; elected officials 62–63, 149–150; employer governments 62; pension administrators 61; taxpayers 63; trustees' constituencies 60–61; unions/employees 63
sufficiency of pension benefits 23, 38–40, **40**, 48–49, 188–190
survival benefits 127–128
sustainability, of pension plan funding 24, 42–44, 49–50, 194–196

taxpayers 28, 63
Tennessee State and Teachers Retirement system 61
Texas Employee Retirement System (TXERS) 115
traditional IRAs 4
trustees 27, 62; constituencies 60–61

unfunded actuarial accrued liabilities (UAAL) 96; amortization methods 100–102, *101–102*
unfunded liabilities 9, 17, 59, 142–146, *144*, *145*
unions 63; contracts 65–66; role of 150

vesting period 3, 119–120

years of service (YOS) 114, 118–119, **119**, 155

Made in the USA
Monee, IL
13 September 2026

62980177R10131